Turning to Practice with Action Research

Labour, Education & Society

Edited by György Széll,
Heinz Sünker, Anne Inga Hilsen
and Francesco Garibaldo

Volume 15

PETER LANG

Frankfurt am Main · Berlin · Bern · Bruxelles · New York · Oxford · Wien

Benedicte Brøgger
Olav Eikeland
(eds.)

Turning to Practice
with Action Research

PETER LANG
Internationaler Verlag der Wissenschaften

Bibliographic Information published by the Deutsche Nationalbibliothek
The Deutsche Nationalbibliothek lists this publication in the Deutsche Nationalbibliografie; detailed bibliographic data is available in the internet at http://dnb.d-nb.de.

ISSN 1861-647X
ISBN 978-3-631-59446-9

© Peter Lang GmbH
Internationaler Verlag der Wissenschaften
Frankfurt am Main 2009
All rights reserved.

www.peterlang.de

Contents

5

Section 3: On the rationality of theories – critical perspectives

Preface and acknowledgements

This book draws on a number of sources of funding, knowledge, and support, and there are many people to thank as what were once intangible ideas and concerns now appear in print. The book springs from a strategic research programme at the Work Research Institute (WRI) in Oslo funded by the Research Council of Norway in the period from 2003 through 2007. This programme made it possible for a group of WRI researchers to relate their own action research and research on work organisations more clearly to other mainstream discourses on theory and methodology. The efforts have produced two anthologies. The first volume to appear was *Action Research and Organisation Theory*, edited by A.M. Berg and O. Eikeland and published by Peter Lang in 2008. It focused on the links between action research and organisation theory. In this volume, however, the key theme is research methods and the contrasts between action research and conventional social science research.

The WRI has an institutional history and tradition of action research in work life that stretches back to the early 1960s, and personal contacts going back even further to American and British action research in the 1950s. Since the turn of the millennium, various ways of "turning to practice" has resurfaced as major concerns of organisational researchers, but apparently without relating to the history and practice of action research. This has made it incumbent on some of us to include the much earlier turn to practice by action research in the discussion.

The first volume on organisation theory was written entirely by researchers from the WRI. In this book, however, we have extended the reach in perspectives by including researchers from other institutions and countries. We are grateful to ISEOR (Socio-Economic Institute of Firms and Organisations, Lyon) for having made us aware of each other, and for providing the opportunity to share experiences and reflect on a number of common dilemmas. Our shared reflections first began at a joint ISEOR and Academy of Management conference in 2007 where many of the following chapters were either best paper winners or nominees. It continued between several of us at the critically important action research track at the conferences arranged by the European Group of Organisation Studies (EGOS) in Bergen in 2007 and in Vienna in 2008. Several of the Norwegian contributors have also re-settled in other institutions than the WRI since the work started. Still, the book reflects the continuous action research concerns springing from our in many ways unique action research experiences at the WRI.

The chapters in this volume each represent specific blends of theories, research methods, and approaches. Each text presents a solution to an experience-based research challenge. However, despite the different national contexts, project designs, and local organisational priorities, the contributions circle around the same dilemmas. How to develop alternatives to the empiricist/positivist bias of management studies? How to move beyond both interpretive and explanatory spectator research? How to devise methods that actually support both practical change and creation of valid knowledge? How to include local knowledge in the research process? Although we have neither sought for common points of reference nor for any general consensus among the contributors, the extensive commensurability of the different contributions stems from the fact that all contributors have an interest in developing actionable knowledge and research methods that can actually contribute relevantly and validly to the concerns of practitioners.

There is something in the constitution of research in general that generates the need to develop our research methods along the lines described above. Differently from much US-based organisational research, we do not search for one best research practice that will eventually emerge as *the* solution to challenges of organisational development and change. These challenges are too complex and dependent on institutional and current settings to be grasped by any one unitary medium. We follow a more context-dependent and pluralistic European approach, to which the form and content of this book attests.

As editors, we would like to thank each other and all the contributors for prolonged patience and efforts in writing and in awaiting the final results. Stig Oppedal has done an excellent and extraordinary job with the proofs, correcting much more than errors of spelling. Our final thanks go to the staff and co-researchers at the WRI, without whose support we could not have finished this book.

Benedicte Brøgger and Olav Eikeland

The contributors

Lucia Alcántara is a seasoned independent consultant with expertise in knowledge management, organizational capacity building, and social development in government, private, and public organizations. As an educational facilitator, she has taught management and multi-cultural relations at Cornell University and Russell Sage College, respectively. She holds a bachelor's degree from the Maxwell School at Syracuse University, a Masters in Public Administration from Baruch College and a Doctorate in Adult Learning and Leadership from Columbia University's Teachers College. E-mail: lalcantara422@gmail.com.

Marie-José Avenier is Research Professor at CERAG, the University of Grenoble Institute for Management Research. She obtained an M.A. in Economics and a PhD in Applied Mathematics from the University of California (Berkeley). She also holds a Doctorate in Economics from the University of Aix-en-Provence. Her research interests are strategic management and complexity, epistemology of management research, and interpretive research methods. E-mail: avenier@free.fr.

Benedicte Brøgger is a postdoctoral fellow at the Norwegian School of Management BI. She also has an affiliation with the Work Research Institute, Oslo. She has a doctoral degree (*Dr. polit.*) in social anthropology from the University of Oslo. Her research interests are social and cultural conditions for (economic) growth. E-mail: benedicte.brogger@bi.no.

David Coghlan is a faculty member of the School of Business, Trinity College Dublin and is a Fellow of the College. He is currently on the editorial reviews boards of *Action Research, Journal of Applied Behavioral Science, Action Learning: Research and Practice, Systemic Practice and Action Research,* and *Journal of Management Education.* The 3rd edition of his popular book *Doing Action Research in Your Own Organization* (Sage) is due to be published in late 2009. E-mail: dcoghlan@tcd.ie.

Trine Deichman-Sørensen is a postdoctoral fellow at Akershus University College, Norway. Previously she was senior researcher at the Work Research Institute, Oslo, working on issues related to work-based learning. Current research interests are novel forms of apprenticeship training, including changes in system regulations as well as orders of learning. E-mail: Trine.Deichman-Sorensen@hiak.no

Olav Eikeland is research director and professor of education and work research at the Akershus University College, Norway. He holds a doctoral degree (*Dr. philos.*)

in philosophy. From 1985 to 2008 he worked as a researcher and research director at the Work Research Institute. His special interest is the relevance of ancient dialogical philosophy for action research and organisational learning, and for the emerging "new production of knowledge". In 2008 he published the book: *The Ways of Aristotle – Aristotelian Phrónêsis, Aristotelian Philosophy of Dialogue, and Action Research,* Peter Lang. E-mail: oleik@online.no.

Siw M. Fosstenløkken is a senior researcher at the Work Research Institute in Oslo. She has a doctoral degree (*Dr. oecon.*) in strategy from the Norwegian School of Management BI. Her current focus is on organization development through innovation, learning, and collaboration. E-mail: siw.fosstenlokken@afi-wri.no.

Rickie A. Moore earned his Doctorate in Management Sciences & Socio-Economic Management, Lyon. He is a Professor of Entrepreneurship, Strategic Management, and Management Consulting, an Associate Professor at EMLYON Business School, Lyon, and currently an Associate Researcher at ISEOR (Socio-Economic Institute of Firms and Organisations), Lyon. He has just co-edited *Board Members and Management Consultants: Redefining the Boundaries of Consulting and Corporate Governance* for Information Age Publishing. E-mail: moore@em-lyon.com.

Jarle Moss Hildrum is a postdoctoral fellow at the University of Oslo and a senior researcher at the Work Research Institute. He holds a doctoral degree (*Dr. polit.*) in innovation studies from the Centre for Technology, Innovation and Culture at the University of Oslo. His research focuses on innovation and organization development processes within inter-firm networks. E-mail: jarle.hildrum@afi-wri.no.

Lars Klemsdal is a senior researcher at the Work Research Institute in Oslo. He holds a PhD in management and organization theory from the Norwegian University of Technology and Science (NTNU). His research interests include the sociology of knowledge and organization science. E-mail: lars.klemsdal@afi-wri.no.

Aoife McDermott is a lecturer in Human Resource Management at Dublin City University Business School and is co-director of the health service management stream of the Learning, Innovation and Knowledge Research Centre at DCU. She holds a PhD from Trinity College Dublin. E-mail: aoife.mcdermott@dcu.ie.

Michel Peron is Emeritus Professor at the University of Sorbonne Nouvelle-Paris 3. He received his PhD from the University of Lyon. He is currently a researcher at ISEOR (Socio-Economic Institute of Firms and Organisations), Lyon and CERVEPAS (Centre for European Research on the Economic Life of Anglo-Saxon

Countries), Paris. He authored and co-authored numerous books and articles with special interest in cross-cultural management, corporate responsibility, business ethics, and the history of economic ideas, coupled with in-depth lexicological research.

Øyvind Pålshaugen holds a doctoral degree (*Dr. philos.*) in sociology from the University of Oslo and is currently research director at the Work Research Institute, Oslo. He is co-editor of *International Journal of Action Research*. Current research interests may be illustrated by the publications "Discourse Democracy at Work - on Public Spheres in Private Enterprises", (*Concepts and Transformation* (2002), and "Reading and Writing as Performing Arts – at Work" (Göranzon, B., Hammarén, M., Ennals, R. (eds) (2006), *Dialogue, skill and tacit knowledge*. Wiley. E-mail: oeyvind.paalshaugen@afi-wri.no.

List of figures

Introduction

Benedicte Brøgger & Olav Eikeland

One of the perennial challenges for modern social science since its inception as an emulation of natural science has been the relationship between "theory" and "practice". More specifically, the relevance of social science theory for the social practice dealt with by this theory has been questioned repeatedly, especially by people outside the guild of professional social theorists but increasingly also by social researchers themselves. This question does not emerge in the same way for natural science, since in social research the known (people) are also knowers, while in natural science the known are *not* knowers in the same way, or more adequately expressed: the objects known in natural science are complete "incommunicados" outside the communicative reach of human researchers, while the human subjects of social research do have something in common with the researchers that can, or could, be shared.

The theories of natural science do not need to be relevant for the objects known (a meaningless request) as long as they make the researchers, i.e. the knowers, able to predict and control (manipulate) those objects in technically better ways. For those known by social research this is altogether different. In a way, natural scientists act on behalf of mankind. It is relatively obvious that advanced natural scientists are pioneers at the frontiers of human knowledge of things that are at the edge of the shared or potentially shared human world (in time and space, micro and macro). Not so in social research, however, since the non-professional human subjects of social research even have their own theories about things happening and things they do, theories that compete with the theories of the social researchers.

This problematique is the broad and recurring background for what seems to be a new and emerging – or merely resurfacing – wave of concern about practice, especially in organization theory and management studies (seen in the Academy of Management, in the European Group of Organization Studies, and in other places). The call is either for a "turn to practice" (e.g. Schatzki and Knorr-Cetina, 2001; Gherardi, 2000; Nicolini et al. 2003, Cunliffe and Easterby-Smith, 2004, Gherardi, 2006; Antonacopoulou, 2008) or for more "actionable" or "practicable" knowledge (cf. e.g. Argyris, 1993, 1996; Reason and Torbert, 2001), although the meaning of these terms is not always clear. These broader, mainstream scenarios also form the background for this book.

The more specific and immediate source of interest for practice comes from action research, however. In the conventional scheme of the social sciences, action research appears as matter out of place between the clearly defined research methods of social science at the academic core, and the equally well defined leadership and organization development and social change efforts that have taken place in the heartland of practice. This position betwixt and between has long been a headache for action researchers. No definite conclusions or agreements on solutions have been reached, but the efforts have produced a large literature on practice that may aid in the recent turn to practice in other fields of research. The two editions of the Handbooks of Action Research provide good overviews of the main strands of the discussions (Reason and Bradbury, 2001, 2007). Although action research is a diverse approach in itself, its common denominator is at least that the different varieties have somehow broken off from mainstream social research and "turned to practice" through several waves over the last 60 years at least.

Over these years, a number of critical charges have been directed at action research. For example, it does not try to establish causal relationships between variables in a test of hypotheses, it is merely "applied research" not "basic research", it is merely a problem solving strategy, without being descriptive and conclusion-oriented, and without trying to generalize. In addition, academically oriented researchers have accused action researchers of not documenting their research sufficiently, making "proper" reliability testing impossible. It is supposedly "sloppy research". Action researchers have also been accused of not relating their work to that of the rest of the research community. Action researchers on their part have countered the charges in two main manners: either through elaborations of the epistemological foundations of action research (Dewey 1989, 2007, 2008; Freire 1970; Habermas 2002; Lewin 2008; Reason and Bradbury 2001, 2007), or by pointing out the difference that action research makes in the practical world (Coghlan and Brannick 2004; Greenwood and Lewin 2006; Gustavsen 1992; Munn-Giddings and Winter 2001; Whyte and Whyte 2001), to mention but a few influential works.

This book approaches the problematique from a somewhat different angle. Instead of discussing action research only on its own terms or only on the terms of conventional science, we use our situated view from action research and explore other discourses on theory and practice in social and organization science. The aim is to contrast and compare in order to draw out lessons that are critical for understanding practice at many levels. The contributions in this volume range from critical evaluations of epistemological foundations and the practice of thinking and writing, to empirical discussions of collaborative sensemaking and the practical impact of research. Each chapter can be read as an independent contribution in itself. At the same time, the chapters complement each other and add to a complex account of what practice is and means – as theory or in practice. The aim of this book, then, is to contribute to our knowledge about theorizing as a form of practice and how practice is informed by theory, and how different theory-practice mixes affect the world of work.

Even though the recent "turn to practice" provides opportunities to approach the theory-practice challenge in new ways, the issues are not new. They have informed action research since it was first conceptualized as a research approach, and they must be thematized every time research is done. In the following first section of this introduction we outline its conceptualizations in the history of action research. In the second section we explicate what it means that research is also a practice. The third section discusses the interdependency between social research and social change, and dilemmas that emerge when research methods are also change methods. The individual contributions to the book are presented in the last section of the introduction.

60 years of action research

Internationally, the 60 years history of action research can be divided into at least two separate phases or waves both in time and in self-understanding (cf. Eikeland, 2006). The first wave lasted from the 1940s to the mid-1960s. Action research was originally conceived as an extension and development of mainstream experimental research inspired by John Dewey's pragmatism and instigated by Kurt Lewin. The first wave thought of itself as an extension of "the scientific attitude" and an expansion of experimental practice from laboratories to everyday activities like work places, schools, and local communities in an undeterred, progressive spirit of enlightenment. This was the self-conception of the first wave of action research. It bred several new disciplines like OD, group dynamics, and evaluation research, before ebbing out in the 1960s. Although springing from the same roots of experiementalism, action research has gradually separated from "quasi-experimentation" as a tendency to think that people could be experimented with or researched "upon" as if they were objects in nature.

The second wave of action research started in the 1970s, mostly without direct continuity with the first wave. Instead of thinking of itself as an extension of a unified science, the second wave was strongly influenced by the counter-cultural impulse within the radicalism of the 1970s, by the anti-positivist winds within the academic world, and by a philanthropic radicalism wanting to serve "the interests of the people" rather than established interests of business and politics. Without any mutual coordination, parallel groups of action researchers seem to have popped up in different places from the general counter-cultural climate of the 1970s. This created action research as an uncoordinated counter-cultural movement in many countries creating a life for itself apart from and as an unmediated alternative to established approaches. Both waves of action research have promoted democratic values. But particularly since the 1970s, action research has developed in more participatory directions, in which participants experiment and explore together what goes on and what to do in order to improve their practices.

Although influential in its ways, action research has a long history of being an outsider in relation to mainstream social science approaches. And although initiated by people like Kurt Lewin and others who were well established and integrated in mainstream social research in the 1940s and 1950s, action research soon became condemned "to a sort of orphan's role in the social sciences shortly after World War II" (Cunningham, 1993:3f) by mainstreamers eager to retain the detached and disengaged purity of science.

In several ways, this was a paradox. One of the most influential and prestigious books on mainstream social research methods – reprinted in many editions over more than 50 years – was initiated by the same circle of authors (Jahoda, Deutsch, Cook, Chein, Festinger, Selltiz, Wormser) around Kurt Lewin that initiated action research in the 1940s. These people were the contributors to the first edition of SPSSI's (Society for the Psychological Study of Social Issues) "Research Methods in Social Relations" from 1951 (Jahoda et al., 1951). In this first edition, the connecting lines to action research are easy to trace. As shown by Eikeland (1998), they are considerably harder to identify in later editions (e.g. Selltiz et al., 1976; Judd et al., 1991).

Other handbooks on social science research methods either do not mention action research at all (Kuper and Kuper, 1998), reduce action to a theoretical concern (Turner, 2006), or, most commonly, they define it as one among many conventional research methods (Birchman and Rog, 1998). Either way, the originality of the action research approach, and the epistemological and practical positioning that provides action research with much of its generative potential for making a difference in practice, disappear from sight.

The practice of social research

Although natural science took the hint from Francis Bacon 400 years ago and became experimental, social research has mostly retained the much older ideal of not influencing its subjects of study. The rationale for this has mainly been that the knowledge sought was knowledge of how things were "naturally", not how they were under some artificial, external influence. Science seeks to understand the "nature" of it subjects of study. Hence, mainstream social science wanted to study societies, groups, and individuals as these subjects of study were by themselves, not only what they seemed to be under the artificial influence of researchers as manipulators, not tainted by the accidental subjective views of peculiar researchers.

18

In addition, the ethical scruples with manipulating human beings and social phenomena have been paramount. But both spectator "idols" and manipulation of the objects of study might create distorted views.

Hence, experimentation has not really become comfortably integrated into mainstream social research. Instead, research methods were for many years carefully devised in order to be unobtrusive and *not* make any practical difference. The effects on the subjects of study of the research activities and the researchers should be eliminated or neutralized. Until recently, this notion has been dominant; witness all the precautions of mainstream methodology textbooks in this respect. Interpretive research approaches may have given up on the quest for finding an objective "view from nowhere in particular", from where those studied can be seen in an unbiased way. Just like anybody, every researcher is situated and positioned in special ways in particular places. As long as this is made explicit, however, it appears to be justified. Still, even interpretive methods are based on a separation between researchers and researched and on not influencing the subjects of study in ways that make their research unreliable.

This "qualitative" view, then, still appears to make methods of social *research* clearly distinguishable from methods of social *change*, even today after several decades of positivist critique. In trying to keep researchers and researched separate, mainstream social research has resorted to constructing formal models or to informal interpretive approaches. But what you see and interpret things *as* still depends on the eyes of the beholder. Intervention may be artificial and unethical. But non-intervention is necessarily referred to the hermeneutically prejudiced and "ideological" viewpoint or position of the observer. It is ultimately subjective, or at least positioned *somewhere* within e.g. a social, economical, psychological, organizational, and historical landscape, different from the world of those studied (cf. Eikeland, 2006).

The established distinctions between the researcher and the researched, and the researcher and the research, have hardly changed over the years, in spite of comprehensive discussions, and the notion of method as a mere tool has surfaced time and time again as the dust settled after the impacts of new theoretical understanding. One aspect of research has, however, become more salient, namely the understanding that any and every method actually does make a change. A questionnaire makes someone reflect on matters that they might not have considered were it not for the questionnaire, an interview does so in an even more profound way. A researcher in the field may try to pretend to be "a fly on the wall", but is made to be part of the local scene one way or the other. In all of social science, there is an increasing realization that there is no way a method can be used in the social world without making an impact beyond the narrowly defined one of a research tool. In this sense, research is revealed as not quite neutral and noninterfering after all. It cannot exist without any practical impact; it does not have to be without any impact; and ultimately, according to Lewin's Baconian dictum, it should not be without any practical impact.

Social science and social change

The question then becomes what practical consequences to draw from insights like the foregoing. Kurt Lewin is famous for the dictum that "in order to understand an organization you have to change it". His dictum contains two key elements: change methods and research methods. This means that not only is organizational content involved in research methods; change methods are involved as well. Neither change methods nor research methods are mere instruments, but neither are the two automatically the same and identical. Although both methods may create both knowledge and change, every change method is not automatically a research method, and every research method is not automatically a change method. Research methods are mostly devised not to make a difference. That they actually do appears as problematic. With change methods the problem is different. They are devised to make a difference, but *how* is knowledge from the process best gained, gathered, and systematized?

The question of how to change an organization can, of course, be answered simply by referring to some organization change method or other. But this alone is hardly an adequate or sufficient answer. Descriptions of technique address an instrumental aspect of method. From such a perspective, method can be likened to any tool, like a hammer or a spade. Tools are used for specific purposes, such as a hammer to nail a floor or a spade to dig a ditch. The normal *tool* is hardly a part of the knowledge needed to do the job, and it is definitely not a part of the result. When it has been used to finish a task, the tool can be put on a shelf and forgotten. Organizational development methods are often presented as tools like these, which in a sense they are, but they are also more than tools. They are intimately connected both with the knowledge regimes from which they emerge, and the contexts in which they are applied. They are part of the knowledge needed to finish the task, and, even more importantly, they often remain as part of the results, almost as "building blocks" of the organization. Organizational change methods involve substitutions, exchanges, and shifts of material resources, people, information, and so on. This makes them far more complex than extraneous instruments to be applied mechanically to a given task.

As anyone who has been a change agent knows, when a change process is in motion it quickly affects a wide range of tangible organizational givens, like buildings, machinery and capital. It also affects intangibles like hierarchies, habits, relationships, and accepted theories. Specific change methods produce specific rebuttals, and it is therefore next to impossible to discuss organizational development methods in the abstract. Still, organization development methods often come disguised as universals, as management systems that can be implemented anywhere or analytical models into which everything can be fitted.

A few examples will illustrate the point. For example, the Quality Circles of the 1970s, the Management by Objectives of the 1980s, the Total Quality Management of the 1990s (or its successor, Business Process Reengineering), and the "corporate religion" movement of the 2000s live on as remnants in the organizational set-up of many companies, but so transformed that they are hardly recognizable as the universals they started out as. They produced change, and were changed by it. And whenever a specific method is thus transformed, there is a new universal method waiting to be implemented. Overall it seems that the appetite for organizational development methods is huge, and the consumption is rapid. But the lessons learned, and the richness of the actual experiences of applying this or that method seems to be quickly forgotten.

As should be clear, the sheer difficulty of handling the multidimensionality of organizational development easily leads to a focus on the simplified "mechanics" and "universals" of change processes. This tendency is strengthened by the conventional idea of method as nothing but an instrument.

But Kurt Lewin's dictum above also challenges research methods that are not simultaneously change methods. If the dictum is true, we need to change things in order to understand them. This was actually the point made by Francis Bacon 400 years ago in promoting experimental research. As already pointed out by Aristotle (SE164a23-b28), mere external spectators are easily fooled by appearances, i.e. by Bacon's "idols" – of the race, of the individual, of the group, or of learned theories – that work as "ideology" hampering realism. In order to be able to see through the ideologically coloured appearances critically, some kind of practical acquaintance is needed with whatever is to be known.

But Lewin's dictum does not say that we should replace research methods for change methods. It does not say we should leave research methods behind. Somehow, knowledge generation needs change or practice, but it does not need just *any* change or practice. It needs something *in addition to* or some *special kind of* change and practice. Hence, the question is not simply "how should we change an organization". In our context it is: "How do we change an organization *in order to* learn as much and as well as possible from the process, in order to get to know the organization?" The challenge is not merely to change an organization, but how do we do research and produce valid and relevant knowledge by changing it or by gaining some kind of practical familiarity with it? The challenge concerns changing the organization *in order to* understand it better.

The contributions

Two main obstacles for the recent (re-)turn to practice, then, are how to deal with the practical consequences of theories of practice, and how to engage in understanding and change simultaneously. These challenges are interrelated. Insights gained from attempts to cope with the first obstacle, invariably inform attempts to deal with the second one, as will become clear from the contributions to this book.

The 10 chapters are grouped according to three main concerns. The first is conventional and not so conventional social science research methods. The second concerns development tools and techniques that at the same time add to the development of general or abstract theory. The third interest is critical comparison and contrasting of action research and prominent organization and social science discourses.

The first section consists of four chapters that deal with research methods explicitly. First, Eikeland's chapter provides epistemological reflection on the conditions for knowledge, and especially the question of validity more generally. Klemsdal and Brøgger's chapters, 2 and 3, analyse how the use of research methods contributes to local change, in other words, the local and not general validity of the knowledge gained. The main theme of Hildrum and Fosstenløkken's chapter is how a specific set of AR methods affects relationship building in network collaboration. Chapter 2, 3, and 4 are all based on a case study, from a municipality, an electronics company, and a network of eight process industry companies, respectively. In chapter 1, Eikeland makes use of an Aristotelian taxonomy to distinguish between different ways of knowing and operating in the world, and in subtle ways the case descriptions help flesh out this discussion, while at the same time each case gains deeper meaning when related to it.

The chapters in the second section address a range of development technologies applied in different institutional contexts ranging from the individual to the sectorial. The common theme is how practical knowledge can be translated to generic knowledge and vice versa. Hence, these chapters, although grounded in empirical work, approach the question of theorizing as practice. The context in Avenier's chapter 5 is the cycle of action and reflections of a top manager in a French company. The chapter presents a generative framework for developing epistemology from reflections on practice. In chapter 6, Peron and Moore present a unique methodology developed at ISEOR in Lyon, France. This is used to gain knowledge applicable for organizational development in individual enterprises *and* for statistical generalization about developmental patterns. Alcantara's chapter 7 thematizes action technologies as they are applied and understood in the context of the education sector in the USA.

The third section collects chapters that explicitly deal with theorizing on the logic and rationality of theories as they are applied in order to understand practice. Each chapter critically relates and deconstructs action research and related fields. These fields are processual approaches by Coghlan and McDermott in chapter 8, actor-network theory (ANT) discussed by Pålshaugen in chapter 9, and socio-technical principles by Deichman-Sørensen in chapter 10. From these chapters, insights emerge on the practical consequences of theories of practice.

Each chapter can be read for the specific insights it conveys, or the papers in each of the three sections may be read to gain a broader and more nuanced understanding of the more general theme of the section. The empirical chapters of the first group may be relevant to anyone interested in work life and industrial relations in Norway. Together with the chapters in the second group and chapter 8 and 10 of the third group, they provide a unique opportunity to compare situations in different European countries and the US. As a whole, the book provides a general overview of critical dilemmas in a (re-)turn to practice.

Section 1: Research practice, effect and validity

Chapter 1. Olav Eikeland: *Habitus-validity in organisational theory and research – social research and work life transformed.* This chapter introduces the concept of "*habitus*-validity", based on the Aristotelian concept of *habitus* or héxis, established within social research over the last decades through the influence of Pierre Bourdieu. Action research requires ways of thinking about validity different from and apparently incompatible with mainstream concepts of validity, whether quantitative, qualitative, explanatory, or interpretive. The article presents and discusses the role of *habitus*-validity in the development of both practical and theoretical knowledge. *Habitus*-validity tries to conceptualize knowledge validity in ways relevant for action research, especially for an action research strengthened through a critical confrontation with the requirements and shortcomings of mainstream research methods. The concept of *habitus* validity is presented as the outcome of such a critical confrontation or immanent critique. The discussion springs from the author's experience through more than 20 years of conducting projects in action research and organizational learning in Norwegian work life and an equivalent number of years of studying conventional methodology, epistemology, and philosophy of science critically.

Chapter 2. Lars Klemsdal: *Making sense of managerial reforms through action research.* The chapter brings together three different approaches to organizational change in order to let them enlighten each other mutually: first, a management reform to be implemented in a public sector organization; second, an action research strategy aiming to learn how processes of organizational development and change can be enhanced in constructive ways; third, a descriptive perspective on how processes of organizational change unfold on a micro level as *sensemaking*. The chapter argues in favour of combining managerial reforms with action research. The action research strategy that is developed is designed in order to address the challenges and possibilities of implementation of managerial reform as they appear through the lens of organizational change as sensemaking.

Chapter 3. Benedicte Brøgger: *Research and change – a comparison of action research and conventional social science research methods.* The key theme in this chapter is a comparison between action research and conventional social science research methods in how and at what level they effect change. The potential for change is identified by using Habermas' three categories of language, work, and power. In discourses on methodology, research methods are conceptualized as means to achieve a predefined end. In conventional social science, the end is knowledge; in action research, the end is the process of learning. In either case, the end is conceived of as being someplace else than the context in which the means are used. The approach in the chapter is somewhat different. The discussion concerns the transformative powers of research methods at the moment when they are neither means to an end, nor ends in themselves, but acts, performances. The action-learning approach of action research is contrasted and compared with the theory-data-method approach of conventional social science in order to better understand their (different) potential for transforming language, work, and relations of power. The discussion is grounded in case material from a development project in a Norwegian electronics company.

Chapter 4. Jarle M. Hildrum and Siw Fosstenløkken: *The action researcher as change agent: On dialogue facilitation and network collaboration.* This chapter illuminates a previously neglected aspect of *industrial action research* (IAR) by focusing on the ways in which the application of a specific set of AR methods affects relationship building in network collaboration. Drawing upon field experiences associated with one specific approach to action research – Industrial Action Research (IAR) – the authors seek to enhance our understanding of the action researcher as dialogue facilitator. The chapter also illuminates a previously neglected aspect of IAR by directing explicit attention to the ways in which the application of action research methods affects inter-community relationship building. The empirical material comes from an action-oriented research programme in the chemical process industry in a region of Norway.

Chapter 5. Marie-José Avenier: *A methodological framework for constructing generic knowledge with intended value both for academia and practice.* This chapter presents a framework for researchers seeking to construct actionable knowledge from practitioners' experience, i.e. knowledge that meets the dual objectives of rigor and relevance to management science *as well as* to management practice. It begins by presenting the notion of actionable knowledge and the constructivist theory of knowledge in which the framework has been developed. Then it provides an overview of the framework. The final discussion focuses on three main issues: the convoluted process by which the methodological framework progressively emerged in the course of doing collaborative research; the differing roles of practitioners and researchers in the various processes involved in the framework; and the position of the framework in the action research perspective.

Chapter 6. Rickie Moore and Michel Peron: *On the axiology and actionability of knowledge creation about organizations in management science research.* The topic of knowledge creation in management science sparks much debate. Knowledge creation and the usefulness and actionability of the research conducted are major subjects of contention. Within the academic community, there has been excessive normatization, inspired by "the hard sciences" approach, with regards to what constitutes knowledge, and the knowledge creation processes. Typical constructs and definitions have been extensively usurped but have been deprived of the richness of their value and abridged in their commonly referred meaning. The complex reality of organizations is often reduced to its simplest components within the pursuit of management research. This denaturing process raises a number of issues about the validity, pertinence, sensemaking, and applicability of the knowledge produced. In this chapter, the authors revisit and explain the axiology of epistemology, the ontology of organizations and the actionability of the knowledge produced in management sciences research. They support their arguments by highlighting the Qualimetrics approach – a balanced quantitative, qualitative, and financial perspective, developed and practised around the world by ISEOR, a Lyon-based French institute that specializes in management sciences research.

Chapter 7. Lucia Alcántara: *Creating practical and operational knowledge from action inquiry technologies.* This chapter offers insights into processes and outcomes associated with the creation of readily applicable knowledge from action inquiry technologies. Action inquiry technologies are a group of inquiry-based research methods which can be used to increase productivity through workplace learning projects, and which offer practitioners the opportunity to support and transform practice, as well as skill development, with timely approaches grounded in lived experiences. A comparative case study of two distinct action inquiry technology programmes is presented. The highly relevant and timely natures of these new understandings develop into readily operational knowledge the moment they are applied in practice or personal domains. Implications for practice and methods are also discussed.

Section 3. On the rationality of theories – critical perspectives

Chapter 8. David Coghlan and Aoife McDermott: *Creating value for scholars and practitioners: Lessons from organization development through action research and the processual approach.* In 2001 in a leading article in the *Academy of Management Journal*, Pettigrew, Woodman, and Cameron commented on the state of the field of researching organizational change. They noted the fragmentation of approaches and some of the difficulties in capturing the dynamism that change involves. They presented partnership between scholars and practitioners as a key challenge and concluded with a call for a new pluralism in the study of organizational change. In response, this chapter considers two approaches to researching change which take account of these factors, albeit in different manners: processual research and organization development through action research. In exploring two approaches which can create valuable academic and actionable knowledge, the purpose of the chapter is to provide insight into research that can create and provide value to both practitioners and academics. The two approaches explored have different understandings of actionable knowledge; respectively focused on generating generalizable guidelines for future action (processual), and real-time guidance for ongoing change (action research). In exploring the implications of pursuing each type of actionable knowledge, the chapter explicates the trade-offs which arise in the nature of the academic-practitioner relationship and the form of actionable knowledge produced. Whilst the two approaches explored have underlying philosophical differences and will never merge, comparison provides valuable insights into the choices facing researchers in designing and undertaking change-related research which creates value for both scholars and practitioners.

Chapter 9. Øyvind Pålshaugen: *The stalemate of organization theory: Ever new frameworks, never new methods – may Actor-Network Theory provide an exception to this rule?* The starting point for Pålshaugen's chapter is the richness in general perspectives and concepts within the discourse on organizations. Nevertheless, this discourse remains too poor in content. Viewed from the experiences and perspectives of action research, this paucity seems to be due to the restricted scope of methods applied in organization studies, and the tiny amount of data they produce. On this background, the following question is posed: Do the theoretical frameworks of organization theory contribute to placing organizational research "outside" the real dynamics of organizations? To test this thesis, several organization studies based on one of the theoretical frameworks which recently has become rather widely applied – the actor-network theory (ANT) of Bruno Latour and others – are subjected to a critical reading.

Chapter 10. Trine Deichman-Sørensen: *Boundary Learning – Work complexities and reflexive practice in action research.* The discussion in Deichman-Sørensen's chapter is based on case material from a network of Norwegian electronics companies. An action research project was set up in order to promote learning between the participating companies, but partly because it was unable to adjust appropriately, the project petered out. In order to make sense of the project experiences, three different theoretical approaches are compared, by Øyvind Pålshaugen, Yrjö Engeström, and Philip Herbst, respectively. The learning experiences from the project were rather unexpected and "non-linear". Deichman-Sørensen criticizes both Pålshaugen's and Engeström's approaches for not really providing space for this kind of unplanned and non-linear learning, and recommends a re-reading of the earlier contributions from Herbst as providing a more adequate understanding.

References

Antonacopoulou, E. (2008), "On the Practise of Practice: In-tensions and Ex-tensions in the Ongoing Reconfiguration of Practices", pp. 112-131 in D.Barry and H.Hansen (eds.), *New Approaches in Management and Organization*, Los Angeles: Sage

Argyris, C. (1993), *Knowledge for Action: A Guide to Overcoming Barriers to Organizational Change*, San Francisco: Jossey-Bass

Argyris, C. (1996), "Actionable Knowledge: Intent versus Actuality", *Journal of Applied Behavioral Science*, 32 (4): 441-444

Aristotle (1955), *Sophistici Elenchi (SE) – Sophistical Refutations*, Loeb Classical Library, Cambridge, MA: Harvard University Press

Bickman, L. and Rog, D.J. (eds.) (1998), *Handbook of applied social research methods.* Thousand Oaks, California: Sage.

Coghlan, D. and Brannick, T. (2004), *Doing research in your own organization.* London: Sage

Cunliffe, A. L. & Easterby-Smith, M. (2004), "From Reflection to Practical Reflexivity: Experiential Learning as Lived Experience", pp. 30–46 in *Organizing Reflection*. Reynolds, Michael & Vince, Russ (eds.) (2004) Aldershot: Ashgate Publishing.

Cunningham, J. B. (1993), *Action Research and Organizational Development*. Westport, Connecticut: Preager.

Dewey, J. (2008) [1916], *Democracy and education: an introduction to the philosophy of education*. Book Jungle, originally New York: Macmillan.

Dewey, J. (2007) [1929], *Experience and nature*. Lightning Source UK.

Dewey, J. (1989) [1939], *Freedom and culture*. Buffalo, NY: Prometheus Books.

Eikeland, O. (1998), *Faglige metamorfoser og immanente konvergenser – opptakt til et nytt kunnskapsforvaltningsregime*, AFI-notat 5/98, Oslo: Work Research Institute

Eikeland, O. (2006), "The Validity of Action Research – Validity in Action Research", pp. 193-240 in Aagaard Nielsen, K. and Svensson, L. (eds.) (2006): *Action And Interactive Research – Beyond Theory and Practice*, Maastricht and Aachen: Shaker Publishing

Freire, P. (1970), *Pedagogy of the oppressed*. New York: Continuum.

Gherardi, S. (2000), "Practice-based Theorizing on Learning and Knowing in Organizations", *Organization*, 7(2): 211–223

Gherardi, S. (2006), *Organizational Knowledge: The Texture of Organizing*, London: Blackwells

Greenwood, D. and Levin, M. (2006), *Introduction to Action Research: Social Research for Social Change*. London: Sage.

Gustavsen, B. (1992). *Dialogue and development*. Assen/Maastricht: van Gorcum and Stockholm: The Swedish Center for Working Life.

Habermas, J. (2002) [1971], *Knowledge and human interests*. Boston: Beacon Press.

Jahoda, M.; Deutsch, M. and Cook, S.W. (1951), *Research Methods in Social Relations – with especial reference to prejudice*, 1st Edition, New York: The Dryden Press.

Judd, C. M.; Smith, E.R and Kidder, L.H. (1991), *Research Methods in Social Relations*, 6th Edition, Forth Worth: Hartcourt Brace Jovanovich College Publihers

Kuper, A. and Kuper, J. (1998), *The social science encyclopedia*. London: Routledge.

Lewin, K. (2008) [1948], *Resolving social conflicts & Field theory in social science*. Washington DC: American Psychological Association.

Munn-Giddings, C. and Winter, R. (2001), *A Handbook for Action Research in Health and Social Care*. With contributions by Cathy Aymer, Peter Beresford, Jane Bradburn, Valerie Childs, Brenda Dennett, Philip Ingram, Philip Kemp, Noreen Kennedy, Richard Lawrence, Cherry Mackie, Vicky Nicholls, Fergal Searson, Michael Turner and Yan Weaver. New York: Routledge.

Nicolini, D. et al. (2003), *Knowing in Organizations: A Practice-Based Approach*, London: M.E. Sharpe

Reason, P. and Bradbury, H. (eds.) (2001): *Handbook of Action Research – Participative Inquiry and Practice*. 1st Edition, London: Sage

Reason, P. and Bradbury, H. (eds). (2007), *Handbook of Action Research – Participative Inquiry and Practice*. 2nd Edition, London: Sage.

Reason, P. and Torbert, W. R. (2001), "The Action Turn – Toward a Transformational Social Science", *Concepts and Transformation*, 6(1): 1-37

Schatzki, T. et al. (2001), *The Practice Turn in Contemporary Theory*, London: Routledge.

Selltiz, C.; Wrightsman, L.S. and Cook, S.W. (1976), *Research Methods in Social Relations*, 3rd Edition, New York: Holt, Rinehart & Winston

Turner, B. (2006), *The Cambridge Dictionary of Sociology*. Cambridge: Cambridge University Press.

Whyte, W.F. and Whyte, K.E. (1991), *Making Mondragon: The Growth and Dynamics of the Worker Cooperative Complex*. ILR Press.

Section 1: Research practice, effect and validity

1 Habitus-Validity in Organisational Theory and Research – Social Research and Work Life Transformed[1]

Olav Eikeland

Introduction

In this chapter I will present and discuss the role of what I believe we could call *"habitus*-validity" in the development and enactment of both practical and theoretical knowledge. The discussion springs from a long-term concern with the role of learning, understanding, and knowledge in organisational settings. What follows may seem theoretical. In some ways it certainly is but not in the most predominant, fashionable, and conventional sense of "theory". The viewpoints I present spring equally from my accumulated and elaborated practical experience since the early 1980s from doing action research in Norwegian work life, and from a corresponding number of years studying conventional methodology and epistemology critically (cf. e.g. Eikeland 1985a, 1986, 1995, 1997, 1998, 2008).

My starting point for thinking about validity is the discussion in Eikeland (2006a). Descriptions, arguments, inferences, concepts, interpretations, explanations, predictions, and conclusions all seem to need validity in the sense of being well grounded on principles or evidence, and able to withstand criticism or objection; so do practices, competencies, and skills. Validity concerns the *status* of *any* arguments and points of view, or, of any practice, competence, and skill, as somehow providing insight into, or mastery of something, that is *better* or more adequate than any arbitrary practice, habit, or opinion about the same thing. Hence, validity is not arbitrary or merely descriptive, just registering what some people in some context happen to accept as the current opinion or established practice. Validity needs justifications, legitimacy, and competence. It is normative, prescriptive, and critically argumentative (discursive), specifying what should and should not rightfully count as standards of truth, justice, fairness, beauty, adequacy, and similar normative dimensions.

Briefly stated, then, the concept of *habitus*-validity tries to grasp and express the structure of a specific *kind* of theoretical and practical knowledge which is genuinely *suited* and *adjusted* to the task, situation, and context at hand – that is, knowledge that "belongs" or "hits the target" in the context. As such, it answers

---

1 This chapter has been partly written within the strategic research programme (2003-2007) at the WRI, Oslo.

to the widespread current call within management and organisation studies for "practicable" or "actionable" knowledge (cf. e.g. Argyris, 1993, 1996; Reason and Torbert, 2001) and for "turning to practice" (e.g. Schatzki et al., 2001; Gherardi, 2000; Nicolini et al. 2003, Cunliffe and Easterby-Smith, 2004, Gherardi, 2006; Antonacopoulou, 2008). For reasons to be presented, recent socio-economic developments also seem to require more "*habitus*-valid" knowledge.

The question is, of course, whether a concept like "*habitus*-validity" is possible or meaningful at all. Current intellectual fashion sometimes seems to imply that every act of cognition could, or even must be understood as the application of a metaphor, that is, as a transfer of meaning to the here-and-now, from something else somewhere else. Metaphors do not really belong *here*. They are brought here – as similes – from somewhere else. Hence, if every cognition can be reduced to a metaphor, knowledge that really belongs as more adequate to *this* situation here and now might be hard to defend principally and enact practically. Then, knowing and understanding what happens here and now, seems to stop at a multitude of metaphors, parallels, and analogies transferred or projected as perspectives from different and particular exterior positions and points of view. Ultimately, only knowing from the outside seems possible. But if *everything* is attempted reduced to metaphors – i.e. that *everything* has to be understood analogically as referred to something else in virtue of its similarity to that something else, *as if* it were something else – an endless regression results.[2]

Metaphors play an important role in *conventional* explanations of phenomena. And they can certainly be useful, revealing, and quite fun in reducing the unknown to something better known, or the "all-too-well-known" and familiar to something new, surprising, and unfamiliar. But they are hardly the whole story concerning concepts, method, and epistemology. Their murkier side is what the scholastics talked about as to explain *obscurum per obscurius*, i.e. explaining something obscure by means of something even more obscure. Metaphors can also be quite misleading if the internal logic of the transferred concepts blocks the view to the present phenomena. Avoiding such bewildering conceptual transmutations has been an important subject in the phenomenological movement of the 20th century and forms the background for the sceptical epokhê or "bracketing" required by

---

2   This is why Aristotle (APo72b5-25, 99b20-100b16) pointed out that basic principles had to be known differently, by means of a kind of knowledge (gnôsis) different from deduction (apódeixis and epistêmê). Strangely, perhaps, the emphasis on metaphor seems to be something scientism or "positivism" and post-modernism ultimately have in common since they both seem to operate with the same concept of science and explanation, the one in favour of it, the other sceptical. Cf. Vaihinger (1924), Hesse (1963), Fiumara (1995).

Edmund Husserl (1936) in order to let the "life-world" appear and become visible from the fog of alien concepts.

Any current utilisation or discussion of the concept of *habitus* has to refer to Bourdieu (1977). As documented and discussed thoroughly by Funke (1961), however, and recognised by Bourdieu (cf. Broady, 1990:236ff.), *habitus* (Latin), héxis (Greek) and related concepts pertaining to gradually acquired habits, routines, dispositions, and inclinations have a very long and continuous history in Western intellectual history, going back to Plato and Aristotle. In explaining and understanding what is implied in "*habitus*-validity", concepts like "topographies" and "grammar" will also be involved in the following discussion, partly inspired by Heidegger (cf. e.g. Malpas, 1999, 2006) and Wittgenstein (cf. e.g. Descombes, 1986, Soulez, 2004) respectively. But although these concepts have their modern theoretical sources, they all hark back to origins within the thinking of Aristotle more than 2300 years ago (cf. Eikeland, 2008).

Habitus-validity is clearly relevant for professional and vocational competence in any field, particularly connected to the current revival of apprenticeship models of learning (Lave and Wenger, 1991; Ainley and Rainbird, 1999; Nielsen and Kvale, 1999 and 2003). In addition, but maybe less obviously, it is relevant for social theory and research in general, and for organisational knowing in particular. An appropriate justification of the concept can hardly be made, however, without indicating how the "normal science" of social research is inadequate. Although what currently passes as "normal" social science has become quite diverse, its basic "form" still has to transform in order to utilise such a concept and to make space for it to unfold. Mainstream social science concepts and divisions between "theory", "method", and "data", between "basic" and "applied" research, and between researchers and researched need to be reconfigured at a quite basic level. To put it somewhat squarely, *habitus*-validity requires a certain kind of action research, that is, a *practitioner* or praxis-research. Furthermore, this action research needs to be nourished and strengthened through an immanently critical confrontation (*Auseinandersetzung* in German) with the requirements and shortcomings, the inner tensions and contradictions of mainstream research approaches, transforming and transcending them from within, based in a radical self-reflection on their ways of doing things (cf. Eikeland, 1997:263ff., 2006a, 2008; Kuhlmann, 1985).

Ultimately, this is how the relevance of the concept for mainstream social research can and should be shown. Such elaborations imply a simultaneous critical suspension of mainstream research approaches, divisions, and institutionalisations, and their subsequent and simultaneous transformation *into* and retention *within* such a "reinforced" action research; a process captured in the dialectical German concept of *Aufhebung* but hardly possible to express succinctly in English. The point is: in order to utilise the concept of *habitus*-validity appropriately, mainstream conventional social research has to transform, in order to save it from itself, i.e. from its inherent self-deconstructive or even self-destructive tendencies, brought to the fore by various critiques; Marxist, feminist, phenomenological, hermeneutical, post-modern, etc.

There are, of course, also many varieties of action research, with equally varied relationships to epistemology and research methods (cf. Eikeland, 2006a). Many of these, often thinking of themselves as no more than applied social research, can hardly sustain such a concept of *habitus*-validity. On a general level, the immanently critical confrontation just mentioned constitutes a dialogical or dialectical process of validation leading up to or revealing "*habitus*-validity" as a necessary constituent of praxis research. Inspired by Hegel's *Phenomenology of Spirit*, I have presented several such dialectical validation-itineraries, pointing towards an emergent *habitus*-validity (in Eikeland, 1985a, 1995, 2006, cf. also Reinharz, 1979). They all point towards what I have called *the methods of methodology* as the most valid and validity securing form of *action* or *practitioner* research, actually even as a most valid and validity securing form of transformed *empirical* social research. But since the methods of methodology are usually thought of as neither empirical nor action-oriented, such a claim may appear somewhat preposterous or, at least, rather theoretical.

Philosophically, "induction" – i.e. somehow generating concepts, theories, explanations, and interpretations "bottom up" and "upwards" from below – is currently a concept held in low esteem. Both plebeian and aristocratic induction (Laudan, 1981:73f.), e.g. both universalising the regularity of the sun rising in the east and setting in the west (plebeian), and trying to infer a theoretical explanation of such extremely regular events from these facts themselves (aristocratic), are generally dismissed in modern philosophy of science as logically untenable. But "induction" is not necessarily restricted to *enumerative* induction, i.e. merely making empirical generalisations about non-essential properties from a number of singular observations (cf. Eikeland, 1997, 1998). Although the following two can hardly be held strictly separate, "from below" in the *present* context means not primarily a) from the knower's extraneous impressions and sense data (*perceptual* observations), but b) from within different forms of the knower's own practice and practically accumulated experience (*practical* observations). Although explanatory and interpretive theories of a certain kind may be inspired and spring from any wild idea, as pointed out by Popper (1980), emerging concepts – the building blocks of theories – are primarily generated from practices as grasped activities at different levels, not from contemplative and distant sense perceptions in isolation.

An *epistemological* turn to practice, then, must mean turning your mind's eye and attention (as an observant practitioner) towards patterns and structures emerging in and from your (and, importantly, from *our*) own practice as knowers, whatever that practice is. Such a practical turn cannot mean merely turning your physical gaze more "close-up" and intensely towards the practices of others. Hence, with such modifications, the present article is an exploration of the necessity, but also of the limits and possibilities of knowledge generation processes working "inductively" from below, since knowledge that "belongs" or "hits the target" must somehow spring from or be adjusted to "the below" here and now.

Setting the Stage

Before proceeding, some preliminary distinctions must be emphasised. They may seem trivial and self-evident. But evident distinctions like these often hide important insights when taken uncritically for granted, as <u>doxa</u>. Conventional social research, whether qualitative or quantitative, operates with a basic trichotomy between 1) "data", "observations", or "experience", 2) "theory", and 3) "methodology" (cf. Eikeland, 1986). These distinctions are internal to any research practice. The different, more general distinction and often bemoaned discrepancy between "theory" and "practice", however, concerns mostly the relations between the end-products of social research and everyday social or political practice; i.e. the external relations of social research, "*post factum*" to its performance. Still, it is internal to *all* professional practice, even to research practice as between normative and descriptive methodology.

Within the trichotomy of conventional social research, then, the "data" and "observations" are what *need* explanation. In the technical terminology of the philosophy of science, they are called *explananda*. "Theories", however, are what explain the observations and data. Accordingly, they are called *explanans*. In less formalised work, corresponding terms could be *interpretanda* (what's being interpreted) and *interpretans* (the interpreting *as*). The basic starting point for conventional research is that some until now presumably badly understood phenomena or processes in nature or society are in *need* of explanation or interpretation.[3]

---

3   "Everything" cannot need explanation all the time. This fact raises questions like "*who* needs this explanation and for what purpose"? In some areas there are clear frontiers of knowledge and competence, e.g. concerning how to travel in outer space, how to manipulate and understand the smallest particles of matter, how to explain the mounting positive evidence for ESP- / psi-phenomena (cf. Radin, 2006), etc. Very few people are able to and allowed to reach most of these frontiers, always *through* specific theories and specific technologies. These pioneers are the *first* human beings to visit these frontiers. But as emphasized in Eikeland (1997:16-17), conventional social researchers working within established divisions of labour, are *never* the first humans arriving. They are

Finally, in this jargon of distinctions, "methods" are rules and procedures for collecting relevant "data" as perceptual observations and bits of information about such phenomena, and for connecting theory and data in valid and reliable ways. The discourse exploring, discussing, and justifying different ways of doing certain things properly or improperly, i.e. what methods to use most appropriately for what purposes, is called "methodology". While data and observations indicate the "what" studied, theories are "things" or "tools" (concepts, statements, assertions, symbols, etc. mostly seen as springing from a different source) *used* to explain, to interpret, or to make sense of the "what" studied. Methodology, however, indicates the *activities* proper to social research, namely its practice; the "how-to-do-it". Hence, methodology is actually the master discipline here; relating, connecting, and ordering the other two parts properly.

In addition to this trichotomy, and for complex reasons based partly on specific, inherited concepts of "theory" and the emulation of modern natural science, conventional social research operates with a fundamental segregation between the researchers (the knowers) and the researched (the [still un-]known). The researched are the naturally exterior or artificially externalised "whats" studied, while the researchers are the doers and the knowers within this regime. Conventional methodology constitutes the self-discipline and self-reflection of the actors-knowers who study some externalised others.

This segregation is hardly "natural", however. It may seem necessary and appropriate concerning the study of *nature* as external to the knower, in relation to which genuine communication is mostly considered impossible. It seems equally contrived and artificial concerning society and other people, however. Or, more correctly, although other *individuals* are external in certain ways (as bodies), cultures, societies, organisations, souls, power, and other typical objects of social scientific study hardly are. There are no strict and unambiguous observable borders between one such "entity" and the next, where the first one definitely and unambiguously ends and another one begins, and exactly when and where we enter or leave one or the other. Hence, since human researchers are hardly external to *any* society, organisation, or culture in any sense relevantly similar to how physical objects are external to us and separate from each other, they have had to do it *artificially*; separate themselves completely and *make* themselves into "incommunicados", and *make* the activities studied into phenomena, in order to emulate and approximate natural science.

---

always the last. The natives have always already been there, constituting the social activities to be studied. The appropriate consequences for social research have still to be drawn. But the question: "Who needs this explanation for what?" is still relevant.

Such conditions of "no-influence-and-no-communication" – *nianoc*-conditions – are, of course, what much social research historically has tried hard to secure and also believed it realised. Hence, even in social research, although hardly real "incommunicados", the researchers are normally temporary or short-term visitors and observing outsiders; they are merely collectors of information trying to avoid influencing what they study in any way, since they want to grasp it in its "natural state". This is how it is and how it should be according to conventional methodological wisdom preaching against the syndrome of "going native", which threatens to dissolve modernist social science as such.

The researched, then, or those who are (still un-)known, are the natives living their daily lives, communicating and influencing things in the cultures, communities, or organisations studied. According to standard research set-ups, the researchers should presumably *not* be natives of the cultures, communities, or organisations studied, for reasons of presumed objectivity and nianoc aims. But even the researchers *are*, of course, natives of *some* culture, namely their own, forming the "background knowledge" they bring along as concepts and constructs in their *explanans* or *interpretans*. They carry with them certain hermeneutical prejudices as "coloured glasses" (or metaphors) through which they observe, interpret, understand, and explain. But they still observe, collect data, describe, analyse, and explain exactly *because* they are *not* natives of the cultures studied; *because* they would like to get to know and understand them better, or at least explain (and predict) certain phenomena or events among the natives better.

The natives, then, are the experienced people described, analysed, and explained. The researchers provide the *explanans* or *interpretans*. For researchers, the doings of the natives constitute the *explananda* to be explained; i.e. the phenomena or appearances. But human natives are not just *explananda*, of course. Natives are not primitive. In this jargon, "native" is merely a relative term designating the human objects studied. We are all natives having our own varieties of *explanans* or *interpretans* as understandings necessary in order to "go on", based in and on our everyday activities and communications, just like researchers (cf. Wittgenstein, 1976:§§150ff., Giddens, 1984:18). But as natives, we are *inside* the researchers' phenomena.

Within the conventional research regime, however, the activities of the researchers are usually not seen as merely a refinement of native ways of knowing, submerged and integrated in their everyday native activities. The activities of research – the research methods – are constituted as peculiar techniques distinctly different in kind from the ordinary activities of the natives. And the explaining theories have, as often as not, been constructed by borrowing concepts and models from mathematics, cybernetics, complexity theory, biology, or other "home-cultures" for researchers which they bring along and presumably already know and understand better than the "whats" they are studying, since if the *explanans* was not better known and understood, it would not explain much. The explanatory theoretical concepts are either imported from somewhere else, or interpreted in terms of things already understood, as metaphors.

Explaining something, then, *is* reducing the observed phenomena to – or subsuming them under – the concepts and theories already possessed and understood by the researchers. And an explanation, if it is adequate to the phenomena and not just some subjective *ad hoc* explanation, presumably enables its possessors, *if* they know and understand these explanatory concepts and theories, to predict the change and behaviour in the phenomena as what normally happens with that *kind* of people in these *kinds* of situations – at a distance so to speak – without necessarily being present as a part of what actually happens, without actually being inside the phenomena.

Hence, although interpretive and ethnographic methods have tried to understand the natives (cf. Eikeland, 2006a), what external researchers actually do methodically inevitably represents a different culture *imposing* its activities and concepts on the native cultures studied (cf. Brøgger, 2009). In physics, the fact that "observing or measuring something *is* influencing it" has been integrated theoretically a long time ago (cf. the Heisenberg uncertainty principle). In social research, different "self-denying" ways of neutralising the effects of the research activity itself have been suggested instead, in order to overcome this "reactivity" of the research methods. But for the purpose of understanding a society, a culture, an organisation, or another individual for that matter, pure *nianoc*-conditions are hardly possible; or, if possible, hardly desirable or very interesting. In fact, people as different as Francis Bacon (1960:20-25), G.W.F. Hegel (1970:78f.), Karl Marx, and Kurt Lewin (1948) all claimed that in order to understand some phenomenon or thing, you have to change it.

Into the conventional methodological regime, then, Bourdieu (1977, 1990) has forcefully introduced the concept of *habitus* (cf. e.g. Broady, 1990; Hillier & Rooksby, 2005). But in being enforcedly adjusted and assimilated to the basic trichotomy of the conventional regime, the concept of *habitus* has been interpreted *too* much as a theoretical concept used by extraneous researchers to explain or interpret the behaviour of others, in spite of Bourdieu's own clear warnings against spectator interpretations (1977:1-2). It then easily becomes culturally deterministic, seeing individuals merely as "products" of their habituation and upbringing within e.g. specific social classes.[4] As these practically institutionalised conceptual distinctions basic to conventional social research – whether "positivist" or

---

4   Cf. King (2000) who joins a number of other critics in seeing the concept of *habitus* as part of an objectivist side of Bourdieu's thinking while there is also a subordinate

interpretive – are becoming increasingly inadequate, however, so is *"habitus"* as a merely "theoretical" concept within the modernist jargon and institutionalisation of social research. The concept should be reclaimed for a more practical approach.

When *"habitus"* is referred back to where and how it was originally coined as <u>héxis</u> by Aristotle (cf. Eikeland, 2008), it emerges as a concept more *methodological* (indicating the self-knowledge, self-reflection, and self-discipline of active knowers) than *theoretical* (explaining external phenomena), to use the modern social research lingo. The concept of *habitus* does not really fit into the trichotomy and the other basic assumptions of conventional social research. In a sense, it does not belong there but to a different "grammar" of knowledge. Paradoxically, then, the concept of *habitus* does not belong properly to the *habitus* of conventional social research. Conventional research certainly implies and enacts a certain *habitus*, but it can hardly handle the concept without dismantling it at the same time. The conventional idiom must be transcended.

As I present alternative categories to work with – deconstructing the trichotomy and introducing a different "grammar" or "topology" of knowing – *habitus* will re-emerge as a concept more *practical* in a certain sense, but also *theoretical* in a sense *different* from the conventional. Methodology specifies and justifies the practices of research, or other practices. And the method of methodology itself – irreducible to the conventional research methods recommended *by* methodology, based on observation, questioning, or experimentation – is the "joint" where the transition from modern methodology to general practice becomes possible and visible (cf. Eikeland, 1990, 1996, 1997, 2001, 2008). Varieties of behaviourism have tried to eliminate every conjecture about events "internal" to the objects observed. Qualitative methods in the tradition from Max Weber interpret opinions and project specific *motives* on to the natives as *explananda*. But *habitus*-based theory requires more: i.e. that the methods of methodology no longer remain a privilege for segregated researchers.

Hence, although my argument may appear theoretical in being distant from how things are immediately perceived,[5] it is really an attempt to facilitate a tran-

---

undercurrent of "practical thinking" in Bourdieu, incompatible with the objectivist *habitus* thinking. As I see it, however, the problem is not the *habitus* concept in itself, but the way and the contextual setting – the *habitus* – within which it is used.

5 This could be more clearly expressed in Germanic languages which differentiate between the momentary experience here-and-now as *Erlebnis (opplevelse)* and the accumulated and acquired bodily embedded experience as *Erfahrung (erfaring)*. *Erlebnisse* can be retained but mostly as memories. Things done, however, are retained as *Erfahrung*. Recollection-work concerns *Erfahrung* more than *Erlebnisse* retained as memories (cf. Eikeland, 1998). *Erlebnisse* are more (not exclusively) perceptually

sition from one concept of theory to another. By the end it will become clear(er) both that and how its theoretical character is different from conventional theory and also intimately intertwined with practically acquired experience. The methods of methodology and the concept of *habitus* establish these connections. A methodologically or practically reconstructed concept of *habitus* is necessary in order to handle both conceptual and practical challenges to conventionally institutionalised social research posed by recent socio-economic developments.

The Challenges

For decades, the standard trichotomy and the divisions of labour within conventional social research have been challenged intellectually, criticising attempts at emulating the natural sciences. More recently the challenge of inadequacy comes also from certain "late modern" socio-economic developments (cf. Beck et al., 1994, Gibbons et al., 1994).

Socio-Economic Validity Challenges

Since World War II, processes of research and learning – knowledge generation and validation – have increasingly expanded *from* being restricted to segregated and specialised academic or scholastic institutions for teaching and research, *to* becoming embedded in work life settings. Concerning the natural and technical sciences, industry has been increasingly research based for at least 150 years (cf. e.g. Bernal, 1969; Reich, 1985). For the burgeoning social sciences of the 19th century, separating the specialised researchers from the "uneducated masses" and "alien cultures" to be studied, may have seemed appropriate even *without* the massive ideological influence from the successful natural sciences, whose subjects of study were of course irremediably "uneducated" incommunicados. But by the beginning of the 21st century, from having been largely socially specialised and monopolised, research and learning processes are becoming increasingly socially distributed (Gibbons et al, 1994, Nowotny et al, 2001). Simultaneously, and as the other side of the coin, the conventional subjects of social research – the natives, or the (knowledge) workers and practitioners – increasingly acquire their own critical research and learning competencies.

---

based. *Erfahrungen* are more practically based. Hence, how something is *erlebt* by someone without *Erfahrung* may be quite different from how people with *Erfahrung* see things.

Personally, I believe a concept like "new knowledge management regime" (Eikeland, 1996, 1997b; 1998a, 1999a, 1999b) is more informative in describing these changes than simply a new "mode 2" of knowledge *production* (Gibbons et al, 1994; Nowotny et al, 2001). But whatever the name, some of the important changes in the social organisation and distribution of knowledge are as follows: 1) an increased distribution of people with higher education, not only at top levels but at all levels of work organisations, making systematic learning and research at work both possible and required in new ways; 2) a greatly increased accessibility (for anyone, anywhere, anytime) of information and formalised knowledge through ICT, making it possible to obtain e.g. expert second opinions from anywhere any time; 3) a rising level of "enforced" reflection caused by an expanding cultural diversity and close-up encounters between cultures (directly or through ICT), producing a corresponding decrease in self-evidence for traditional standards in any field (music, clothing, food, religion, ethics, etc.), making it necessary for individuals themselves to "define" who and what they are, and why (cf. e.g. Bauman, 1993, Beck et al, 1994); 4) the increased knowledge and competence intensiveness of work-processes and products through increased competence and technology requirements at every stage, all the way from the acquisition of raw materials to the finished consumer products; and 5) the rising demands for "tailor-made" customisation by informed and educated customers and users of products and services made possible not the least through ICT.

These developments are interconnected and mutually reinforcing. They strain and challenge old paradigms for organising work hierarchically. In addition, the intellectual challenges to conventional epistemology have moved from the academic philosophy departments, to the emerging knowledge-based work places. All attempts at measuring "quality" in work life refer implicitly or explicitly to age-old discussions in the social sciences about how to measure social phenomena. In product development and market research, focus groups, field work, and participant observation, and other social research methods are utilized. MTV and others hire anthropologists to conduct field research into the hippest local music scenes. Knowledge management and organisational learning are central catchwords in every management course. Knowledge and competence are being discussed like never before in almost every ordinary work place.

Hence, when educated, knowledgeable, and reflective workers and production lines using extremely flexible ICT meet equally educated, knowledgeable, reflective, and demanding users and customers (same people, different roles), new hybrid contexts are produced for knowledge production and development interspersed in, "in-between", or "surrounding" traditional work life and conventional institutions for research and teaching. The transfer and generation of learning and knowledge find new ways and means in these encounters while traditional teaching institutions have trouble staying relevant and keeping up with social, organisational, and technological changes in work life. It seems obvious, then, that these hybrid contexts also challenge age-old divisions of labour between "us" (the researchers as knowers), "them" (the natives known and researched), and the conventional mediators in educational institutions. The challenge is no longer simply the application by practitioners of knowledge produced by others, or the transfer of such knowledge. If that was ever an ideal standard for social research and organisational practice, its self-evidence and relevance has all but evaporated.

As increasing numbers of natives are becoming researchers and life-long learners, or at least conscious of their knowledge claims and ways of knowing, natives and researchers increasingly face *the same kind* of challenges in knowledge creation, justification, and "application" – as native practitioner researchers. Hence, altered relationships and changes are required in the division of labour between institutions a) of research, b) of teaching and learning, and c) of practice and performance. Their relationships are in fact already transforming rapidly (cf. e.g. Teare et al., 1998), requiring a different infrastructure to be established between them which is more symbiotically learning (Eikeland, Work in progress).

For mainstream social research, still mostly based on a division (of labour) between knowers and known, these developments produce major and peculiar challenges, for example: What happens to the distinction between the researchers and the researched when members of both groups do similar things, i.e. when the known are (fully recognised as) knowers and colleagues, and the researched become researchers themselves? If we all become researchers and knowers facing the same kind of challenges and participating in the same kind of discussions, and the radically "others" disappear as subjects of research, who or what remain as the subjects "known", what happens to causal inferences, etc? What are adequate and reasonable ways of doing research on / with / within such changes?

For both theoretical and practical reasons, then, neither the discussions nor adequate answers can be regulated by conventional boundaries between methodology, theory, and data. The discussions about knowledge and knowledge forms, research methodologies, and divisions of labour are no longer only part of a philosophical or methodological "meta-discipline" among insulated researchers in research institutions studying others. They become part of what goes on in work life and in society itself as these try to adjust to new conditions. Discussing this, we cannot continue making the traditional assumptions separating researchers and subjects of research. Increasingly, these kinds of discussions about knowledge generation and validation become part of a substantial understanding by practitioners of dynamic, knowledge intensive, organisational forms. They are no longer merely "meta-discourses". A different grammar of knowledge is needed.

This makes the methods of methodology directly relevant for what happens in work life. Methodology constitutes the self-discipline and self-reflection of actors-knowers. Hence, practically, in the action research projects I've been part of since the 1980s, we have tried to draw some consequences of these new constellations by collaborating to organise and establish permanent organisational learning capacities in work life – i.e. the ability to learn and improve collectively, by emulating *not* natural science but rather the methods of methodology (cf. e.g. Eikeland 1985b, 1987, 1989, 1990; Eikeland & Lahn, 1995; Eikeland & Berg, 1997; Klemsdal et al, 2002, Eikeland et al, 2005). The current situation also means, however, that these discussions must somehow become part of mainstream organisation *theory*, transforming it in the process into a different kind of theory. Conceptual transformations of conventional distinctions are needed, suspending and transcending them.

Hence, most conceptual and institutional distinctions basic to conventional social research are challenged *both* by socio-economic developments *and* for more intellectual validity reasons. What, then, does an appropriately transformed organisation theory look like? How would it be different? What kind of knowledge will it represent? I have already indicated that it has to become more "methodological", "practical", and "experiential" in specific senses of these words. In order to meet the challenge, some kind of "turn to practice" is needed. But neither "practice" nor "*habitus*" can be reduced to the "theoretical lenses" of still segregated but "close-up" researchers within the trichotomy of conventional research, through which to observe the social world and social actors "with microscopes", while the framing research practices or methods – the grammar – remain unchanged. We have to critically study our research practices and the methods of methodology *as* research practitioners. These knowledge generation practices become increasingly relevant for other advanced practitioners in work life. Hence, although the concrete *habitus* of conventional social research is becoming increasingly out-dated and unsuitable, the general methods for articulating, developing, and transforming this *habitus* contains interesting suggestions. They therefore need to be scrutinised for validity and relevance. Methodology needs to be transformed and transferred.

Validity Challenges from Methodology and Philosophy of Science

Here, I will only discuss some basic insufficiencies and inconsistencies intrinsic to conventional methods of observation, questioning, and experimentation (cf. Eikeland, 1985a, 1995, 2006a). Such insufficiencies do not mean that methods like these could or should be abandoned. But in order to be part of the solution, they need to be reinterpreted and transformed critically.

Varieties of observing, questioning, and experimenting are generally recommended as empirical by the discipline of social research methodology. But at least since Francis Bacon, 400 years ago, experimentation has generally been seen as the most basic and reliable method. Bacon's famous idols – *idola tribus* (of the race), *idola specus* (of the individual), *idola fori* (of the group), *idola theatri* (of learned theories) – were all invalidating distortions bothering receptive and passive observation through the senses from afar. Bacon knew that everything received passively through the senses is thoroughly interpreted through particularly positioned, prejudiced perspectives – the very same idols. Today, however, after both empiricist and phenomenological attempts at eliminating all theoretical contamination – getting behind or below the idols – this "idolatry" seems to be generalised into a kind of post-modernistic stalemated and indifferent absolution and suspension of all perspectives. Except for parts of psychology (still emulating natural science), the social sciences have marginalised experimentation as both too impractical and too unethical. But experimentation needs to be re-conquered and transformed by practitioner research and organisational learning.

To repeat, then, we make sense of *explananda* by seeing or interpreting them *as if* they were similar to something we already understand. We explain and interpret perceptions by means of whatever knowledge and understanding we bring along, *assimilating* whatever is perceived to what we already have. The standard structure of explanation seems to make the universe thoroughly metaphorical and prejudiced by idols. Everything seems to be understood by means of something else transferred, ending up in an endless regression.

But somehow this regression has to stop. How are the concepts we "already have" in the *explanans* known? Our understanding of any explanation or interpretation is ultimately based in and referred to our practically acquired and accumulated experience – *Erfahrung* not *Erlebnis* (cf. Eikeland, 1997, 2008). This experience is generated and formed over a certain time, placed somewhere specifically, repeating things over and over. It is getting to *know* something by learning how to *do* something. Practice has to *accommodate* to whatever is encountered. Repetitions create practical patterns at different levels, i.e. generalities transferred as accumulated experience, habits, and skills from one situation to another. Grasping these patterns engenders concepts *in nuce*, which, in turn, does *not* produce another *explanandum* needing explanation; rather it produces new basic understanding, i.e. a new *explanans* that can and will be used to understand or interpret new assimilating sense-perceptions.

Hence, experimenting with whatever subject is studied, deliberately intervening and changing it in controllable ways, was and is an attempt at moving beyond or below the "idolatry" of arbitrary spectator interpretations by non-participants from afar. In moving beyond metaphors, then, Bacon's idols need to be deconstructed phenomenologically and put aside in order to reach basic experience, not punctual sense experience as singular impressions but adequately habituated and skilled patterns. Experimentation in the wide sense – trying things out again and again – is gaining new experience first-hand with whatever our knowledge, interpretation, or explanation is about. Hence, the regression stops here, not necessarily at the standard experiment of natural science but at a certain kind of concept-generating experimentation.[6]

The insufficiencies of conventional social research methods are indicated by a number of specific objections well-known within methodology and the philosophy of science. Roughly, there are two sets of arguments, one concerning the quality of data or relevant experience, another one concerning the quality of explanations or interpretations. Data collection depends on theories, often implicit as basic assumptions or hermeneutic prejudices, in at least two different ways.

Data collections are *selections* of data. The relevance of data depends on some kind of *theory* of relevance. For example, in explaining or interpreting social conduct, most social researchers ignore the positions of the planets and stars as irrelevant. For astrologers, however, they are the most relevant data. Their theories of relevance differ widely, no matter who is right. But data are not only theory *dependent*. Data are also theory-*saturated*. Again, hardly anyone considers heavenly bodies divine. 2000 year ago, even the most educated did. But they were not stupid. Many understood logic and basic principles of knowledge better than most modern social researchers.

The examples emphasise the thoroughly interpreted nature of all perceptual observations. They are chosen and interpreted according to what we as interpreters bring along (idols or metaphors). Hence, there really is no solid foundation made of un-interpreted data, the way the logical positivists presupposed. Data are *not* given. The question is *how* we interpret what we perceive and how some interpretations may be said to be more adequate than others. Merely "unbiased" sense-perception from any distant position is insufficient, and so are interpretive positions arbitrarily chosen, since basic experience is not merely sense-perceptual but practically patterned ways of doing things.

The reactivity of the data collection procedures also invalidates conventional data collection. The way data are collected is a socially defined activity. Different social contexts influence people in different ways. Neutral contexts hardly exist, since eliminating everything social is impossible and at least not neutral. The very consciousness that something called "data collection" is going on will influence

---

6   Cf. the discussion in Eikeland (1997:150-152) of Wartofsky's (1968:200ff.) difference between "experiments of discovery" and "experiments for testing the consequences of hypotheses".

everyone involved. But what is sought for are not data "contaminated" by the abnormal activity of data collection; the researchers want to know how things are when they are *not* present and influencing (cf. Eikeland, 1985a), i.e. "naturally" or normally, recommending different self-obliterating ways of eliminating research effects. But conventional research stumbles in its own feet, since it is literally standing in its own way. Researchers cannot be eliminated from the research processes. Hence, different ways of *utilising* the interactive effects as relevant information instead of trying to eliminate them have been suggested. But such utilisation involves radical self-reflection and moves conventional research closer to the methods of methodology or to what emerges as "hard-core" action research.

Finally, concerning data and the realities studied by social research, there is the challenge of what might be called indicator research. Conventional research concepts of "experience" are inadequate (cf. Sandelands & Srivatsans, 1993; Eikeland, 1997). Most subjects studied by social research are out of reach for the "experience" of conventional research, normally interpreted perceptually. Hardly anything studied by social research can be observed perceptually and delimited as objects in the world the way e.g. stars, rocks, plants, or animals can. Neither "a state", nor "an organisation", nor "the soul", nor "power" can be seen, heard, smelled, tasted, or touched.

The emergent current orthodoxy sees this as indicating how almost everything is socially constructed and "un-real", not "out there". But claiming that e.g. organisations, states, and souls are unreal is absurd for everyday practitioners who have to observe *practically* the rules and regulations of these very real powers. They are not "just theory" or "theoretical constructs" simply because they cannot be perceived by the five senses. For researching but non-participating observers or visitors these things may seem unreal and arbitrary. But *they* themselves observe other rules and regulations practically that seem equally invisible and incomprehensible for those visited or observed. None of this is unreal, however. You just have to be a native – inside the phenomena – in order to experience their reality. They are the patterns of basic practical experience imperceptible to non-natives but still not out-of-reach for practitioners' experience. They *are* the native experience. "Going native" is not a distortion, then, it is a precondition. The things you have to do as a "native" employee in a company or public bureaucracy are as real and influential as the rules of research are for "native" researchers. In either case the basic rule is: drop the rules and you are out of the game. *You* become unreal.

Only one problem concerning explanations and interpretations will be mentioned; the challenge of theory pluralism. For 2000 years, theory pluralism has been associated with the explanatory principle of "saving the phenomena" (cf. Duhem, 1969). For ancient astronomers what mattered was saving the phenomena by means of any logically consistent model able to predict – and *eo ipso* explain – the movements of the lights in the heavens. Theoretical realism – i.e. believing theoretical concepts and models were real and "out there" – was *out* before Galileo. Instrumentalism – i.e. considering theories merely as tools – was *in*. Instrumentalism makes *adequacy* in the sense of similarity between concept and object meaningless, since tools do not have to be *similar* to their objects as long as they fulfil their instrumental tasks. Today, inspired by filmmaker Akiro Kurosawa, instrumentalism has re-entered social research as the Rashomon syndrome in anthropology (Heider, 1988): The same phenomenon can logically and legitimately be interpreted and explained in totally different ways. Bacon's idols have returned with a vengeance, since *any* given set of data can be explained in logically valid ways by an unlimited number of true and false premises, i.e. theories. True conclusions – e.g. true descriptions – can follow from utterly false premises. If all "fishes" are warm-blooded (false premise), and all whales are "fishes" (false premise), it follows logically that all whales are warm-blooded (true conclusion). Exchange fishes with Xs, and you have your logical proof of theory or idol pluralism. Any X will explain that whales are warm-blooded.

The "abduction" of Charles S. Peirce (1868, 1878) has been suggested as a solution for developing good explanations. But abduction works *first* by means of constructing *any* "reasonable" explanation that will produce observations as consequents in logical inferences, and *then* confirming the consequent, i.e. by confirming observables like "all whales are warm-blooded" or "the sun always rises in the east and sets in the west". But completely false premises may validly produce true conclusions. Confirming such consequents says absolutely nothing about what the true antecedents are, e.g. it says nothing about whether geocentric or heliocentric theories best explain the observed movements of the sun, and nothing about whether fishes or mammals are proper to whales. Also, it says nothing about whether the sun is divine or not. Quine's (1961) claim is that such theories are radically underdetermined by the data.

Ways of Knowing – Knowledge Forms

But the problems described are connected to specific concepts of theory, methods, and experience. In order to transcend them, these concepts must be transcended and transformed. A broader perspective on knowing is necessary. Therefore, I will present and discuss a number of alternative ways of knowing. They cut the cake differently from the modernist divisions.

Distinctions between tacit and articulate ways of knowing (Polanyi, 1958, 1966) and between novices and experts in apprentice models of learning (e.g. Dreyfus and Dreyfus, 1986; Lave and Wenger, 1991; Nielsen and Kvale, 1999 and 2003) are important. So are basic relational ways of knowing extracted from the *Corpus Aristotelicum* (cf. Eikeland, 1997, 1998, 2001, 2006b, 2008), together with the Aristotelian concepts of *habitus* (héxis) and virtue or excellence / virtuosity (aretê). The relational concepts of knowing are summarised in Table 1.

Basis	Way of knowing	Associated rationality	English equivalent
Aísthêsis (*perception*)	Theôrêsis = epistêmê₂	Deduction, demonstration, didactics	Spectator speculation
	Páthos	??	Being affected passively from the outside
Empeiría (practically acquired experience)	Khrêsis	Tékhnê (calculation)	*Using*
	Poíêsis		*Making*, manipulating
	Praxis₂	Phrónêsis (deliberation)	*Doing*: virtuous performance, practical reasoning
	Praxis₁	Dialectics / dialogue. The way from *novice to expert*, from *tacit to articulate*	Practice, training for competence development and insight (theôría)
	Theôría = epistêmê₁	Dialogue, deduction, deliberation	Insight

Table 1: Ways of knowing

Before presenting and discussing the concepts, however, their status as *existentials* (Heidegger, 1927) must be explained briefly. Understanding the status of existentials is part of the announced transition from one kind of theory to another. Generally, every practice has some kind of identifiable pattern to it, some *form* which is achieved or realised to a greater or lesser extent. Such patterns are emergent, both individually and socio-historically, as individuals and collectives learn and acquire the ability to perform certain tasks better or merely differently. Hence, the patterns are more or less explicit, both in our minds and in our practices, and they may be more or less perfectly realised in actual practice. The performed patterns constitute our acquired practical experience.

Existentials are simply the most general or universal practical patterns, or forms, and relations presupposed and implied in everything else we do. This makes them inevitable. Like Kantian "transcendentals" and Aristotelian "commons" (koiná), they are general (ways of doing) "things" (distinctions, concepts, activities, relations, patterns, "pragmata") our more specific practices have in common. Hence, existentials represent quite basic practical patterns and distinctions we have to perform and relate to as acting human beings in the world. The conceptual acquisition of existentials *is* the gradual grasp and recognition, and the retrospective or reflective awareness, of their practical presence as patterns repeated in our lives, making their full implications and ramifications explicit.

Modern mainstream epistemology has been one-dimensional. Knowledge is knowledge, only more or less precisely so. Measured along one dimension and according to the same standard, certain kinds of knowledge are considered insufficient, others are "good". *Scientific* knowledge has been considered superior, while the insufficient and inferior knowledge forms have been all the ways of knowing – traditional, practical, tacit, emotional, experiential, intuitive, etc. – that are not yet infused with modern "science". Accordingly, in order for practical knowledge to improve, it must somehow "apply" scientific methods or the results of scientific research. Otherwise it will remain on a level of untested habit at best, and stay full of prejudices, superstitions, imprecisions, lack of factual knowledge, and so forth. But this one-dimensional approach is insufficient for understanding knowledge.

Modern epistemology can be traced to both Plato and Aristotle. But Aristotle, especially, was more differentiated. He did not start with knowledge as such, differentiating only one-dimensionally by degrees of exactness. His thinking about knowledge is fundamentally and explicitly *relational*. There is always a *knower* and something *known* related to each other in specific and different ways. Certain relationships between means and ends specific to the different ways of knowing are implied. As explicitly relational, the ethico-political implications of different ways of knowing are also immediately brought to light. Ethics is an aspect of what should be called the *gnoseology* of Aristotle, since epistêmê is just one form of gnôsis (a wider category of knowledge). Ethics deals with relations between people, and the ethical aspects of the different relational knowledge forms emerge when they are implanted among people. They make relations visible that are normally kept in the dark in modern ways of thinking about knowledge, as if knowledge and ethics really *were* completely separate departments that could be treated independently from each other.

The relational starting point brings out several fundamentally different ways of knowing, impossible to reduce to one basic form along one dimension only. The ways of knowing are mostly independent from each other, with their own ways of acquisition, and with their own validity criteria. The modernist unity-of-science dream of transforming and reducing all kinds of knowledge to one basic form was alien to Aristotle. But so was the opposite "post-modernist" tendency of making all kinds of knowing indifferently valid or equivalent.

The most current "applied" way of presenting Aristotle on knowing is to separate epistêmê from tékhnê and phrónêsis (cf. Flyvbjerg, 2001; Toulmin, 1996a,

1996b, 1996c, 2001; Schwandt, 2002; Ramírez, 1995; Dunne, 1993; Polkinghorne, 2004). This is usually done in order to emphasise phrónêsis as an independent alternative to epistêmê and tékhnê, or to "science" and "technology". Phrónêsis is deliberation connected to praxis, interpreted as approximately our everyday activities, contrasted to science and technique. Often, rhetoric is also mustered as the deliberative rationality most appropriate for everyday practice, in the attempt to transcend modern reductionist science.

This interpretation is not mine, however (cf. Eikeland, 1997, 1998, 2006b, 2008). Epistêmê cannot be equated with modern science. There are differences both in kind and of degree only, *within* the Aristotelian epistêmê. The concept of praxis, on the other hand, is much more specific than our everyday activities. It is also much more specific than most modern concepts of "practice". But still different aspects of praxis must be distinguished even in its specialised Aristotelian sense.

But I start by explaining epistêmê. There are two concepts of theory and epistêmê, one at either extreme of Table 1. They share similarities making them theoretical in an Aristotelian sense. The principles of movement, change, or development in the subjects studied reside in those subjects themselves, not in anyone or anything external. Things studied theoretically move, change, and develop by themselves, not because or as some external knower makes them move or change. We might say they move, change, and develop naturally, not artificially. An Aristotelian theorist, then, is interested in knowing and understanding things without artificially altering them. This separates both forms of theory from the intermediary non-theoretical knowledge forms. But the two forms of theory are still fundamentally different and should be kept apart.

The first form, called theôrêsis, epistêmê$_2$, or "spectator speculation", is based on observation at a distance. Theôrêsis relates to separate external objects. It is based on aísthêsis or sense perception, or, rather, on a *combination* of perceptual knowledge and knowledge from other sources. The relation implied is one of difference, distance, non-interaction, and non-interference – basically "nianoc" conditions. In its deductive form, astronomy has served as a paradigm. For social and historical reasons, this paradigm conquered the whole field of science from the 17th century on. It has formed the institutions of modern science and research quite fundamentally. Its experiential base is collections of "data" as bits of information or observations taken at face value. Its non-critical and non-interventionist relationship to "data" – collecting them without influencing them – is phenomenalistic, not phenomenological. As indicated above, "saving the phenomena" instrumentally has been its objective.

The way of generating theoretical explanations within theôrêsis is somewhat mystical and creative (cf. Popper, 1980). But theories are required to provide falsifiable models (mathematical, graphical, physical, or linguistic) for predicting the behaviour of the observed phenomena or events. The explanatory principle consists in reducing or assimilating the data or *explananda* to an *explanans* or *interpretans* as something already and better understood, subsuming the data as instances of something general. Here, within the structure of theôrêsis, is where the use of metaphors and analogies really is at home. Although an attitude of theoretical realism has accompanied theôrêsis in the modern age, theôrêsis is more suited for the instrumentalism of pre-modern astronomy.

The movement "down" in theôrêsis, *from* theory *to* "data", experience, or practice, is primarily formal and deductive. But even interpretive and qualitative social research remains mainly within this model of theôrêsis, although it normally does not formalise its theories, and although it has long since expanded the repertoire of data collecting techniques to include interviewing or questioning in different forms, generating "reactivity-challenges" in its wake. The people studied are still the *others*, not the actors-knowers themselves. The people known are not the researchers. It is important not to intervene, and to neutralise any unintended effects (reactivity) of the research activities. Because of its status as scientific paradigm in the modern period, however, almost all philosophy of science and research methodology has made theôrêsis under different designations (covering law, HDM) its starting point and framework (cf. e.g. Hacking, 1983).

But theôrêsis was not the only model for epistêmê, that is, for knowledge that was stabilised and pretty secure, about subjects that were for the most part or always stable and regular themselves. At the lower extreme we find the other epistêmê form, which in certain ways represents the extreme, contrary knowledge form to the first. With Aristotle, not only what *we* normally consider sciences were forms of epistêmê: boxing, music, grammar, orthography, medicine, and other skills and disciplines were also called epistêmê, because there was a certain patterned stability and regularity in what they represented.

We may use grammar as the paradigm example for this other kind of epistêmê₁ or theôría (cf. Aristotle, and Wittgenstein, 1974). Theôría translates as "insight". In grammar the *relation* between the knower and the known is different from the corresponding relation in astronomy. Grammar is basically about us as native speakers of a language. It expresses and organises certain aspects of our linguistic practice, the more or less stable patterns that repeat themselves in certain ways in our performance. Grammar is descriptive and analytical, but it is also normative, since it sets standards for correct speech and writing, describing topographies of language use. The *basis* for grammatical knowledge is not primarily hypothetical conjectures about artificially collected "data" of sense perception observed from the outside, but the practical competence, or patterns and structures in the acquired practical experience of the knower herself. It is based on empeiría (= *Erfahrung*

53

not *Erlebnis*). *Adequacy* only gains meaning on this basis. There is no distance between the knower and the known as there is between the researcher and the heavenly bodies in astronomy. In some sense, we are internal to grammar, or grammar is internal to us.

This means that the subjects studied – our own forms of practice – must be "reified" reflectively in order to be grasped. They are not really outside us or outside our practices at all, the way stars are, and the way external nature is in general. In grammar, the knowers and the known are really the same. Principles of movement, change, and development are in the known and in the knower simultaneously. In theôrêsis, they are in the known but outside the knower (who, therefore, must project models and metaphors). In the in-between forms of khrêsis and poíêsis, the principles of movement, change, and development are in the knower but outside the known. Grammar coordinates aspects of our practice, and all language users – the practitioners – have the same relationship to grammar. We may be novices or experts in using the language and at different levels of tacitness or articulation of the common forms. But as practitioners, we have grammar in common, and we relate to the grammar of our spoken language as equals. Knowledge forms like grammar organise and structure the competence of their carriers, within a certain field or in general, and become primarily a qualification of their carriers themselves, individually and collectively. They produce a specific *habitus*.

Grammar also exemplifies what is called praxis knowledge in Table 1, where the relationship between the starting point, the means, and the end or objective for our actions is one of formal equality. As in playing an instrument or in dancing, what we do as novices, what we do on our way to perfection – as means – and what we do as perfected virtuosos are all formally the same. The end or objective is entailed in the activity itself as its perfection. Praxis forms are autotelic. They are not merely technical means for external and separate ends. There is no technical "method" formally different, in-between, and separate from the starting point and the end. In perfecting a practice or in attempting to perform virtuously (as in acting courageously, fairly, or honestly), the aim and end is carried with and inside the activity. We dance or play our instrument all the way, but we do it gradually better over time. The general form of the activity, getting *into* the form, emerges as *habitus* and experience as we practice. Grasping the practice constitutes the emergent concept. Praxis knowledge is the primary base for theôría.

For Aristotle, praxis knowledge represents a relationship between colleagues sharing common standards for how to go about their professional activities. But our common and equal relationship to practical standards even sets an ethical standard *both* for practical political communities of equals *and* for a political science very different from one based in theôrêsis. It could also serve as a gnoseological paradigm for a different form of organisational science, one that is very relevant for practitioner action research and for our current search for a different kind of theory. Praxis knowledge regulates, or organises, the relationships between equals. It constitutes a "we" literally as a community with common standards (as in grammar), and it regulates relations among "us". All those with an equal practical relationship to the common standards make up the relevant "we" as a community. In fact, the modern discipline of methodology must be understood basically as praxis.

What, then, about the *methods* of methodology? For both Aristotle and Plato, the way of learning or research, moving *"up" from* how things appear to us phenomenologically *to* an articulated insight in basic principles of grammar or of any other fields of activity we relate to in similar ways, goes through critical dialogue or dialectics (cf. Eikeland, 1997; 2008). By searching actively for patterns, comparing and sorting similarities and differences in our accumulated practical experience, and in how we use language, dialogue helps articulate what we carry with us as habituated tacit knowledge – our *habitus*. It helps us on our way from novices to experts and to virtuoso performers; it helps the form emerge in us and for us as it helps us perfect our practice.

This dialogical articulation from within practice and practical experience is what is called praxis$_1$ on the second lowest row in Table 1. It is *inductive* in a wide and non-enumerative sense. Dialogue is a form of praxis in itself, *common* to all other forms, even to the knower side of the non-practical knowledge forms in the table. Our own practices, as with grammar, we articulate and make explicit from the inside out, as natives from inside the phenomena, as producers of phenomena. Hence the way to principal insight is not mystical as with theôrêsis. It goes via the gradual development of habits, *habitus*, and experience into virtue or virtuosity, mastery, and insight. Dialogue needs relief from immediate pressure to act, however. The articulation of emerging insights is a task of its own in need of *leisure*. Leisure is skholê in Greek, the word that became "school" in most European languages. But the original skholê was primarily a space for reflection interspersed in practical contexts. It was neither a didactic didaskaleíon for instructive teaching nor an external observatory or "theôretêrion".

In theôría, the way down from "theory" to "practice" is also different. With grammar the practical enactment is often spontaneous in proficient speakers. We usually do not think twice before speaking. But in other fields where the practice is not equally standardised and "automated", for example in ethics, the "application" of general competence or knowledge of principles provided by virtues like justice, courage, friendliness, and honesty, needs deliberation, practical reasoning or phrónêsis, trying to find out how to act in the most just or fair way towards someone here and now. Perfecting a practice needs dialogue on "the way up" from particulars to general competence. It needs phrónêsis on "the way down" from acquired competence – "applying" or enacting it – to the proper consideration of particulars. This way down is what is called praxis, in the third row from below in Table 1. The transition from theory to practice within this kind of knowledge is *not* deductive, nor does it go by some form of application of merely efficient causes and technical calculation of effects. It was intended to be deliberative by Aristotle, not rigorously deductive or calculative based on strictly formalised knowledge.

Khrêsis is competence in using external or reified things as *instruments* or *tools* for the user's purposes. It is an independent competence, as for example in driving a car. This is not a vague and insufficient form of science in astronomical form. In order to become good at driving, you do not need any of the other knowledge forms first. You do not have to be able to build a car, or understand the principles of a carburettor engine. You need to practice in the specific relation as a user of this specific kind of thing. Khrêsis is possible and even prevalent in human relations too, of course. Some are even very good at it. But the ethics of using other people as instruments for achieving your own interests is hard to defend *generally*.

With poíêsis the case is similar. It is competence in manipulating external objects as *material* according to the manipulator's own plans and intentions, forming them and making something out of them. In poíêsis, movements and changes in the external object depend on us as knowers-manipulators. It is not natural. Poíêsis *intervenes* artificially in its material. Trees do not become chairs naturally. A carpenter intervenes in wood. *Qua* carpenter he is only interested in those aspects of wood relevant for making houses, tables, chairs, and other artefacts from it. His interest is not theoretical, and he needs very little botanical theory in order to become a good carpenter.

When this poíêsis relationship is transferred to human relations, it does not always look as attractive, however. The art of manipulating others is hard to defend ethically on a general basis, although it exists, and many people are very good at it. The conventional *experiment* is a variant of poíêsis, and the art of medicine is clearly poíêsis in relation to the human body, ethically defensible for sure. As an art of rhetoric, persuading and seducing, it is sold to business executives as competence in making people e.g. do what you want, see things your way and support you, and work with you not against you. Páthos is knowledge created from being passively affected and formed by external sources, maybe less cognitive and more as embedded and embodied patterns of emotional reactions. I will discuss it no further here.

Both khrêsis and poíêsis are based on technical calculation of effects in instruments and materials for reaching the aims of the actors. Their articulation is tékhnê. Both khrêsis and poíêsis relate to external things (even to human beings) as material or as instruments. Both khrêsis and poíêsis employ means (instruments, tools) that are different formally and in kind both from the starting point and from the end or objective for the act. Both have their aims outside the activities themselves. They are both heterotelic. Although modern jargon tends to assimilate all of them into "practice", this makes khrêsis and poíêsis different from praxis in important ways.

The common denominator for both forms of epistêmê is that they are both non-interventionist and theory-directed. Neither one is practical in the sense of being *directed at* the generation of specific actions of any kind. The second one, theôría, is action *based*, however. Although it is *directed* towards developing theôría, it is necessarily developed from a *base* in acquired practical experience. Theôría is generated from within practice, training, exercise, and habituation. It emerges from the *habitus* springing from practical experience (empeiria) as an articulation of its patterns (sifting differences and similarities). Its primary source is praxis$_1$, but since praxis$_1$ is inherent in all the other ways of knowing as well, it includes all the action-based knowledge forms khrêsis, poíêsis, praxis, and even theôrêsis considered as an activity. The ways of knowing differ in their relationship to what is known, but the fact that there is a praxis-aspect internal to all, makes praxis more universal. Each way of knowing has its *habitus* specific to its particular relation to what is known and to its particular structure of means and ends. Hence, transferring a poíêsis *habitus* or a theôrêsis *habitus* to a context requiring praxis, produces a certain *habitus*-invalidity. This is what modernist social science has done in emulating natural science uncritically. But *habitus*-validity does not require just one kind of knowledge. In order to adjust suitably, it needs several.

Praxis$_2$ and phrónêsis as practical reasoning are both action-*based* and action-*directed*, then, and so are the intermediate knowledge forms in Table 1 (except páthos). Praxis regulates relations among some "us" having an equal relationship to standards of conduct that some "we" have in common. But in human relations both theôrêsis and the other intermediate forms regulate relations between some "us" and some "them". The known is separate from the knower(s). In a way, theôrêsis creates and requires total ideal apartheid. Where we cannot communicate with whatever we study, as with stars and planets, this may be the only possibility. But reducing social knowledge to this form is unnecessary, artificial, and highly problematic.

We can discuss how much of conventional modern social research that has produced and produces knowledge in the form of theôrêsis (spectator speculation), khrêsis, or poíêsis. It may not be all of it. But a large part has been doing it and still does. As indicated, there are fundamental insufficiencies of validity inherent in all social research approaches based on "othering" (cf. Eikeland, 2006a). At least, the table of knowledge forms suggests that "othering" ways of doing social research are not necessary, natural, or the only possible ways. The emergent, socially distributed mode of knowledge production, where distinctions between natives and researchers are dissolving, also requires "non-othering" knowledge forms. Praxis and theôría are possible ways of knowing with great potentials in providing standards more adequate for a socially distributed knowledge production. They make it easier to clarify what praxis research as practitioner research might imply.

Conventional social science, even its interpretive forms, still carries the marks from its inception and its attempts at emulating the natural sciences of modernity. It is mostly a form of theôrêsis. This has not made social research more scientific, rather less, in any basic sense, since the knowledge form has been inappropriate and unsuited to its "object". In the most profound sense, objectivity does not mean treating everything as an external and delimited thing or object. It means an "adequation" to the peculiarities of the "object", or becoming "pragmadequate" (cf. Eikeland, 2008).

The conventional scientific experiment is mainly a form of poíêsis, however, intervening consciously in whatever it studies in order to produce effects. Although in a scientific experiment, the point is not really to reach manipulated results but to generate knowledge, the *kind* of knowledge generated is of a poiêsis kind, in *habitus*-conformity with manipulative purposes. Action research springs historically from experimental social research. But experimentation does not have to be poiêsis. It could be either khrêsis or praxis, and it could be concept-generating rather than hypothesis-testing. In addition, a praxis-based experiment would not be based on manipulating others. It would be based on experimenting – trying things out – together, where everyone becomes an experimenter, not an "experimentee". The transformation of organisation theory, then, must be conceptualised as a transformation both from theôrêsis, and from poíêsis-tékhnê, to praxis-theôría constituting the basis for operational, practicable knowledge. For social knowledge, the break with the natural sciences must be completed, then, not by abandoning completely the scientific and experimental attitude, but by emulating the really common practices of science and research – the methods of scientific methodology.

The Transition to Habitus-Based Theory

Praxis and theôría may appear to have been expelled from modernist social science and to be struggling to re-enter it from the *outside*. But theôría has not been completely neglected or expelled. As an *existential* it hardly can. In *methodology*, researchers study themselves and their own activities from *within*, as professional practitioners, normatively and reflectively, but experientially based, *not as* a phenomenon, i.e. not as some thing or some body external to themselves. Basically, the *method* of methodology is necessarily and primarily reflective, like grammar and practitioner action research (cf. Eikeland, 1995, 1996, 1997, 2001, 2006a, 2008). Methodology is or contains theôría as reflectively reified generalities. The methods of methodology bring this out. Methodology is the reflective, practically based self-consciousness of professional researchers, just like the professional self-consciousness of other professional practitioners is contained in the rules, and lies latent in the embodied competence or *habitus*, of their professional conduct. For "modernist reasons" this self-reflective method of methodology is normally interpreted as "non-empirical", since it does not base itself on a remote and alienating observation of strangers by strangers.

But the craft of methodology presupposes and entails certain conditions as real in what it controls for in its procedures (cf. Eikeland, 1985a, 1995). When professional and experienced researchers self-reflectively, critically, and dialogically analyse the structures of their own *habitus* and acquired experience incorporating the patterns in their ways of doing things, the immanent relational presuppositions and historical-institutional preconditions of these patterned ways of doing things emerge and become visible empirically as an implied topography. Everything that competent ways of doing things – i.e. competent methods – heed and take into consideration, emerges as the implied social reality more or less taken for granted, making this examination of *habitus* the most empirical way of studying human realities. The different ways of knowing inherent in specific ways of doing things emerge and become visible *with* and *within* their embeddedness in historical, social, institutional, economic, and cultural moulds, with their ethico-political implications, etc. As in a hologram, specific institutions, organisational forms, interpersonal relations, former individually accumulated experience, common history, and so forth are all implied. By showing what is implicit and implied in personal *habitus*, then, the split between different levels of theory (micro, meso, and macro) has a chance of being overcome from a practical and native starting point.

Instead of seeing societies, cultures, organisations, and professional and everyday practices as external "things", or activities of others, to be studied descriptively, interpretively, and explanatorily by theôrêsis, they could and actually do need to be understood and analysed from the inside as activities by practitioner-researchers. The aim of theôría is to make the practical methods and standards of such social activities explicit from the inside for and by native practitioners, *including* all the social realities – the topographies – that need to be heeded, the way methodology does it for the specific activity of research. The aim is to grasp the general but topographically adjusted *forms* of these activities as competencies, not the private aims, motives, or emotions – the final and efficient causes – of any particular performers or actors. The seeds of theôría are, of course, everywhere to be found in native practitioners' spontaneous sensemaking and self-interpretations of their lives and activities. The methods of theôría are the methods of methodology and the methods of practitioner research. They are critically dialogical, analytical, and empirical. *Habitus*, then, is a *methodological* praxis-concept engendering theôría – a different kind of theory – when analysed correctly.

If doing (praxis), making (poíêsis), and using (khrêsis) produce something epistemic, then, it is as reflectively reified methodological rules or ways of proceeding and doing things, extracting the more or less stable elements or patterns present and presupposed in the activities, which remain as performance standards for practitioners. *Habitus* as a modern theôrêsis concept may tend to predetermine its subjects as passive products of culture. But as a methodological concept it does not. Instead, it is the necessary base and starting point for developing practically relevant and adjusted knowledge and ways of knowing, for developing habits into competent and adjusted excellences or virtues dialogically and phronetically. Hence, epistemic results are not algorithms to be performed technically or mechanically. They are topologies, grammars, and guidelines for practitioners practising and performing, to be taken into account and consideration, "applied", enacted, and adjusted to the particular circumstances of a situation with proper deliberative phrónêsis by each and every practitioner.

Skholê (as the necessary leisure and reflective space), dialogue, and phrónêsis need to be established in work life emulating *not* the special theôrêsis and poíêsis of modern natural science but the methods of methodology as the *general* preconditions for learning and professional performance. They need to be developed as practitioner action research and organisational learning. They need to be explored further *in* an attempt to find ways of knowing suitable to a "post-modern knowledge condition" (Lyotard, 1979) where the distinction between knower and known has all but evaporated, and *as* an attempt to organise and establish permanent organisational learning capacities in work life – i.e. the ability to learn, theorise, improve, and improvise collectively. This will certainly imply major changes and transformations in both organisations and organisation theory. Research institutions have been modelled as insulated and external "observatories", or "laboratories" researching other humans as "natural objects" receiving treatment and manipulation, explaining their behaviour with "covering laws" and statistics. The subsequent interpretive turn has not turned enough, that is, to praxis and theôría. Instead, practitioner researchers should provide standards and methodological guidelines from the inside for each and every autonomous practitioner, as "grammarians" and methodologists of social practices.

References

Ainley, P. and Rainbird, H. (1999), *Apprenticeship – Towards a New Paradigm of Learning*, London: Kogan Page.

Antonacopoulou, E. (2008), "On the Practise of Practice: In-tensions and Extensions in the Ongoing Reconfiguration of Practices", pp. 112-131 in D.Barry and H.Hansen (eds.), *New Approaches in Management and Organization*, Los Angeles: Sage.

Argyris, C. (1993), *Knowledge for Action: A Guide to Overcoming Barriers to Organizational Change*, San Francisco: Jossey-Bass.

Argyris, C. (1996), "Actionable Knowledge: Intent versus Actuality", *Journal of Applied Behavioral Science*, 32 (4): 441-444.

Bacon, F. (1960) (orig. 1620), *The New Organon*, Indianapolis: Bobbs-Merrill Educational Publ.

Bauman, Z. (1993), *Postmodern Ethics*, Oxford: Blackwell.

Beck, U., Giddens, A. & Lash, S. (1994), *Reflexive Modernization – Politics, Tradition and Aesthetics in the Modern Social Order*, Cambridge: Polity Press.

Bernal, J.D. (1969), *Science in History*, 4 Vols., Harmondsworth: Penguin Books Ltd.

Bourdieu, P. (1977) (French original,1972), *Outline of a Theory of Practice*, Cambridge: Cambridge University Press.

Bourdieu, P. (1990) (French original, 1980), *The Logic of Practice*, Cambridge: Polity Press,.

Broady, Donald (1990), *Sociologi och epistemologi – Om Pierre Bourdieus författarskap och den historiska epistemologien*, Stockholm: HLS Förlag.

Brøgger, B. (2009), *Research and Change – a Comparison of Action Research and Conventional Social Science Research Methods*, Chapter 3 in this volume.

Cunliffe, A. L. & Easterby-Smith, M. (2004), "From Reflection to Practical Reflexivity: Experiential Learning as Lived Experience", pp. 30-46 in *Organizing Reflection*. Reynolds, Michael & Vince, Russ (eds.) (2004) Aldershot: Ashgate Publishing.

Descombes, V. (1986), *Objects of all sorts – A philosophical grammar*, Oxford: Basil Blackwell.

Dreyfus, H.L. and Dreyfus, S.E. (1986), *Mind over Machine – The Power of Human Intuition and Expertise in the Era of the Computer*, Oxford: Basil Blackwell Ltd.

Duhem, P. (1969) (orig. 1908), *To Save the Phenomena – an Essay on the Idea of Physical Theory from Plato to Galileo*, Chicago: University of Chicago Press.

Dunne, J. (1993), *Back to Rough Ground – "Phronesis" and "Techne" in Modern Philosophy and in Aristotle*, Notre Dame: University of Notre Dame Press,.

Eikeland, O. (1985a), "H.W. Smith og jakten på den skjulte mening eller: the actual meaning of triangulation", pp.173-208 in Østerberg, Dag and Otnes, Per (eds.): *Sosiologisk Aarbok*, 1985, Oslo: Institute for Sociology, University of Oslo.

Eikeland, O. (1985b), "Jobbskaping i lokalmiljø – perspektiver og muligheter", pp.12-13 in *Studienytt*, no.4.

Eikeland, O. (1986), "I en modellbyggers kaotiske 'virkelighet'", *Sosiologi i dag*, 16(1): 65-80.

Eikeland, O. (1987), *Rapport til Hovedavtalens bedriftsutviklingstiltak (HABUT); Bilbransjeprosjektet*, AFI-notat 31/87, AFI, Oslo: Work Research Institute

Eikeland, O. (1989), *Bedriftsutvikling i bilbransjen 1984-1989; en oversikt.* Rapport til HABUT, Oslo: Work Research Institute.

Eikeland, O. (1990), *Historisk-teoretisk grunnlag for forståelsen av praksislæring*, Paper presented at the conference on Work Life, Vocational Education and Training, May 21-23, 1990, Oslo: Statens Yrkespedagogiske Høgskole.

Eikeland, O. (1995), "Aksjonsforskningens horisonter – et forsøk på å se lenger enn til sin egen nesetipp", pp. 211-268 in Eikeland, Olav & Finsrud, Henrik Dons (eds.) (1995), *Research in Action – Forskning og handling – søkelys på aksjonsforskning*, AFIs skriftserie nr.1, Oslo: Arbeidsforskningsinstituttet.

Eikeland, O. (1996), *Kunnskapsproduksjon i endring – to bidrag*, AFI-notat 8/96, Oslo: Arbeidsforskningsinstituttet.

Eikeland, O. (1997), *Erfaring, dialogikk og politikk – Den antikke dialogfilosofiens betydning for rekonstruksjonen av moderne empirisk samfunnsvitenskap. Et begrepshistorisk og filosofisk bidrag*, 3rd ed., Oslo: Universitetsforlaget.

Eikeland, O. (1997b), *Demokrati og medvirkning under et nytt kunnskapsforvaltningsregime*, AFI-notat 5/97, Oslo: Work Research Institute.

Eikeland, O. (1998), "Anamnesis – dialogisk erindringsarbeid som empirisk forskningsmetode", pp.95-136 in O. Eikeland & K. Fossestøl (eds.) (1998): *Kunnskapsproduksjon i endring – nye erfarings- og organisasjonsformer*, AFIs skriftserie nr.4, Oslo: Work Research Institute.

Eikeland, O. (1998b), *Faglige metamorfoser og immanente konvergenser – opptakt til et nytt kunnskapsforvaltningsregime*, AFI-notat 5/98, Oslo: Work Research Institute.

Eikeland, O. (1999a), *From training to learning – new trends and future perspectives*, AFI-notat 3/99, Oslo: Work Research Institute.

Eikeland, O. (1999b), *Mot et nytt kunnskapsforvaltningsregime?*, AFI-notat 7/99, Oslo: Work Research Institute.

Eikeland, O. (2001), "Action Research as the Hidden Curriculum of the Western Tradition", pp.145-155 in Reason, P. and Bradbury, H. (eds.) (2001): *Handbook of Action Research – Participative Inquiry and Practice.* 1ˢᵗ Edition, London: Sage.

Eikeland, O. (2006a), "The Validity of Action Research – Validity in Action Research", pp. 193-240 in Nielsen, K.Aa. and Svensson, L. (eds.) (2006): *Action And Interactive Research – Beyond Theory and Practice,* Maastricht and Aachen: Shaker Publishing.

Eikeland, O. (2006b), "Phrónêsis, Aristotle, and Action Research", *International Journal of Action Research,* (2)1: 5-53.

Eikeland, O. (2007), "From Epistemology to Gnoseology – Understanding the Knowledge Claims of Action Research", *Management Research News,* (30)5: 344-358.

Eikeland, O. (2008), *The Ways of Aristotle – Aristotelian phrónêsis, Aristotelian philosophy of dialogue, and Action Research,* Bern: Peter Lang Publishing Company.

Eikeland, O. (Work in progress), *Symbiotic Learning Systems,* Paper presented at the OLKC conference in Amsterdam, 26-28 April, 2009.

Eikeland, O.; Lahn, L. C.. (1995), *Organisasjon og arbeidsmiljø ved Avdeling for historie, Universitetet i Oslo,* AFIs rapportserie nr.2/95, Oslo: Work Research Institute.

Eikeland, O.; Berg, A. M. (1997), *Medvirkningsbasert organisasjonslæring og utviklingsarbeid i kommunene,* Oslo: Kommuneforlaget.

Eikeland, O.; Ausland, L. H.; Enehaug, H.; Klemsdal, L.; Widding, S. (2006c), *Har systematisk læring på arbeidsplassen noe med livsfase- og seniorpolitikk å gjøre?,* Rapportering fra Forsøks- og Utviklingsprosjektene i Nasjonalt Krafttak for seniorpolitikk i arbeidslivet (2001-2005), AFI-rapport 6 / 2006, Oslo: Work Research Institute.

Fiumara, G. C. (1995), *The Metaphoric Process – Connections between Language and Life,* London and New York: Routledge.

Flyvbjerg, B. (2001), *Making Social Science Matter – Why Social Inquiry Fails and How It Can Succeed Again,* Cambridge: Cambridge University Press.

Funke, G. (1961), *Gewohnheit,* Archiv für Begriffsgeschichte, Band 3, Bonn: H.Bouvier u.Co. Verlag.

Gherardi, S. (2000), "Practice-based Theorizing on Learning and Knowing in Organizations", *Organization,* 7(2): 211-223.

Gherardi, S. (2006), *Organizational Knowledge: The Texture of Organizing,* London: Blaxkwells.

Gibbons, M. et al. (1994), *The New Production of Knowledge – The Dynamics of Science and Research in Contemporary Societies,* London: Sage Publications.

Giddens, A. (1984), *The Constitution of Society – Outline of the Theory of Structuration*, Cambridge: Polity Press.

Hacking, I. (1983), *Representing and Intervening – Introductory Topics in the Philosophy of Natural Science*, Cambridge: Cambridge University Press.

Hegel, G.W.F. (1970), *Enzyklopädie der philosophischen Wissenschaften I*, Frankfurt a.m.: Suhrkamp Verlag.

Heidegger, M. (1986) (orig.1927), *Sein und Zeit*, Tübingen: Max Niemeyer Verlag.

Heider, K. G. (1988): "The Rashomon Effect: When Ethnographers Disagree", *American Anthropologist*, 90(1): 73-81.

Hesse, M. (1963), *Models and Analogies in Science*, London: Sheed and Ward

Hillier, J. & Rooksby, E. (eds.) (2005), *Habitus: A Sense of Place*, Aldershot & Burlington: Ashgate Publishing.

Husserl, E. (1936), *Die Krisis der europäischen Wissenschaften und die transzendentale Phänomenologie*, Hamburg (1977): Felix Meiner Verlag.

King, A. (2000), "Thinking with Bourdieu Against Bourdieu – A "Practical" Critique of the Habitus", *Sociological Theory*, 18(3): 417-433.

Klemsdal, L.; Eikeland, O. & Teig, I. L. (2002), *Hvordan gi et allment begrep individuelt innhold gjennom dialog – medvirkningsbasert utviklingsarbeid i Hordaland fylkeskommune*, AFI-notat 9/2002, Oslo: Work Research Institute.

Kuhlmann, W. (1985), *Reflexive Letztbegründung – Untersuchungen zur Transzendentalpragmatik*, Munich: Verlag Karl Alber Freiburg.

Laudan, L. (1981), *Science and Hypothesis*, Dordrecht: D.Reidel Publishing Company.

Lave, J. and Wenger, E. (1991), *Situated Learning – Legitimate Peripheral Participation*, Cambridge: Cambridge University Press.

Lewin, K. (1948), "Action Research and Minority Problems". In: K. Lewin, *Resolving Social Conflicts*. G. Lewin (ed.), New York: Harper & Row.

Lyotard, J. F. (1979), *La Condition Postmoderne – Rapport sur le Savoir*, Paris: Les Editions de Minuit.

Malpas. J. E. (1999), *Place and Experience – A Philosophical Topography*, Cambridge: Cambridge University Press.

Malpas, J. E. (2006), *Heidegger's Topology – Being, Place, World*, Cambridge, MA: The MIT Press.

Nicolini, D. et al. (2003), *Knowing in Organizations: A Practice-Based Approach*, London: M.E. Sharpe.

Nielsen, K. and Kvale, S. (1999), *Mesterlære: læring som social praksis*, Copenhagen: Hans Reitzel.

Nielsen, K. and Kvale, S. (2003), *Praktikkens læringslandskab: at lære gennem arbejde*, Copenhagen: Akademisk Forlag.

Nowotny, H. et al. (2001), *Re-Thinking Science – Knowledge and the Public in an Age of Uncertainty*, Cambridge: Polity Press.

Peirce, C. S. (1868) & (1878): "Some Consequences of Four Incapacities" (1868), "Deduction, Induction, and Hypothesis" (1878), both in Houser, N. & Kloesel, C. (eds.) (1992), *The Essential Peirce – Selected Philosophical Writings, Vol.1. (1863-1893)*, Bloomington & Indianapolis: Indiana University Press.

Polanyi, M. (1958), *Personal Knowledge – Towards a Post-Critical Philosophy*, London: Routledge & Kegan Paul (corrected version from 1962).

Polanyi, M. (1966), *The Tacit Dimension*, Gloucester, MA: Peter Smith.

Polkinghorne, D.E. (2004), *Practice and the Human Sciences – The Case for a Judgment Based Practice of Care*, Albany: State University of New York Press,.

Popper, K. R. (1980) (German original 1934), *The Logic of Scientific Discovery*, London: Hutchinson & Co.

Quine, W. v. O. (1961) (orig. 1953), "Two Dogmas of Empiricism", pp. 20-46 in *From a Logical Point of View – Logico-Philosophical Essays*, New York: Harper & Row.

Radin, D. (2006), *Entangled Minds Extrasensory Experiences in a Quantum Reality*, New York: Paraview Pocket Books.

Ramírez, J.L. (1995), *Skapande mening – En begreppsgenealogisk undersökning om rationalitet, vetenskap och planering*, Stockholm: Nordplan.

Rapaport, R. N. (1970), "Three Dilemmas in Action Research – With Special Reference to the Tavistock Experience", *Human Relations* 23(6): 499-513.

Reason, P. and Torbert, W. R. (2001), "The Action Turn – Toward a Transformational Social Science", *Concepts and Transformation*, 6(1): 1-37.

Reich, L. S. (1985), *The Making of American Industrial Research – Science and Business at GE and Bell, 1876-1926*, Cambridge: Cambridge University Press.

Reinharz, S. (1979), *On becoming a Social Scientist – From survey research and participant observation to experiential analysis*, San Francisco: Jossey-Bass Publishers.

Sandelands, L. E. & Srivatsan, V. (1993), "The Problem of Experience in the Study of Organizations", *Organization Studies*, 14(1): 1-22.

Schatzki, T.R; Knorr Cetina, K & von Savigny, E. (eds.): *The Practice Turn in Contemporary Theory*, London & New York: Routledge.

Schwandt, T. (2002), *Evaluation Practice Reconsidered*, New York: Peter Lang

Soulez, A. (2004), *Wittgenstein et le Tournant Grammatical*, Paris: Presses Universitaires de France.

Teare, R.; Davies, D., and Sandelands, E. (1998), *The Virtual University – An Action Paradigm and Process for Workplace Learning*, London: Cassell.

Toulmin, S. (1996a): *Introduction*. In: Toulmin/Gustavsen (eds.) (1996): pp. 1-4

Toulmin, S. (1996b): *Concluding Methodological Reflections: Élitism and democracy among the sciences*. In: Toulmin/Gustavsen (eds.) (1996): pp. 203-226.

Toulmin, S. (1996c): "Is Action Research Really 'Research'"? *Concepts and Transformation*, 1(1): 51-62.

Toulmin, S. (2001): *Return to Reason*, Cambridge, MA: Harvard University Press.

Toulmin, S.; Gustavsen, B. (eds.) (1996): *Beyond Theory – Changing organizations through participation*, Amsterdam / Philadelphia: John Benjamins Publishing Company.

Vaihinger, H. (1923), *Die Philosophie des Als Ob*, Leipzig: Felix Meiner Verlag

Wartofsky, M. W. (1968), *Conceptual Foundations of Scientific Thought – An Introduction to the Philosophy of Science*, New York: The Macmillan Company.

Wittgenstein, L. (1976) (orig. 1953), *Philosophical Investigations*, Oxford: Basil Blackwell.

Wittgenstein, L. (1974), *Philosophical Grammar*, Oxford: Basil Blackwell.

2 Making Sense of Managerial Reforms through Action Research[1]

Lars Klemsdal

Introduction

In organisational change, action research is often framed as an alternative strategy to implementing ready-made managerial reforms and organisational models. While managerial reforms are often perceived as imposing a new organisational structure specifying a new way of organising work top-down, the strategy of action research is framed as involving the employees in developing new ways of organising and improving work based on their own practice and their primary tasks (Greenwood and Levin, 1998; Coghlan and Brannick, 2001). This chapter investigates how the two strategies might combine in fruitful ways. I will analyse an attempt at implementing a top-down managerial reform through a bottom-up action research strategy in a municipal organisation. The conceptual key for merging these two presumably opposing strategies is provided by the theory of organisational sensemaking as coined by Karl Weick.

Weick's (1979, 1995) theory of sensemaking says that organisational change happens as the members of the organisation (the practitioners) encounter new situations that they are forced to make sense of. This sensemaking happens as the practitioners improvise in these situations (that is, deal with the new situations ad hoc) and then retrospectively justify these actions in plausible terms. From this it follows that change through sensemaking often happens in coincidental and accidental, and sometimes even blindfolded, ways. The theory of sensemaking thus makes us aware of the importance of paying attention to what we actually do about new situations, instead of "buying", so to speak, our immediate retrospective justifications (and rationalisations) of what we did. From this perspective, planned

1 This chapter has been written as part of the strategic research programme (2003-2007) at the WRI, Oslo. I would like to thank the following persons for their instructive and supportive comments on both recent and earlier drafts of this text. Thanks to the editors of the book, Benedicte Brøgger and Olav Eikeland. Thanks also to my other colleagues at the SIP Group at WRI, Siw Fosstenløkken, Jarle Hildrum and Øyvind Pålshaugen. Thanks to two anonymous reviewers who commented and approved of an earlier version of the text delivered at the conference on research methods, arranged by the Research Methods Division of the Academy of Management and the ISEOR, in Lyon, April 2007. Thanks also to the audiences at this conference for their comments.

organisational reforms contribute to organisational change primarily by creating a new and thus unknown situation that calls for being made sense of by the organisational members or practitioners (Klemsdal, 2008).

This view of how processes of organisational development and change unfold is contrary to what is often presupposed by theories of planned change. Practical theories of reforms presuppose that plans can be implemented by e.g. being *translated* more or less straightforwardly from plans to practice.[2] Also the so-called action research cycle of diagnosing, planning, acting and evaluating (cf. Coghlan and Brannick, 2001; French et al., 2005) presupposes that new actions are tried out on the basis of deliberate plans, and then evaluated. Through the lens of sensemaking, the importance of planning action, of interpreting plans in order to translate them practically and so forth, is played down. Instead, improvised enactments are emphasised as the basis for understanding new ways of working when implementing reforms.

This gives us a rationale, in a double sense of the word, for enhancing and thus leading processes of change when implementing reforms. On the one hand, it gives us a specific understanding of what is to be enhanced, namely the way and "the what" the participants talk about when discussing the new way of organising (the reform), not least their way of improvising in the new situation. On the other hand, it highlights the importance of focusing on the way they are dealing with the situation, rather than on what they should be doing, as they otherwise end up implementing the new way of organising rather blindly. The theory of sensemaking thus gives action research, understood as literally speaking *researching* the organisational members' *actions* during processes of change, a specific rationale. On the other hand, the action research cycles, in their modified way, present a solution for practitioners to deal with the challenges and pitfalls of sensemaking.

As for the managerial reform, it gives us an opportunity for investigating how processes of sensemaking can be enhanced through cycles of action research. At the same time, it gives us the opportunity to explore in what way action-research must be focused specifically in order to work fruitfully. This chapter thus argues in favour of a concept of action research as primarily engaging the practitioners in doing research on their own actions (cf. Eikeland, 2006). It argues in favour of combining the descriptive theory of organisational sensemaking with the normative perspective of certain forms of action research. And ultimately, the chapter

---

2   There is a vast range of literature that can be classified within this very broad category, ranging from the most hardcore "implementation theories" (cf. Hill and Hupe, 2002, for an overview of different positions within the so-called implementation studies) to the rather constructivist translational perspectives (cf. Røvik, 2007; Christensen and Lægreid, 2007; Lozeau et al., 2002). See Klemsdal, 2008, ch. 10.2 for further elaboration of this argument.

argues in favour of combining processes of managerially induced planned change (or reforms) with processes of action research, in order to enhance the unavoidable processes of sensemaking that finally end up constituting the new way of organising that the reforms propose.

Following a Process of Planned Change in a Town Hall

In November 2004 I was invited to follow a process of organisational reform in a medium-sized Norwegian municipality. Over the two preceding years, I and a colleague had already been conducting a course for the municipality on *Organisational learning and doing action research in your own organisation*. The managers, as well as the internal group responsible for the development activity within the organisation, were thus acquainted with and recognised action research in general as a fruitful way of working with organisational development. Initially, though, the management had not planned on hiring external assistance in facilitating the reform. When I received a grant from the Research Council of Norway for taking a PhD on the general topic *Public Sector Innovation*, however, they invited me to join them as a researcher in their implementation process. In the contract with the organisation it was loosely stated that as a researcher I was supposed to participate actively in their change process.

As part of the reform, all the central services in the municipality, formerly organised as separate units located in separate buildings, had been moved into *a new town hall* with a so-called open landscape design. At the same time, new principles for organising and management had been introduced. The former hierarchical structure was eliminated, and people were no longer employed in specific service units, but instead in so-called *networks* in accordance with their field of competence. With the network as a basis, the employees were thus part of several work teams organised around tasks; these work teams were in principle flexible, with the idea being that they could be changed according to what would optimise task performance at a given time. Neither the networks nor the work teams were supposed to have managers. The basic principle of the new way of organising was so-called *empowered employees* who were able to manage their own performance of their primary tasks (the principle of self-management) and shared responsibility for the common tasks with their work team colleagues. Each work team had a *work team coordinator* and each network had a *network contact*. These roles were *not* supposed to substitute for the management roles, rather, according to the plan, they were defined as "mediators" and "messengers" between the top management and the networks / work teams. The roles were supposed to rotate every third month between the members of respectively the networks and the work teams.

The process of implementation was as generally and abstractly formulated as the plan. In accordance with the new principle of empowered and self-managed employees, the employees were given a large degree of freedom of figuring out how to work in a new way in practice. There were hardly any plans for facilitating the process of implementation as such.

If we believe Brunsson and Olsen (1993, Pp. 33-43), the reform at the new town hall is typical for administrative reforms in public sector organisations in its formal sense, where

reform ideas consist of principles rather than detailed descriptions, theories rather than perceptions, i.e. reforms present ordered ideas which cannot encompass all the complexity of the real world, but which therefore seem more clear than reality.

This was also what quickly became the general experience at the new town hall. The ideas were clear enough at an abstract level; they were experienced as meaningful when they were discussed in general terms at the level of planning. But when they were to be concretely enacted, they were immediately experienced as being rather fuzzy and unclear. For instance, the abstract definitions of the new roles did not respond very adequately to the concrete tasks that needed to be done. The process of implementation, or *organisational change and development*, turned out to be basically about clarification. Or in other words, *the new way of organising had to be made meaningful or sensible in practice*.

But this general insight about the change process was also only clear on an abstract level of understanding. The conceptualisation of the essence of the change and development process had to be made concretely meaningful in practice. It was thus not only the new way of organising that needed to be made sense of; also the process of *making sense* of the new way of organising had to be made sense of.

This is the point where I came in as a researcher with the general task of following the process of implementing the reform. Before I present the double sensemaking process that followed from this point in the change process, with me as a participant researcher together with the practitioners, I will elaborate my research strategy in terms of the theoretical framework that informed it: on the one hand, a repertoire of research strategies from action research, and on the other hand, the concept of organisational sensemaking as coined by Karl Weick.

Method and Theory

Aspects of the Scandinavian Action Research Tradition

The way I positioned myself and framed my role in this project drew on a framework of related research strategies developed within the Scandinavian field of action research, particularly represented by Eikeland (1997, 2001, 2006), Pålshaugen (1998, 2002) and Greenwood and Levin (1998).

A distinctive and common characteristic of these research strategies, one that is central to my approach, is that they combine the practice of organisational development with researching processes of organisational change. As organisational change and development is perceived as improved practice, something that is internally connected to an improved understanding of how to perform the given tasks, the outcome of the change process and the outcome of the research process are perceived as similar: both outcomes are about improved understandings about how to perform the tasks. These understandings are not necessarily *shared* among practitioners and researchers (nor among the practitioners themselves). Nonetheless, it is a common endeavour where researchers and practitioners bring their respective competencies and interests in: "bridging local knowledge and scientific knowledge", in Greenwood and Levin's terms; where the researchers bring the "discourse of social science" and practitioners "the discourse of their practice", in Pålshaugen's terms (1998, p. 19); or in Eikeland's terms, their different "native practices" (2006, Pp. 19-21).

The research strategy of action research is, according to Pålshaugen (1998, Pp. 20-25), to intervene in the organisation by connecting the discourse of social science with the discourse of the organisation. This is not done by introducing abstract organisational solutions (or *simulated solutions*, as Pålshaugen labels them) into the organisation. Rather, it is done by helping to develop and enhance the established discourse within the organisation in order to make this discourse incorporate richer understandings of what is going on in the organisation, as well as how one could act in different or improved ways (ibid., p. 22).

For Greenwood and Levin (1998) the important intervention for the action researcher is to engage in dialogues with the practitioners about their situation, contributing with general theoretical knowledge in order to elevate and enhance the local knowledge. This coupling of general theories with local knowledge is also expected to help enhance the researcher's general theories, either by rejecting them, making them more nuanced or even confirming and expanding them. The research process is thus about creating both change in the organisation and new knowledge about social phenomena.

Eikeland (2006) dissociates himself explicitly from the notion of "intervention", conceiving an action research strategy where the researcher and the practitioners operate in a peer group relationship where both act as "both masters and apprentices, going the same way" (2006, p. 18). Thus, for a researcher to become familiar with a field, he has to take the natives' position, learning to master the world as a native does; optimally he should *become* a native. Within such a paradigm, it follows that the researcher operates as an apprentice in the field, while the practitioner is the master. On the other hand, in order to change or improve the way the practitioner masters his world (going about his daily work), the practitioners' knowledge must be made explicit through collective reflection on action. And here the researcher can return something to the practitioner, namely a special skill in making tacit knowledge explicit when articulating experiences in order to communicate them scientifically.

The three perspectives have in common the idea that organisational change and development, as well as research on such change and development, is best off where there is *mutual participation* between researchers and practitioners who meet in *a space for independent inquiry about practice* (performance of tasks). Eikeland (1997, 2001, 2006) and Pålshaugen (1998) conceptualise this space for independent inquiry as a "development organisation" dealing with the "development tasks", to be distinguished from the work organisation, dealing with the organisation's primary tasks.

While the research process and change process are intertwined in this space for independent inquiry, the outcome of the process can be separated in two distinctive products: a) change or improvements in the concrete situation, and b) general knowledge about social phenomena.

If we try to specify which development tasks should be dealt with in the space for independent inquiry, according to the three approaches, several distinctions emerge. Both Pålshaugen (1998) and Greenwood and Levin (1998) seem to build on the so-called "action research cycle", originally introduced by Kurt Lewin (cf. Coghlan and Brannick, 2001; French et al., 2005). The point of these cycles is that "[t]he researcher and the client engage in collaborative cycles of planning, taking action and evaluating" (Coghlan and Brannick, 2001, p. 10). In other words, practitioners and researchers in the development organisation should plan the content of the new way of organising, plan how to enact this new way of organising, enact the new way of organising, and then evaluate how the actions turned out or how the planned measures worked. The case used in Pålshaugen's book is about how the employees are engaged broadly in developing the plan for the new way of working, and further in the process of implementing this plan experimentally. The point of this kind of action research as strategic organisational development is thus to develop ideas together, based on the general situation of the organisation, and then "test" these ideas in practice. As Pålshaugen expressed it in a personal communication: "It is about experimenting under real life conditions." Greenwood and Levin (1998) also build on the action research cycle as the basic structure for the action research activity, but downplay strategic development in favour of continually involving the organisation in action research cycles in order to promote and enhance incremental change. Eikeland (2006) seems to depart from the action research cycle, instead arguing in favour of action research as literally *researching our actions* (2006, Pp. 210, 219) in order to learn how to improve our practices. In other words, the point of action research is not the planning of new actions as such, but the investigation of established actions or practices in order to discover how they work and how they are likely to be improved.

The exact differences between the three approaches are hard to set in theory. It is by studying their different practices that the differences and distinctions might be assessed precisely, and this is not the task of this chapter. Still, the three approaches provide me with a conceptual repertoire to draw on when actively researching the change process at the new town hall.

A Double Agenda: a Shared Action Research Approach

Framed within this horizon of the Scandinavian action research field, I initially formulated two general aims and ambitions for the research project. On the one hand, based on the expectations from my funding source, I was supposed to study a case of *innovation in a public sector organisation.* On the other hand, the Innovation Network, the municipality's internal organisation development group – my gatekeepers as well as "inside partners" in the new town hall – helped me define a second purpose for my participation: I should be a researcher *in* their change process. That meant that the research process should *contribute* to the change process, not merely study it. They specified their expectations towards me as being a *critical friend* from the outside, asking critical questions about what they were doing and what was happening, helping raise their own critical awareness towards what they were doing, as well as giving feedback about what I experienced as a participant researcher.

As the organisation consisted of 220 employees belonging to more than 20 areas of competency and participating in about 128 different work teams, I had to restrict my participation in the change process at the new town hall, in terms of either intensity or scope. As the point of my study was to participate closely in their longitudinal change process, the best way of making restrictions was in terms of scope. Thus, I decided to follow practitioners from mainly one field of competency during the change process, namely social service workers organised in the so-called *Social*

Network as well as in various work teams (which included members from other service fields and thus networks of competency). I participated regularly in the Social Network's internal meetings, and in internal meetings with several of the relevant work teams; I also participated in meetings with the clients and external collaborators of these work teams. In addition, I participated in regular meetings with the top management group of the municipality and the small administrative management team of the new town hall, as well as with the Innovation Network, which had the practical responsibility for "running" the change process.

Based on the abovementioned ambition of participating in the change process not only as a researcher but also as a critical friend, I defined my research strategy as taking part in and working to enhance a space for independent inquiry regarding what was going on in the change process. In practice this meant that I was trying to create a space for critically evaluating what was going on in the change process among the different groups I was following (from the top management to the work teams of the social services). More specifically, the aim of this strategy was to make the new way of organising meaningful in practice, for the practitioners as well as in terms of organisational research. But how do we make concrete sense of a plan for a new way of organising? *What do we do and what do we talk about in the space for independent inquiry?* As coined by Karl Weick (1979, 1995, 2001a-e), the theory of sensemaking in organisations turned out to be a constructive basis for answering these questions, as it presents a theory about how practitioners enact change on a micro level in order to make their world meaningful.

Sensemaking

Sensemaking is the core concept in Karl Weick's perspective(s) on organisations as primarily continuous processes of *organising* (1979, 1995, 2001a-e). By the focus on organisations as primarily organising, Weick wants to direct our attention towards how the daily performance of tasks in organisations also involves a component of (re)organising the way of performing the tasks, for instance due to changes in the surroundings. Even though the process of organising is a continuous aspect of practice in an organisation, it becomes especially precarious and visible in transition phases, such as during processes of planned change. It is important to emphasise that the planned part of the change process does not represent the process of organising as such, but must be perceived as changes in the surroundings of the daily practice that the practitioners need to make sense of in practice. The (re)organising is primarily this activity of sensemaking. Sensemaking is in this sense almost synonymous with organising; it is a specification of what organising is about.

According to Weick (1995, p. 5), sensemaking is a process that is evoked when we are interrupted in our ongoing daily activities by our expectations not being met. In other words, sensemaking is about making sense of *a situation*, an event or a phenomenon that is new to us and experienced as ambiguous.[3] Sensemaking is then about practically *making* these events, situations or phenomena sensible by "*enacting* them" (that is, dealing with the situations ad hoc) and then interpreting this enactment retrospectively in order to conceptualise it. In other words, the relationship between action and interpretation in sensemaking is *not* primarily that we sit down and interpret the situations or events, and then act upon this interpretation. Even though we try to do it this way, this strategy will not bring us far enough in making sense of the new situation. There is always a gap between the ideas about and interpretations of the new situation and the answer to what to do about the situation. In line with the theory of sensemaking, this gap must be filled with actions, i.e. improvisational actions that can again be interpreted retrospectively, thereby constituting the new open situations and ideas as specific situations and ideas (see Weick, 2001d, 2001e). As Weick puts it, the seeming order of the action is imposed in retrospect, as a spurious order on an indeterminate past (2001a, p. 13):

> Meaning is retrospective and only elapsed experience is available for meaningful interpretation. [...] Action when viewed retrospectively clarifies what the action is doing, what business it is in and what its projects may be. (Weick, 1979, p. 245)

The retrospective interpretations tend to be informed by a need to *justify* our actions according to what is acceptable to the social context that the action has taken place within. The interpretation has thus a tendency to *explain* what we did in socially legitimate terms (1995, 2001a, 2001b).

This is the most challenging aspect of the sensemaking process, according to Weick. The process of establishing meaningful interpretations of our enactments post factum is often *not* a process of explicit, deliberative reflection. Rather the opposite, which means that an important challenge in sensemaking is that the interpretations of enactments tend to justify enactments. This means that unfortunate enactments tend to be reinforced, rather than disclosed and altered, during the process of sensemaking. As Weick formulates it, "an enacted [situation] becomes rather quickly a plausible guide for subsequent action and interpretation" (1979, p. 229). It

---

3   There are several authors who point to the need for a crisis or state of ambiguity, or at least an extraordinary situation, to initiate and motivate change and innovation within an organisation (Brown and Duguid, 1991; Gioia and Chittipeddi, 1991; March, 1991; Weick, 1995, 2001). In the words of Brown and Duguid, there has to be a situation (either created or arising more subtly) that allows, or even requires, the practitioners to step out of their inevitably limited core world view and try something new (1991, p. 51).

becomes quickly established as a scheme for "how we do things around here", and thus, *"[t]he enactment perspective implies that people in organisations should be more self-conscious about and spend more time reflecting on the actual things they do"* (Weick, 1979, Pp. 168-169, my emphasis).

In terms of change and development processes, if we are aware of how the sensemaking process evolves by improvised enactments, on the one hand, and by justificatory post factum explanations of these enactments, on the other, we are in a better position to see when the enactments take off in one direction while the retrospectively explanatory discourse takes off in another; the risk in such a case is that we end up institutionalising malpractice that we in addition lack an adequate concept of.

From this insight in the logic of sensemaking, we can derive the following practical advice in order to make the sensemaking process more constructive: focus more on analysing what we actually do, primarily trying to understand it as a specific way of dealing with our situation, instead of trying to explain it by subsuming the actions under a socially plausible general category.

This analytical framework and its practical implications proved after a while to be very productive, when trying to figure out how the change and development activity could be organised and enhanced in the abovementioned municipal organisation. It highlighted the importance of acknowledging that the basis for the process of change, in both constructive and destructive terms, was to be found in what the practitioners were already doing when dealing with the new situation. Thus, it represented a rationale for turning the focus of the discussion about the "new way of organising" away from what to do towards what we have already done.

Making Sense of the Research Process on Organisational Change

Experience of Chaos and Unclarities

To return to the case of the municipal organisation, the ideas in the change plan had, as mentioned above, seemed clear enough on an abstract level. But as the employees started to work concretely within the new town hall from the beginning of January 2005, the situation turned out to be unclear. It became apparent that instead of providing answers for how to perform the tasks in a new way, the plan for "the new way of organising" led to a lot of confusion and a sense of chaos among the employees. Viewed from the perspective of sensemaking, the change plan made two contributions to the change process. On the one hand, by eliminating three central structural features of the "old organisation", namely the middle managers, 10% of the man-years, and the formal and physical boundaries between the services, the change plan *introduced a new situation*. With Weick (2001f, p. 210) we can specify the eliminations of the three structural features as *loosening the organisational structures* "by transforming strong situations which used to be well defined by structured salient cues, into weak situations that are now ambiguous with fewer salient guides for action". From this perspective, the change plan can be perceived as an "ambiguity by design" (Gioia and Chittipeddi, 1991) that primarily breaks up the equilibrious stream of the practitioner's daily way of going about performing the tasks. On the other hand, the change plan contributed with a reified image of a new way of organising, thereby providing many new abstract *cues* (see Weick, 1995, Pp. 49-55), such as "empowerment", "self-managed work teams" and "network contact role", that steered the practitioners towards certain aspects of the new situation that had to be dealt with in order to make the new situation more strongly defined.[4] As cues rather than as prescriptions or specifications, however, they gave little direction about how to enact the new way of organising. But this was not clear to the practitioners at that point in time; they searched for answers in the change plan that could solve the confusion.

It was especially the elimination of the professional management roles that seemed to create confusion. The CEO had from the beginning explained the decision to eliminate all the professional middle manager roles on the grounds that the employees were competent professionals and did not need any managers to tell them what to do or how to perform their tasks. In addition, the CEO said, the tasks are simple and clear enough for the employees to manage their daily work without managers. He also emphasised that the new way of organising without managers promoted empowerment among the employees, made the work situation more flexible, and released personal initiative and creativity in the organisation.

From the beginning, the employees of the Social Network (the group I paid particular attention to) had questioned the decision of eliminating the middle managers, and they contested the CEO's framing of the management role. They said that the CEO was right about them being able to perform their own primary tasks without managerial supervision. As far as they could remember, the manager role in their service area had never been about telling the employees what to do and how to do it. Rather, the middle managers had dealt with many other tasks, such as talking to the media, attending meetings with external partners, making overall priorities on behalf of the service, and so forth. Thus, the challenge of the new situation was not about the individual professional taking responsibility for performing his or her primary task, as the CEO's framing implied, but about taking part in a collective responsibility for performing the former *management tasks*. This way

---

4 See Klemsdal (2008) for a further elaboration of this perspective on how change plans contribute to organisational change.

of framing the elimination of management highlighted a particular consequence of this situation, namely that as the former management tasks were delegated collectively to all the employees, no one would take responsibility for them. As they said, "When everybody is given the responsibility, nobody takes responsibility."

The employees' reframing of what the elimination of management was about (namely distributing the management tasks to all the employees) was based on their experiences with the management tasks "popping up" after the manager had been abolished; their identification of the consequences of this situation was, however, not based on such experiences. Already before they moved into the new town hall, the maxim "when everybody is given responsibility, nobody takes it" was presented as the major consequence of the new way of organising. But this was merely a folk theory. As I will demonstrate shortly, it was not based on experience.

Looking for Concrete Possibilities for Enacting the Reform in Practice

So far, we can say that the discourse about the change process is characterised by the CEO *framing* (Bean and Hamilton, 2006) how the employees (and other, external audiences) were supposed to understand the new way of organising. In the terms of Gioia and Chittipeddi (1991), the CEO tries to *give sense* to the plan for the new way of organising. This sensegiving has the character of general folk theories, bordering on myths, about management, empowered employees, and so forth. In this sense, sensegiving functions more as general justificatory explanations for the new way of organising than as guidelines for the concrete sensemaking of the employees.

This became very clear as the employees responded by challenging the CEO's theories and explanations by showing more specifically what the manager used to do. When it came to how they should proceed for themselves, though, they resorted to a general folk theory of why nobody would take responsibility for the management tasks. Thus, both discourses on the change process (the managers' and the employees') were very weakly coupled to actual practice (except for the employees' descriptions of the former management tasks), primarily referring to general theories and explanations. Their attempts at interpreting and translating the reform plan/ ideas as such did not seem to bring the change process any further.

At this point in time, I thought that the way this abstract, general *discourse on the change process* could be more connected to (and productive for) the change in practice, was to encourage the employees to analyse the possibilities of performing the tasks on their own terms, supplementing the analyses of the challenges. This way of thinking was in line with the action research cycle. The idea was to engage the employees in a process of figuring out what the different ideas of the change plan could concretely mean in their practice, and then deciding on what to do in order to enact this meaning (diagnosing – micro-planning – acting – evaluating). In this way, the abstract ideas of the reform could be translated locally by the practitioners, first discursively and then enacted.

An important task for the few remaining top-level managers would then be to ask for and study the employees' analyses of the challenges and possibilities related to the new way of organising. In this way, I thought, the inquiry around the change process could guide and drive the process of changing practice by helping the practitioners figure out how to enact the new way of organising.

The management followed this up by arranging meetings with all the network contacts, in order to jointly develop common guidelines for how to enact the network contact roles. This was due to signals that this role was enacted in different ways among the different networks, and that the employees felt that the role was unclear in terms of expectations and tasks. I perceived this effort as one step towards establishing a more thorough, independent discourse (an independent space for inquiries) around issues concerning the organisation's change and development process.

In line with the same way of thinking, I arranged evaluation meetings during the spring in order to thoroughly analyse the challenges and possibilities of the new way of organising, with the intent of figuring out how to deal with the challenges and enact the possibilities. The discussions seemed to work fine. The employees were engaged, coming up with extensive lists of challenges, thinking creatively about new possibilities of working, suggesting ideas for new work teams to be established, and so forth. Even though the analysis of possibilities was abstract, the brainstorming proved inspiring and energising and showed that the employees were very capable of proposing future solutions regarding the challenges and performance of the tasks. They said that thinking in terms of new possibilities made the situation clearer to them. This was, in my view, promising. It demonstrated that there was a lot of potential for change in the new way of organising. We saw this as a manifestation that the practitioners could drive the organisation development process themselves, by inventing new ways of performing the tasks according to what they found useful in professional terms.

The management, for their part, was happy, as the focus on exploring possibilities within the new situation (rather than challenges) corresponded to their way of thinking about how organisations "are on the move, by focusing on future possibilities rather than on the past". Thus, during the spring, the purpose and content of the space for independent inquiry for researching and developing the organisational change process became more and more concretised for me: it could work as a space for continuously identifying challenges and possibilities and how to deal with them in order to develop the organisation further.

This did not last, however. Soon it would be clear that inventing solutions and possibilities in discussions and on paper was, literally speaking, easier said than done. The sensemaking perspective made it easier to see that the solutions, with enough momentum for changing practice, were what had already been enacted. This turned the practitioners and my own focus towards what *had happened*, rather than towards what was supposed to happen.

Looking Backwards instead of Forwards

This second change of focus came "naturally", so to speak, as I returned to the field in the early autumn after being away for four months. The clarifying conversations and discussions from the previous spring had, in fact, not clarified much. Contrary to my expectations, my first meeting with the Social Network in the autumn displayed even more confusion about the new way of organising. It was thus natural to ask *what had happened since last time*. The way of framing the question was not only "natural". It was also in line with the sensemaking perspective's way of perceiving how people make meaning out of their world. This perspective thus seemed to work as a better basis for a specific development strategy than the action research cycle, starting with what has been done rather than what to do as a basis for figuring out how to deal with the new situation. At the same time, the following experiences did frame my reading of the sensemaking perspective, helping me make concrete sense of the enactment and retrospective interpretation of the concept of *sensemaking*.

I thus had the sensemaking perspective of Weick in mind when I asked them what had happened since the last time. This question seemed to correspond with what was on the employees' minds, and they eagerly started talking about what they had been doing. The retrospective mode of discussing the new way of organising seemed very energising.

In my first meeting with the Social Network after coming back, the big issue was that they had just missed an application deadline for extra funds that were to be spent on dental care for the municipality's clients. Since the Social Services budget had already been greatly exceeded, that meant that they were about to forego a large amount of sorely needed money.

The network contact turned to me and said that this typified the vagueness concerning responsibility within the new way of organising. For was it actually he who was responsible for this application, he asked rhetorically, before answering the question himself:

> Yes, it was me. In practice it's me who deals with these things, but since this isn't a task that is formally delegated to me and clarified as part of my role, I end up giving it low priority. Since I'm actually supposed to be mainly engaged in the client

work, I just glance briefly through all the incoming mail, and thus risk missing a lot of important information. The delegation of authority has definite weaknesses. One is that the distribution of responsibility melts into air, so to speak. Another weakness is that information is spread around more or less by accident, without anyone being responsible for taking the initiative to act on the information. We all end up sitting and waiting for all the others to take responsibility.

A second participant continued by saying that incoming mail is delivered to a common mailbox for the whole network:

But who is responsible for checking it? Everyone is. But it's very random who ends up taking the responsibility. The present network contact takes a big responsibility, while the work team coordinators take a small one. But he doesn't actually have that responsibility. The functions of both the coordinator and the network contact have been unclear and ever changing.

I asked if it could be a good idea to at least compile a comprehensive list of all the fluctuating management tasks that need to be taken care of, and then distribute these tasks among every member of the work teams. The network contact responded quickly:

We've tried putting things down on paper. We've been holding seminars, but it doesn't help us much. Before we moved in to the new town hall, we were invited to say what we meant that the network contact and the work team coordinator roles should be. What kinds of tasks and responsibilities they were supposed to have. But we didn't relate to these roles at that point in time. We didn't relate to "the new way of organising", either. Then it turns out that different networks and work teams have different needs and concepts of management, different manager roles and tasks. That means that we can't use the same model for every network, like the top-level management did when designing the reform plan. That's something you see immediately in practice if you take a trip around the town hall and look at the different interpretations of the two roles that are being enacted in the different networks and work teams. The roles must be developed individually within each network and on their own terms.

I continued:

But what about now? Now you have experiences. Maybe it would be more meaningful and adequate to be engaged in figuring out, making sense of or developing these new roles by evaluating the experiences you have now after ten months? That could also be to make a list of all the tasks that the old unit leader had and discuss how they could be distributed.

They all seemed to agree with me that this could actually be of interest and even fruitful. "But who is to take the initiative for doing this?" a third participant asked. "It's a problem that we don't have anyone who is particularly responsible for prioritising the initiative of starting such a process." "And then we just talk without coming any further in practice", the second participant said.

What has happened?

The above excerpt reveals the following about the change process, as perceived with the help of the theory of sensemaking: The cognitive/ discursive understanding of the new way of organising has not been advanced much. The enactments, however, have continued full steam, especially through the enactment of the network contact role that increasingly appears as the central focus point for making sense of the "new way of organising". This is probably due to the fact that the network contact had been able to, or rather "forced" to, enact this role for ten months, rather than rotate it after three months as prescribed.

What has happened, then, is that all the minor and major tasks that the former unit leader handled himself have gradually "popped up" and come to the attention of the members of the Social Network. And their emergence required that someone must deal with them: more or less accidentally, the person who has in practice been handling these tasks is the network contact, "since someone had to do it". He has been representing the Social Services in official meetings outside the organisation as "a manager"; he is the one who has to make sure that letters and other enquiries to the Social Services, for instance concerning special applications for funds, were answered. In this way, more or less coincidentally and ad hoc, he has enacted the network contact role into a full-fledged manager role. We can even put it more strongly: he has ended up creating a monster of a network contact role, that no one – not even himself – feels capable of mastering; it is a role that appears completely without limits and clarity and that no one dares release him from.

Thus, instead of being clarified by being enacted in practice, the new situation seems instead to have been enacted into something even less sensible[5] than it originally was experienced. The question, then, is how they can make sense of it again.

From Weick's theory of sensemaking we can draw the following suggestions. First, the practitioners, by having enacted the new situation, are already on their way to making sense of it. Now they need to adequately interpret and conceptualise the enactment. Instead of talking about how the new way of organising is a bad idea in general terms (for instance by the abovementioned maxim about distribut-

---

5 Read *sensible* both in terms of *comprehensible* and *functional*, as is the point of the concept of making sense in Weick's terms, namely making something comprehensible by making it work in practice, even if the way of working might turn out to be dysfunctional.

ing responsibility), while at the same time studying the plan for what to do in the new situation, they can begin interpreting and conceptualising what they actually *have* done in dealing with the situation, and use that as a further basis for figuring out how to act in the new situation.

This insight was partially expressed by the network contact at the end of the excerpt from the meeting. In line with the logic of the sensemaking perspective, he points out how it is no use "getting things down on paper"; they had tried that before in the preliminary seminars where the employees were supposed to be involved in developing the plan of the new organisation, and also during the spring evaluation meetings that focused on the possibilities of the new situation. The reason the network contact gave is that they had no preconditions for understanding what was required and what this would look like in practice.

Further, he emphasised that the network members must have space for enacting the network contact role differently in different service fields. Interestingly, he says this on the basis of concrete observations of practice. Through regular meetings between the network contacts, the different practices and understandings – in short the different enactments – of the network contact role within the different networks have been displayed. The problem is that the way of framing and conceptualising these roles in these general network contact meetings has not focused on the real enactments, but on attempts at creating shared guidelines for how these roles should be enacted, based on the initial minimum definition. Because they still hang on to the initial minimum definition (specification) of the network contact role, the situation with all the differently enacted network contact roles becomes very unclear.

In other words, the roles as defined by the change plan are not unclear – the definitions are clear enough, but very simple, and not at all adequate for how the roles have been enacted in practice. In terms of sensemaking, what is encountered here is interesting. According to the logic of sensemaking, new ideas and concepts such as the network contact role start out as *cues* for actions that again become what the concepts and ideas *mean* when interpreted retrospectively. The network contact role gets its specific content by how it is enacted in practice *as this enactment is interpreted in retrospect*. This retrospective interpretation of a more practically specific network contact role gives new and more "salient cues" for the further enactments of the network contact role, and gradually the role literally becomes what the practitioners have made out of it in practice. In this particular case, however, the concrete enactment of the network contact role was not retrospectively interpreted. The only material for interpretation was the minimum descriptions of the role in the original plan. This shows the importance of retrospectively interpreting the enactments in sensemaking. If situations or roles are only enacted, without being retrospectively interpreted and conceptualised, there is a big risk that a discrepancy will develop between what we do in practice and our notion of what should be done. Even though abstract concepts are "plastic", in the sense that they can be enacted in many different ways, there is still a limit to what a concept might designate (Tsoukas and Chia, 2002). The further away the enactment of the concept is from the kernel of its abstract definition, the less able people are to grasp their own enactments in any meaningful way. Thus, in cases such as the monstrously enacted network contact role, the network contact role sorely needed being reformulated and reconceptualised (see Klemsdal, 2008). The unclarity of the roles and the plan of the new way of organising is thus not due to the plan as such, it is the enactment of the roles that have created unclarity. But the way of clarifying and making sense of the role is not primarily about enacting the role differently. It is about literally *coming to terms* with how the role has been enacted and using that as a starting point for deliberately and reciprocally adjusting the enactments and the conceptualisations of the enactments.

The problem is actually not that they "just talk without coming any further in practice", as one of them says, but that they stop taking action and discussing their actions. Rather than searching for how ideas or principles can be enacted in local practice, as is implied in much organisation development and action research literature (Cummings and Worley, 2005; Emery, 1998), this emphasises the importance of retrospective interpretation (formulations and conceptualisations) when trying to make sense by improvising new situations. What I thus suggested in the meeting, after experiencing this, was that the practitioners, in order to progress in their development process, primarily needed to clarify what they had actually been doing and thereby make sense of the new situation at the new town hall.

Making the Sensemaking Process Explicit and Deliberate

Already in February 2005, it seemed like the discourse about the change process had moved away from discussing the intentions and possibilities of the plan as such. Further, Weick's theory of sensemaking helped me explain and understand why all my attempts in March to engage the various practitioners in diagnostic analyses of new possibilities did not pay off in practical terms. These diagnostic analyses provided additional abstract ideas about how we could take advantage of the new situation, but they were never enacted in practice. They merely added new abstract cues to an already large set of abstract cues. In light of the sensemaking perspective, the focus on identifying and analysing future possibilities became less important. Instead, the sensemaking perspective suggested that in order to understand how to work in a new way at the new town hall, the practitioners had to focus more on what they were actually doing in the new situation and use this as a further basis to figure out how to act. My reframed hypothesis was that they needed to articulate and systematise their experience with enacting the new way of organising in practice.

We started working actively together on what I thought of as *making their sensemaking process explicit*. By reframing the inquiry about the change process towards making concrete, descriptive and critical analyses of the practitioners' own enactments, the practitioners and I were able, during different meetings and seminars, to deconstruct the monstrous network contact role and break it down to simple tasks and practices. On that basis we discussed which of these tasks could be distributed to the rest of the employees in the network, and what arrangements were required to enable them all to take part in the management tasks. These discussions were also based on concrete enactments. For instance, by analysing the successful experiences of a group of three persons who collaborated on applying for funds for a new project, they discovered that it was easier to distribute the management tasks to different groups rather than to individuals. This idea was tried out further and adjusted on the basis of practical experiences.

Thus, when the enactment of the new way of organising without managers was laid out for critical scrutiny, it was possible to discover new possibilities with the role, as well as find solutions to how it could be manageable. The way of clarifying the role was to extend the comprehension of how it was enacted in practice. We thereby also enacted the research strategy of enhancing spaces for independent inquiries as a process of mutual sensemaking.

The space for independent inquiry about the new way of organising unfolded in discussions and conversations that took place in several meetings during the autumn. But it really took off in a two-day seminar in January 2006, one year after the central services moved into the new town hall. At this seminar, all the members of the Social Network were gathered together with some of the few remaining managers, and they went through a process of reviewing very concretely what had happened during the year. The aim was to collect and systematise the analysis that had been going on during the autumn, and elaborate further on it in group works and plenary sessions. In addition to enhancing further the abovementioned process of *managing the process of making sense of the new way of organising*, the seminar also improved the collective commitment, creating consensus that the process was a collective responsibility and endeavour (see Klemsdal, 2008).

Concluding Discussion

The practitioners reported that the situation was radically changed, especially after the seminar in January 2006. Through the socially binding mechanisms of the group process, combined with the deconstruction and concrete clarification of how to take responsibility for the management tasks through the elaboration of already enacted "solutions", the distribution of the management tasks was working much better. Everyone was taking responsibility for the collective responsibility they had distributed (see Klemsdal, 2008, for elaboration and documentation). Nonetheless, despite these improvements in the management tasks and the general sensemaking, after two years of practice it was still difficult to assess whether the performance of the primary tasks had improved as a result of the reform. The new way of organising seems to have become concretised on the terms of the local practice, and it has changed practice; it is not yet clear, however, whether it has improved the services of the municipality.

What did we Learn from the Process?

The most important lessons learned by the practitioners, and by me as a researcher, from applying the sensemaking perspective *in* the process of change in the municipal organisation are as follows: The change plan is a set of abstract cues, rather than a blueprint or a set of specifications, for how to work in a new way. It must therefore be treated accordingly in order to be made meaningful in practice: what appears as specifications of the plan must be treated as *cues* to be improvised in the concrete context where they are supposed to be enacted, and then interpreted retrospectively in order to attain specific contextual meaning. For instance, the new roles, such as the network contact role, can hardly be enacted according to an abstract definition of being "a messenger", even though a messenger role is elaborated more thoroughly on paper. The role must be enacted in accordance with, or at least in relation to, what needs to be done in the concrete work situation. Sensemaking can thus be described as unfolding as a dialectic between cues that are introduced as part of a new situation or an event and that catch the attention of the practitioners, by selecting out aspects, elements and parts of the situations and events that are to be enacted, leaving other parts out. These enactments are then understood and made meaningful for the practitioners in retrospect, where the enactment can be conceptualised concretely. New inventions for how to deal with new situations must happen in practice before they can be adequately conceptualised in discourse. Through the activity of retrospective interpretation, we may draw out the implications of the enactments, extract more cues for further enactments and refine our discursive understanding of our way of going about.

Retrospective interpretations of enactments occur more or less constructively and productively, and it is both an individual and a collective effort, as it largely unfolds through people talking and trying to find plausible explanations for the enactments or the problems and possibilities that the enactment creates. The retrospective interpretations tend to invoke already established and justificatory discourses that deliver general, socially plausible explanations for what has happened (i.e. been enacted). In order to grasp the newness of the enactments, or even avoid that the retrospective interpretations become inadequate as conceptualisations of the enactments (which would merely create more confusion rather than impose a meaningful order on the enactments), the retrospective interpretations should be made explicit and organised as critical, descriptive examinations and analyses of the concrete enactments.

This is where action research can help us, especially in the literal variant of *researching our actions* (cf. Eikeland, 2006). When people sit down together and systematically and critically review their way of dealing with their situations, analysing them by thoroughly describing and then conceptualising them (as is what social scientists are supposed to do), the following happens:

Together they concretely describe how the new way of organising is enacted, which enables them to discover common conceptualisations of the concrete (enacted) manifestations of what the new way of organising is about. When the enactments are deconstructed into concrete elements, rather than "constructed" into a simplifying and reductive explanation, it is possible to evaluate and deal systematically with the enactments by figuring out what works and what does not: How shall we deal with what does not work? How shall we enhance further that which does work?

By this way of talking concretely and thoroughly about the enactments, the participants are likely to focus their attention on what is actually happening and will be forced to validate their meanings about it explicitly and bindingly. The explicit analysis helps enhance common and mutual understanding, as it is much easier to either agree with or at least understand others' viewpoints when the discussion is based on thorough descriptions of concrete events, rather than on general viewpoints on concrete events. By thoroughly discussing the enactments together, different practitioners create an updated common discourse about the new way of organising.

In this way we can say, in line with Eikeland (1997, 2001, 2006), Pålshaugen (1998, 2002) and Bushe and Shani (1991), that the analysis of the new way of organising is a way of organising itself; it is a way (method) of figuring out how to perform the tasks in a way that is updated to the new surroundings that are imposed on us.

The perspective on how to implement "the new way of organising" at the new town hall changed twice during the process of change, as I have interpreted it. In the beginning, the reform process was initiated and dealt with as the ideas of the reform (the plan) were focused on as specifications to be deconstructed and translated to local actions by the practitioners. This was the change strategy of the management of the new town hall, and it was in line with much of the recent literature on change management (cf. Bean and Hamilton, 2006; Balogun, 2003; Balogun and Johnson, 2005). After a short while, this strategy seemed insufficient as a way of changing organisational practice "in line with" the reform, basically because what the reform was supposed to be in practice was not clear at all when the practitioners started to "implement" it. In March 2005 I tried to intervene in this unclear situation, by establishing a discourse among the practitioners about what to do in order to deal with the *new situation* that had occurred when the reform plans were introduced to the organisation. This strategy was in line with the so-called action research cycle, where the point is to diagnose the situation in order to figure out what to do with it, and then do it. This search for possibilities for how to work in a new way was experienced as promising. But even though the further steps were decided on, this way of guiding the practice did not gain much momentum. This became clear after the summer, in September 2005, when I returned to the organisation after being away for four months. The situation was not much clearer. The attempts had just dissolved during the spring, something that was particularly clear as viewed in retrospect. From this retrospective perspective, however, it also became possible to see what the employees had *actually* done in order to deal with the new situation. This represented a second turn of focus in the alternative change management strategy I was trying to figure out together with the practitioners. This change of focus on what to talk about and pay attention to, in order to enhance the process of "implementation", was guided by Weick's (1995) concept of sensemaking; this sharpened the focus and clarified both what kinds of pitfalls to deal with in such processes of planned change, and laid out a basis for formulating a new strategy for how to deal with the change process.

Through this process of changing the focus on and of the change process, it was also possible to learn more about processes of planned change, as well as about action research as a way of researching and enhancing processes of planned change and organisational sensemaking. As for the action research approaches, I ended up with a version that can be precisely framed by Eikeland's (2006) cue of action research as researching our actions. The rationale of this variant of action research, as I applied it, was connected to a process of dealing with the consequences of a planned effort of strategic change in an organisation. The theory of sensemaking connected the planned change effort to the action research strategy.

From the perspective of planned change, the theory of sensemaking gives us a specific understanding of the coincidental and "un-linear way" (Greenwood and Hinings, 1996) that processes of reform implementations move in. It helps us understand the unfolding of the process in a way that allows us to deal with and enhance the process more specifically. Action research contributes with a constructive repertoire of frameworks for dealing with this enhancement of the process, particularly with providing insight into how all the members can participate in the processes of change. Action research contributes with the "space for independent inquiry" about organisational matters, where the process of sensemaking, which is the core of the change activity, can be enhanced by replacing either general, plausible explanations or simply mere confusion with more thoroughly critical analysis, when retrospectively interpreting the enacted events, surroundings and cues.

References

Argyris, C. and Schön, D. (1996), *Organizational learning II*. Reading, Massachusetts: Addison-Wesley Publishing Company.

Atkinson, J. (1984), "The flexible firm and the shape of jobs to come." *Labour Market Issues* no. 5. Oxford: The Trade Union Research Centre, Ruskin College.

Balogun, J. (2003), "From blaming the middle to harnessing its potential: Creating change intermediaries." *British Journal of Management*, 14(1): 69-84.

Balogun, J. and Johnson, G. (2005), "From intended strategies to unintended outcomes. The impact of change recipient sensemaking." *Organization Studies*, 26: 1573-1601.

Barley, S. R. and Tolbert, p. S. (1997), "Institutionalization and structuration: Studying the links between action and institution." *Organization Studies*, 18(1): 93-117.

Barret, F., Thomas, G. and Hocevar, S. (1995), "The central role of discourse in large-scale change: A social construction perspective." *The Journal of Applied Science*, 31(3): 352-373.

Bartunek, J., Krim, R., Necochea, R. and Humphries, M. (1999), "Sensemaking, sensegiving, and leadership in strategic organizational development." In Wagner, J. (ed). *Advances in qualitative organizational research, Vol 2*. Stanford, CA: Jai Press.

Bartunek, J. M. and Spreitzer, G. M. (2006), "The interdisciplinary career of a popular construct used in management. Empowerment in the late 20th century." *Journal of Management Inquiry,* 15 (3): 255-273.

Barzelay, M. (2003), "Introduction to the process dynamics of public management policymaking." *International Public Management Journal,* 6(3): 251-282.

Bean, C. J. and Hamilton, F. E. (2006), "Leader framing and follower sensemaking: Response to downsizing in the brave new workplace." *Human Relations,* 59 (3): 321-349.

Brunsson, N. (1985), *The Irrational Organization. Irrationality as a Basis for Organizational Action and Change.* Chichester: John Wiley & Sons.

Brunsson, N. and Olsen, J. p. (1993), *The Reforming Organization,* London: Routledge.

Bushe, G. R. and Shani, A. B. (1991), *Parallel learning structures: increasing innovation in bureaucracies.* Reading, Mass.: Addison-Wesley.

Christensen, T., p. and Lægreid, p. G. (2002), *New Public Management: The transformation of ideas and practice.* Aldershot: Ashgate.

Christensen, T., Lægreid, P., Roness, p. G. and Røvik, K. A. (2004), *Organisasjonsteori for offentlig sektor. Instrument, kultur, myte.* Oslo: Universitetsforlaget.

Coghlan, D. and Brannick, T. (2001), *Doing Action Research in Your Own Organization.* London: Sage.

Cummings, T. G. and Worley, C. G. (2005), *Organization Development and Change.* 8th edition. Mason, OH: Thomson South Western.

Daft, R. L. and Weick, K. E. (1984), "Toward a model of organizations as interpretation systems." *Academy of Management Review,* 9: 284-295.

DiMaggio, p. J. and Powell, W. W. (1983), "The iron cage revisited: Institutional isomorphism and collective rationality in organizational fields." *American Sociological Review,* 48: 147-160.

Eikeland, O. (1997), Erfaring, dialogikk og politikk. Oslo: Universitetsforlaget.

Eikeland, O. (2001), "Action Research as the Hidden Curriculum of the Western Tradition." In Reason, P. and H. Bradbury (eds), *Handbook of Action Research.* London: Sage

Eikeland, O. (2006), "The validity of Action Research – validity in Action Research." In Nielsen, K. A. and Svensson, L. (eds), *Action Research and Interactive Research. Beyond Practice and Theory.* Maastricht: Shaker Publishing.

Emery, M (1998), *Searching. The theory and practice of making cultural change.* Amsterdam: John Benjamins Publishing Company.

French, W. L., Bell, C. H. and Zawacki, R. A. (2005), *Organization Development and Transformation. Managing Effective Change* (sixth edition). Boston: McGraw-Hill.

Gagliardi, p. (1986), "The creation and change of organizational cultures: A conceptual Framework." *Organization Studies*, 7: 117-34.

Gioia, D. and Chittipeddi, K. (1991), "Sensemaking and sensegiving in strategic change Initiation." *Strategic Management Journal*, 12, 443-448.

Gioia, D. A. and Thomas, J. B. (1996), "Identity, image and issue interpretation: Sensemaking during strategic change in academia." *Administrative Science Quarterly*, 41, 370-403.

Gioia, D. A., Thomas, J. B., Clark, S. M. and Chittipeddi, K. (1994), "Symbolism and strategic change in academia: The dynamics of sensemaking and influence." *Organization Science*, 5: 363-383.

Greenwood, D. and Levin, M. (1998), *Introduction to Action Research*. London: Sage.

Greenwood, R. and Hinings, C.R. (1996), "Understanding radical organizational change: Bringing together old and new institutionalism." *Academy of Management Review*, 21(4): 1022-1054.

Hall, p. and Taylor, R. (1996), "Political Science and the Three New Institutionalisms". *Political Studies*, 44, 936-958.

Hammer, M. and Champy, J. (2001), *Reengineering the Corporation. A Manifesto for Business Revolution*. London: Nicholas Brealey Publishing. (Originally published 1993.)

Hatch, M. J. (1997), *Organization Theory. Modern, Symbolic and Postmodern Perspectives*. Oxford: Oxford University Press.

Hearn, G. and Ninan, A. (2003), "Managing change is managing meaning." *Management Communication Quarterly*, 16(3): 440-445.

Herbst, p. G. (1974), *Socio-technical Design. Strategies in Multidiciplinary Research*. London: Tavistock Publications.

Hovik, S. and Stigen, I. M. (2004), *Kommunal organisering i 2004. Redegjørelse for Kommunal- og regionaldepartementets organisasjonsdatabase*. Notat 2004: 124, Oslo: NIBR.

Kanter, R. M., Stein, B. A. and Jick, T. (1992), *The Challenge of Organizational Change: How Companies Experience It and Leaders Guide It*. New York: Free Press.

Klemsdal, L. (2006), *Den intuitive organisasjonen. Forny virksomheten med de samme menneskene*. Oslo: Gyldendal Akademisk.

Klemsdal, L. (2008), *Making sense of "the new way of organizing". Managing the micro processes of change in a municipality*. PhD thesis, Department of Industrial Economics and Technology Management, NTNU. Trondheim: Tapir.

Lozeau, D. and Langley, A., Denis, J-L. (2002), "The corruption of managerial techniques by organizations". *Human Relations* 55(5). 537-564.

Levin, M. and Klev, R. (2002), *Forandring som praksis*. Bergen: Fagbokforlaget.

March, J. G. (1981), "Footnotes to organizational change." *Administrative Science Quarterly*, 26: 563-577.

March, J. (1991), "Exploration and exploitation in organizational learning", *Organization Science*, 2/1: 71-87.

Marshall, C. and Rossman, R. B. (1995), *Designing Qualitative Research*. Thousand Oaks: SAGE Publications.

Mills, C. E. (2000), "The interfaces of communication sensemaking and change." *Australian Journal of Communication*, 27(1): 95-108.

Mills, C. E. (2002), "The hidden dimension of blue collar sensemaking about workplace Communication." *The Journal of Business Communication*, 39 (3): 288-314.

Mizruchi, M. S. and Fein, L. C. (1999), "The social construction of organizational knowledge: a study of the uses of coercive, mimetic and normative isomorphism." *Administration Science Quarterly*, 44: 653-683.

Morris, T. and Lancaster, Z. (2005), "Translating management ideas." *Organization Studies*, 27(2): 207-233.

Mueller, F. and Carter, C. (2005), "The scripting of Total Quality Management within its organizational biography." *Organization Studies*, 26(2): 221-247.

Orlikowski, W. J. (1996), "Improvising organizational transformation over time. A situated change perspective." *Inform. Systems Res* 7(1): 63-92.

Pålshaugen, Ø. (1998), *The end of organization theory? Language as a tool in action research and organizational development*. Amsterdam: John Benjamins Publishing Company.

Pålshaugen, Ø. (2002), "Creating internal public spheres in private enterprises." In Ennals, R., Fricke, W. and Pålshaugen, Ø. (eds), *Concepts and Transformations*. Amsterdam: John Benjamins Publishing Company.

Ragin, C. C. (1994), *Constructing Social Research*. Thousand Oaks: Pine Forge Press.

Ramsdal, H. and Skorstad, E. J. (2004), *Privatisering fra innsiden. Om sammensmeltningen av offentlig og privat organisering*. Bergen: Fagbokforlaget.

Reason, p. and Bradbury, H. (eds.) (2001), *Handbook of Action Research*. London: Sage.

Reed, M. I. (1988), "The problem of human agency in organizational analysis." *Organization Studies*, 9/1: 33-44.

Robertson, p. and Seneviratne S. J. (1995), "Outcomes of Planned Organizational Change in the Public Sector: A Meta-Analytic Comparison to the Private Sector." *Public Administration Review*, 55: 547:588.

Røvik, K.A. (1998), *Moderne organisasjoner*. Bergen: Fagbokforlaget.

Røvik, K. A. (2007), *Trender og translasjoner. Ideer som former det 21. århundrets organisasjoner*. Oslo: Universitetsforlaget.

Schön, D. (1983), *The Reflective Practitioner.* New York: Basic Books.

Skattum C. (2006), *Stab/støtte i to-nivå kommuner.* Sluttrapport. Bærum: Asplan Viak.

Sutcliffe, K. M., Brown, A. D. And Putnam, L. L. (2006), "Introduction to the special issue Making Sense of Organizing: A special issue in honor of Karl Weick." *Organization Studies,* 27(11): 1573-1578.

Tsoukas, H. and Chia, R. (2002), "On organizational becoming. Rethinking organizational change". *Organization Science,* 13/5: 567-582.

Waterman, R.H. (1993), *Adhocracy.* New York: Norton.

Weick, K. E. (1979), *The Social Psychology of Organizing.* 2nd Edition. New York: McGraw-Hill.

Weick, K.E. (1995), *Sensemaking in organizations.* London: Sage.

Weick, K.E. (2001a), "Introduction." In *Making Sense of the Organization.* Malden: Blackwell. Pp. ix-xi.

Weick, K.E. (2001b), "Sensemaking in Organizations: Small structures with large Consequences" In *Making Sense of the Organization.* Malden: Blackwell. Pp. 5-31.

Weick, K.E. (2001c), "Sources of order in underorganized systems: themes in recent organizational theory." In *Making Sense of the Organization.* Malden: Blackwell. Pp. 32-56.

Weick, K.E. (2001d), "Organizational redesign as improvisation" In *Making Sense of the Organization.* Malden: Blackwell. Pp. 57-91.

Weick, K.E. (2001e), "Improvisation as a mindset for organizational analysis." In *Making Sense of the Organization.* Malden: Blackwell. Pp. 284-304.

Weick, K. E. (2001f), "Enactment and the boundaryless career: Organizing as we work." In *Making Sense of the Organization.* Malden: Blackwell. Pp. 207-223.

Weick, K.E. and Quinn, R. E. (1999), "Organizational change and development." *Annual Review of Psychology,* 50: 361-386.

Weick, K. E. and Sutcliffe, K. M. (2001), *Managing the Unexpected.* San Francisco, CA: Jossey-Bass.

Weick, K. E., Sutcliffe, K. M. and Obstfeld, D. (2005), "Organizing and the process of Sensemaking." *Organization Science* 16: 409-421.

Weick, K. E. and Westley, F. (1996), "Organizational Learning: Affirming an Oxymoron", in Clegg et al. (eds), *Handbook of Organization Studies.* London Sage. Pp 440-458.

Weisbord, M. (1991), *Productive Workplaces. Organizing and Managing for Dignity, Meaning and Community.* San Francisco. Jossey-Bass Publishers.

Yin, R. K. (1994), *Case Study Research. Design and Methods.* Thousand Oaks: SAGE Publications.

3 Research and Change – a Comparison of Action Research and Conventional Social Science Research Methods[1]

Benedicte Brøgger

Introduction

In this chapter I compare action research and conventional social science research to draw out their similarities and differences in how they effect change. I will show that action research is much more than merely a tool in the kit of conventional social science, and this is also why it is not possible to say that one approach is better than the other.

Two separate research situations provide the empirical material for the discussion. The context of the research is the same, namely a research and development (R&D) project in a Norwegian electronics company. One research situation was based on participant observation combined with a survey based on qualitative, semi-formal interviews. This research was informed by a combination of socio-technical and social-anthropological methods, and the aim of the research was to identify the dynamics of the company's socio-technical system. In the other situation, the method was participatory inquiry, and the research was informed by action research theory. The aim of this research was to bring the disconnected discourses of the company out on a public arena where they could be worked on by the participants themselves. The effects of research are different when researchers, as a distinct type of practitioners, deal with each other, for example in the form of decisions about research design, application for funding, peer-reviews of papers, presentations at conferences and so on. In this paper the focus is on the interface between two types of practice, industrial production and research, in order to gain practical knowledge of how the latter influences the former.

The data gathering part of each case lasted about two days, and the analysis, reporting and discussion of the findings took about a month. The research situations were simple, straightforward and of short duration. Therefore, they are well suited for the purpose of drawing out and comparing their salient features. Although the features were particular to the given situation, they also have relevance for the

1 This chapter has been written as part of the strategic research programme (2003-2007) at the WRI, Oslo. The project described was funded by the Norwegian Research Council through the program Value Creation 2010 (VS 2010).

general discussion. Emphasis is on the practice of research, that is, what researchers actually to do when they "use" research methods the usual topic for textbooks on research methods. The discussion centers on occurrences while a researcher is "in the field", that is, during interaction mainly with non-researchers.

In the following section comes first an outline of the general principles that inform the concluding discussion of the relationship between research and change, and then a discussion of why the imagery of performance serves well to bring out the salient features of the two research situations. An ethnographic account of the two situations follows in section two. In the discussion section, I first discuss the effects the different research methods had on the development of the company.

Research and Change

Research refers to both the practice and content of science. It is a general term for a range of quite different activities designed to bring forth legitimate, public knowledge within the framework of a scientific paradigm. Even if social science in the beginning tried to emulate the natural sciences, at least since the middle of the last century, the "human condition" – the understanding that all knowledge is socially situated and interpreted in human terms – has been acknowledged as a sine qua non for all types of social research (Arendt 1989). In one of his earlier works, Habermas used his awareness of the interested and situated nature of any process of inquiry to discuss their potential for emancipation (Habermas 2002:308ff). In this volume, Habermas distinguished between three forms of inquiry: empirical-analytic, historical-hermeneutic and the systematic sciences of social action. The dividing lines between different types of science are contested, but these will serve the purpose here, as the main interest is in the difference between the last one and the first two. According to this schema the first of the research processes in the company, the survey, would be recognizable as a combination of the first two forms of inquiry, the empirical-analytic and the historical-hermeneutic. The second research process, the dialogue conference, would belong to the systematic sciences of social action.

Habermas identified three media through which situated interests take form: work, language and power. He states, "the specific viewpoints from which, with transcendental necessity, we apprehend reality ground three categories of possible knowledge: information that expands our power of technical control; interpretations that make possible the orientation of action within common traditions; and analyses that free consciousness from its dependence on hypostatized powers" (Habermas 2002:313). Work, or labor, is the means by which humans engage with and transform the external forces of nature, the material forces. Language is the means by which humans work on their understanding of each other and themselves, in short, the medium of communicative action. Power refers to the "ideologically frozen relations of dependence that can in principle be transformed (Habermas 2002: 309), that is, the institutional webs that connect people. Even though the knowledge-constitutive interests take form in these three media, their configuration is not the same in the three categories, and it is only the medium of language that raises humans "out of nature". Emancipatory cognitive interests then must aim at the pursuit of reflection through language. Habermas has developed this line of reasoning much further and has inspired a vast literature on language and communicative action and the potential for interest-free discourse (Habermas 1984-1987).

The focus on language has tended to leave material conditions and institutional webs in the background, as they are thought to be mediated by language and therefore cannot be but meta-media. Studies from other fields indirectly or directly contest this order of priority. Rituals are shown to consist of embodied knowledge, and the non-verbal aspects have as much political force as the spoken word (Connerton 1989); the planting of a tree is a way to alter a physical landscape in a manner that resonates with the improved socio-economic standing of a group (Winslow 2002); and human society develops as much from "biased cultural transmission" in the form of imitation as from direct logical reasoning (Henrick 2002:252ff), to mention but a few examples. The question of language versus material conditions resonates with much more complex issues than will be dealt with here. It resonates with deep and long disagreements in the history of philosophy, for example in the debate on rationality versus experience, as well as in economics, in the debates on the priorities between base and superstructure or on the role of homo economicus, the rationalist per excellance. Here, the general question is what happens when researchers, in a recognized social role as researchers, interact with non-researchers in order to generate knowledge, and more specifically, what kinds of changes are generated when the research design is action research versus when it is conventional social science research.

Nevertheless, Habermas' economical and comprehensive distinctions between work, language and power are particularly meaningful for the discussion in this paper and I therefore continue to use them. I identify the effects of research in the company in terms of the three Habermasian forms: changes in work, in the discourses or in the relations of power. For example, does participation in a survey change how work is done or the tools with which materials are worked upon, and if so, how does it happen? Or, do reflections on work experiences in a dialogue setting affect the organizational hierarchy, and if so, how? Or what happens when new concepts are introduced into an existing discourse?

When researchers interact with research subjects they not only mechanically execute tasks according to a method book, they actively perform the tasks, and the performances are as much part of the "scripts" of science as of the local conditions and the actual interaction between specific persons. Through performance, research becomes manifest as a social presence. In order to identify the particularities of how this occurred in the two research situations referred to above, a means for sorting out the different elements of the given situations is needed. For this purpose I will use situation analysis, which is a limited form of a case study. In a case study, "[the]…analysis treats each case as a stage in an on-going process of social relations between specific persons and groups in a social system and culture" (Gluckman 2006: 16), and cases are more than "apt illustrations" of theoretical points (Gluckman 2006:15); rather, the general points are developed from the case studies. Therefore, I will present the development of the two research situations in some detail below. The survey and the dialogue conference are analyzed as separate situations consisting of a limited set of events.

A case study is "essentially heuristic; it reflects in the events portrayed features which may be construed as a manifestation of some general abstract theoretical principle" (Mitchell 2006:28). Here, that constitutive principle is the notion that processes of inquiry have different potentials for change and that it is only in self-reflection that knowledge and interest is one. This is another reason why Habermas' schema is particularly suitable here. He uses a convoluted phrase to make his point: "my thesis is … that the knowledge-constitutive *interests take form in the medium* of work, language, and power" (Habermas 2002:313, emphasis added), and it is the combination of the words "interests", "medium" and "form" that is so powerful. By this move Habermas collapses theory's epistemological position either as an instrument for reflection on absolute truth (medium) or as truth itself (form). And by his reference to the knowledge-constitutive interests, he also collapses the distinction between practical and theoretical knowledge. Work on the premises for arriving at legitimate knowledge may take place in a factory just as well as in a university. In the case discussed here the reflection takes place in a company where science was one among several knowledge-constitutive interests, each of which contributed to the changes that did occur, some instant and elusive, others of a more lasting nature, and all related to the company's work, the discourses and the relations of power.

Research as Performance

In order to grasp the potential for change in the two research situations, I will describe a series of acts that were performed. The perspective on research as performance is inspired by Goffman, who was the first to systematically make use of this type of perspective in the social sciences (1959). He portrayed social action as occurring on a stage, with actors, props and scripts, and where the actors are also the audience to each others' performance. An audience emerges every time the participants' ongoing, non-public reflections about the performance itself are spoken out loud, and such situations are critical for the direction of the performance. The outcome of the performance depends on the sum total of the participants' actions and interpretations. Goffman's concern was how we become social persons through our presentation of self and others' responses to it. He looks for clues to how that occurs in all aspects of a performance (body posture, language, use of objects, etc.) and devotes much attention to the definitions of a situation and what happens when someone does not "play their part" or "creates a scene". Through this perspective it is possible to approach what the "part" or "scene" is as far as research is concerned.

In order for *research* practice to have effect, it must be recognizable as a distinct type of activity. Therefore, in order to work, research needs to establish its conditions while at the same time being at least on some level understandable and relevant in a foreign social setting outside the bounds of the scientific community. A research situation consists of a series of performative acts. A performative act is a statement that in the saying is also doing, and which makes it clear that the act is performed (Austin 1975). Austin used marriage ceremonies as an example. When the bridal couple says "I do", they are not just saying something; they are actually getting married by saying it. Austin's discussion concerns a specific form of speech act and the logical conditions under which it operates. However, he also presupposes specific material and institutional conditions necessary for the performative to work, although these are not his analytical concern and he only deals with them in passing. All of the conditions relate to accepted, appropriate and specific procedures, circumstances and participants (Austin 1975:14f). Certain people must be someplace at certain times and utter statements in the expected order. There may also be requirements for specific objects, like documents, food or jewelry, or more intangibles like sounds, colors, tastes or smells. After the performative has been enacted there is a range of prescribed occurrences, and the change takes effect. In many instances the now-married couple may no longer act as if they are two independent individuals. For example, there are situations where their material resources are defined as belonging to their unit, in matters of taxation, getting bank loans, health care, writing wills and so on. In other words, for the performative to work there must be a situation in place and there must be social patterns that exist before and after it has been enacted. And through the performative, that social order that it needs to perform is also reproduced.

Establishing the performative's social conditions is particularly critical in a research situation, which does not have the support of legal institutions or the pomp and circumstance of ceremony. After all, the props consist mainly of paper and pen, or occasionally a laptop. The burden of establishing its own conditions is something for which social research is poorly prepared. The effort is undermined from within social science in several ways. One is as the result of the efforts to democratize the process of inquiry of the systematic action sciences. In this approach the taken-for-granted assumption of the superiority of research/scientific theory over other types of knowledge-generating processes and concepts is challenged. That generates the dilemma that if research is equal, how can it establish itself as different? Another dilemma appears in the acknowledgement of all horizons of meaning of the historical-hermeneutic sciences. How do we distinguish between "folk" theory and "proper" theory? Is there any use in making such a distinction? How do we deal with the fact that only the researchers' write the scientific papers about the experiences and perspectives of others? In addition to these epistemological dilemmas, there are a range of practical ones. The script is hard to explicate because the process is open. The activities go on outside the home turf of the researchers. The stage is set for other productions and the participants are busy with other tasks. Nevertheless, research does contribute to change, although action research and conventional social science research achieves that by different means.

The Company and the Background for the R&D project

The two research situations were part of a collaborative research and development (R&D) effort between the Work Research Institute (WRI) and a Norwegian company I will here call Electron Ltd. Electron is a family-owned electronics company that produces emergency communication equipment for the air and maritime industries. The main plant is located in the heart of the electronics industry on the south coast of Norway, and there are other plants abroad. In all, the company employs about 200 people. Electron is a global market leader in its line of industry. The products are high-quality, complex, integrated systems and the company has highly skilled and competent workers. It is also distinctly market driven, and new products are developed as new markets develop throughout the world. This results in a very internationally oriented company constantly dealing with the challenges of globalization. At the same time, the relations in the company are explicitly anchored in the national patterns of industrial relations, with a strong union that cooperates in all aspects of the development of the company, while it at the same time opposes and negotiates changes that are experienced as detrimental to the interests of the workers. The company is also firmly local in its priorities. The vagaries of the market forces are mediated both by the industrial and the regional relations. Thus, the company's development is not the direct result of decisions made elsewhere and by people not directly involved in the business. In short, it was a relatively well-delineated and self-contained unit, and while the project lasted no unexpected external events created upheaval in the ordinary flow of activities.

The links between Electron and the WRI were many and had been established over a number of years. WRI researchers had engaged with managers from Electron in two networks, one devoted to regional development, the other to development of human resource management practices in a number of electronics companies. Other links were through the unions, especially Fellesforbundet (the Norwegian United Federation of Trade Unions), which is a member of the main national union, Landsorganisasjonen (LO). WRI had assisted in several training sessions for union representatives, among them Electron's main union representative, contributing with methods for enterprise development. Hence, the research activities in the company were based on a comprehensive knowledge of its local context, but less on knowledge of the inner workings of the organization.

When the project started, the company had grown rapidly for several years. All indicators showed a company in good shape. The financial situation of the company was good, productivity or uptime had increased, and the rate of sick leave was below the national average. As mentioned above, a number of organizational changes had been made a few months before the start of the project. The most important of these were the introduction of team-based production, and that the plant had been split into two different lines of work – logistics and production. The logistics workers were organized in one unit where all employees reported to the logistics manager. The remaining production workers had been organized into three semi-autonomous teams. Each team was responsible for one product line, and each was coordinated by an appointed team leader who reported to the plant manager. The other units of the company were the engineering department, the procurement department and the service department. As the project was to address production issues, these units were marginal in the project apparatus and activities. The plant manager and the logistics manager reported to the managing director/owner. These three comprised Electron's top management. The organizational structure was fairly flat with only one organizational level between the top management and the workers – the team leaders. One of the recently appointed team leaders was also the main union representative.

Establishing the R&D Project

The R&D project was the direct result of discussions between the plant manager and the WRI researcher during the human resource network meetings. The plant manager had learned about "self-learning organizations" from his colleague, the logistics manager of Electron, and was intrigued by the concept. He had also recently reorganized the production workers into teams, but felt that as no one had yet experienced the full potential of the organizational change, a self-learning organization might help. (In this context, the concepts of "self-learning organization" and "team" did not gain their meaning from their position in a theoretical landscape, but from the practical context in which they were used. I once asked the managers for references, but they said they did not remember any. As I was more interested in how the terms came to be realized in the company than what the textbooks said, I did not pursue the topic any further.)

A project team was set up to support and research the establishment of a self-learning organization involving the logistics and production workers. The team consisted of 6 representatives from Electron and WRI: two managers, two union representatives and two researchers. The set-up of the project team was in itself part of the social change in the organization: First, it broadened the scope of people involved in discussions about participation – for example, it took a while before the composition of the project team became clear. Second, it generated new experiences with collaboration between employees and employers. The existing formal arenas where they interacted were part of either the organizational hierarchy or the committees established for negotiations. In order to establish the project organization, both management and workers had to reflect on their patterns of interaction in the context of collaborative enterprise development. Third, the different interests – between management and workers, between employers and employees and between researchers and others – were made manifest and acknowledged, but also contested and redefined in the course of working out the practical details.

As soon as the project was under way, the journey toward the fairly abstract goal of developing a self-learning organization ran aground on more immediate obstacles. Discussions soon centered on problems with product quality and backlog in the production, rather than on developing new ways of knowing. Everyone in the project team had their own opinions about the production problems and corresponding solutions. The discussions revealed an impressive breadth and depth of the efforts to gain knowledge about the situation and ways to improve it. The top management had made several attempts to analyze the problems, but said they never had time to do it thoroughly. The engineering department, busy working on new products or correcting flaws in the old ones, did not have time either. The procurement department worked hard to get suppliers to deliver on time. The workers were trying out small, significant changes in routines and modes of cooperation, both within the teams and across the new dividing line between logistics and production workers. And every day the same fight started anew – to make enough quality tested products, and get them out the door in time. People were getting tired of it.

The First Research Situation – Fieldwork and Survey

In line with conventional thinking about research, the company representatives in the project team wanted from time to time to outsource the analytical work to the researchers. As our involvement with the company was based on action research, which is based on participatory inquiry, that was not a viable solution. However, being educated as a social anthropologist, I saw the benefits of an opportunity to move about the premises unrestrained by the formalities of meetings. A brief period of participant observation, a type of empirical-hermeneutic approach, would give me another inroad to understand the workings of the company (Pelto and Pelto 1978; Bernard 2005; Berg 2007). I would then be able to examine the products, the layout of the building and the production equipment. I could experience the flow of activities at different times of the day, and most importantly, I could speak with anyone who wanted to speak with me. This would allow me to explore people's interpretations of what was going on and the categories and ideas of connections in this social world. As a response to the expectations of analyses from us, I therefore suggested a mini-fieldwork, and the project team agreed to this.

The material was to be presented in the form of a socio-technical map of the company. A socio-technical mapping is a technique developed to identify the connections and missing links between a technical and a social system (see the appendix by Per Engelstad in Emery and Thorsrud 1976; Trist 1981; Qvale 2002). For that purpose, the plant manager brought a flow chart of the production lines and an organizational chart to one of the project team meetings. The drawings were used by the company representatives in the project team to describe and explain the workings of the company. In the same manner as the considerations of the team leader-cum-union representative, the charts brought to the forefront differences in interpretations and opinions of the actual workings of the company, but this time they were interpreted as part of a research process and the conclusion was to wait for the findings.

Participant Observation

I started the fieldwork by donning a helmet and safety boots. The fieldwork had been publicly announced at the monthly information meeting at the plant, and as we had been around for a while, I assumed that most people had an idea who I was. I planned to start by just "hanging around" as anthropologists do in the field, although my aim was to speak with about one-third of the people who worked in logistics and production, and cover all levels of the hierarchy, teams and functional units in order to ensure a breadth of perspectives.

The most obvious place to start was at the smokers' corner, but when I spoke with the people there, they only responded when I spoke about the weather, family life or events in the local town. My every attempt to talk about work was met with abrupt silence from the one I spoke with, while all others were keenly listening. I therefore proceeded to walk around the plant to observe the layout of the building, the positions of components and products and the flow of activity, pieces of information that I jotted down on the flow chart I had brought for that purpose. I walked from the smokers' corner through a corridor between the plant and the administrative building and from there into the warehouse, a huge room with maze-like shelves stacked high with items. At the far end of the room, I followed behind a man who carried a cardboard box and walked through a little door into the production hall. There I walked along row after row of workbenches where each worker was surrounded by an assortment of components, wires of different colors, and some tools. Each seemed to be working at his or her own pace, and occasionally someone would move about. I could see no apparent pattern to their movements. There was a low hum of noise, but nothing like an incessant roar of an unyielding automated assembly line. There was a test chamber in the middle of the room and beyond it were workbenches with complicated machinery for further testing. Getting back toward the corridor, there was a little hallway where a number of people labeled and packed the products and loaded them onto a forklift to wait for the trailer. I returned to the smokers' corner, which was empty. Then I did another circuit.

As I did my circuits, it was quite apparent that about 50 people were following my every move and waiting for whatever was supposed to happen. Simply "hanging around" was not feasible. The use of time and space was so regimented by the flow of the production, and in order to get ahead I had to somehow instigate a beginning. I did this by walking up to the man who worked at the first workstation in the production process, taking out my notebook and pen and asking if he had time to talk with me. He had, and so it began. At that moment, the conditions for the research had to be established, not only in the eyes of the people following my every move, but between him and me. The unsaid definition of the situation was research, which meant that I was supposed to give directions. In order to do research I had to realize that social form, but the content of the knowledge was to be about his work. Therefore, the definition could only be explicit for an instant; if not, he would be little more than a prop in my drama. Concretely, I told him about the project in a few sentences and asked him if he had any questions. He just nodded and continued to work, which confused me. I therefore asked him to explain what he was doing.

He told me that he had worked in the company for many years, under two generations of owners, and had held different positions. Then he told in vivid detail about the nature of his work. He demonstrated the operations of the machine he used and the electronic workflow system. He showed me the work manual where the actions he was supposed to take were listed in great detail, but told me that he did not have time to read it, and it was not really useful anyway. People passed by all the time, and often stopped to ask for something or just listen in on the conversation. I surmised that he was an unofficial leader, and when I asked him about it, he gave me a lopsided smile and said that he had announced his interest in a team leader position, but the plant manager had chosen someone else. Having started with work, we had entered the medium of power. We began to discuss the team organization, but I soon realized that the definition of the situation had changed. I was treated as if I somehow had the power to further this man's interests, making me a prop in his drama. What had happened was that our interests became visible, and his and my interests were at odds. This would have been an ideal occasion to reflect on the nature of these interests, and also to reflect on the content of the knowledge that their conflict produced. However, this was contrary to the chosen form of research, and neither the stage, nor the script or the participants were appropriate. The research method of participant observation was developed to study the workings of a community's local affairs as they unfold on their own accord, not to stage them for the purpose of research and certainly not in order to bring on change of any kind. I had performed the research according to my participant observation script, and was faced with the invitation to do something else, an invitation I was in no position to accept.

For a moment I wondered what to do, and then I decided on a middle way. I told him why I needed to remain outside and apart, explained again the goals and organization of the project, and said that I could contribute in sorting out what *he* could do, and, using my knowledge of the company, I gave him some examples. That brought the conversation over to opportunities and restraints the workers faced when they wanted to improve something in the company. There were no other opportunities than those directly relevant for the performance of their allotted tasks, and occasionally in informal collaboration with co-workers. He complained that with the organizational changes he was not even supposed to interact with the production workers, and certainly not the computer people, even though he knew a thing or two that could help reduce the backlog. For me, that was a nice prompt to bring up the self-learning organization issue, and I intended to follow that up with questions of what type of organizational set-up would allow him to make better use of his experiential knowledge. However, the concept of a self-learning organization was outright alienating. He had heard of it, but that was all. For a while, it floated about our conversation as an unwieldy item. Neither of us managed to make sense of it in the context of his work. Resorting to a presentation of the general properties of the theoretical model would not have helped. This disruption in the flow of the conversation served as a natural point to break it off as now several people were waiting for him to sign some papers.

This was the first event of the research situation. The exchange had taken about 15-20 minutes. Through the work to establish the conditions for the research, the play of interests was revealed, and new knowledge about the workings of the company had been generated for both of us through our exploration of the work, power and language of the company.

The Interview-based Survey

Thus caught in the social machinery, but needing to think, I left the stage and headed for the canteen for a cup of coffee. The participant observation script for the research had turned out to be unsustainable, and I therefore decided to fall back on a more hardcore empirical-analytic approach so that there would be less doubt about the definition of the situation. My hypothesis was that the production problem was a result of the new division between logistics and production, and I devised a very short interview guide to uncover the links, or lack thereof, between the different stations in the production process.

As I walked out of the canteen, it was time for the two o'clock coffee break and the smokers' corner was full of people. They saw me come out of the canteen and teased me about my freedom to come and go as I pleased. I was happy to be included in their banter, to be put in my place, any place. I had little doubt that my first conversation had been the theme for other conversations, and in that manner at least something had changed because people commented the production backlog in general terms, and a couple of people mused about self-learning organizations. The rest of the day was spent talking with the logistics people. Again the conversations consisted of demonstrations of equipment and machinery and reflections on work experiences and the hierarchy. Each story was unique, and at the same time hovered around the same base – the backlog in the production and ways to improve it, the workings of the organization, the hazy meaning of the term "team", and the limited scope for participation.

The next morning, I came in with the morning shift and systematically worked my way through the production hall. I also discovered an inconspicuous door, which lead into a workshop-cum-test site. The man in charge bluntly stated that he was not at all interested in an interview, but would teach me how to handle the products as if I were an apprentice, if I was interested. He asked me to leave my papers on his desk and come over to a large tank. The room was apparently somewhat of a free zone, for people drifted in and out of the room to check on the products, get a tool or discard some item, to talk about he products and the flow of the production, and to correct what I was doing. My fallback to participant observation was unintended, but I welcomed it, tired of having acted for a whole day in accordance with a rigid, alienating methodological schema. My props were taken from me and the definition of the situation had changed radically. The purpose was still knowledge and learning, but now it informed an entirely different form of inquiry. For me the most important factor was that we followed the flow of *their* tasks and topics, not mine. Through the mutual performance of the research these days, the distance between their knowledge and categories and mine was being reduced, even though they remained. Some half-joked that I better come work with them, others that they could do this research themselves now they had seen that it was not such a great deal.

The final interview was at a workstation I was curious about, the last in the line. It was located in the hallway, and seemed to be a kind of no-place, which was quite significant because by being nothing, it revealed what was "something" in the social and material topography of the company. In front of the workstation was the corridor and to the back were the doors to the production hall. To the left was the entrance to the warehouse, and to the right a plastic-covered opening to the outdoors loading area, which made the hallway pretty cold.

Having interpreted these signs of the topography of power in the company without being aware of it, I was surprised and moved when the worker who stood there proudly greeted me with the following statement: "I am the last link in the production chain. It is the result of my work that the customers first see". The place might have been a no-place as observed from the material conditions, but there was certainly someone who thought better of it. He smilingly added that I did not have to tell him about the research, he knew what I was doing. His workstation was made up of four old work tables of unequal height. Over the tables were rough homemade shelves made from leftover planks. He said that it was difficult to find a comfortable work position due to his back problems, and he had asked for new, moveable tables and shelves and a different kind of chair, like they had in other factories. "Never mind," he continued, "I have to run around a lot anyway." He walked me through one of his rounds. The printer he needed for the labels was in the warehouse. The machine for gluing was old and he had to bend to adjust it with a screwdriver. He also said that he walked the stairs whenever he needed to check a document with the procurement people, and they were located one floor above. He did not trust the workflow system to get it right, and they were under so much pressure with the backlog and all.

As the conversation proceeded I got the impression his idea of the situation did not match mine. Feeling the need to explicate the research context, I asked him what he thought about the research. He said he thought it was some kind of health-and-safety assessment and that he wanted me to know more than I would probably learn from the management, because not everything was fine. I told him that the health-and safety issue was only one among several influencing the socio-technical system, and although I would include something about it in the report, it would not be the main topic. After that he became far less talkative. When the conversation became a monologue on my part, I asked him again what he thought I was doing. He stopped working and looked intently at my face for an instant, and then asked if I was doing some kind of productivity study. (He referred to a type of Tayloristic productivity study that is used as background material in wage negotiations, and for which the procedures are explained in great detail in the agreements regulating industrial relations in Norway). I explained why our conversation could not possibly be part of such an endeavor. In addition I reminded him, as he had earlier told me that he was a union member, that the R&D project was based on the collaborative tradition developed as part of the industrial relations, and that this was separate from the wage negotiations. His suspicions were laid to rest, but it also became clear that he had no other idea of why I could possibly want to talk with him. Fearing that his patience was wearing thin, I did not want to describe the R&D project again, and telling him about participant observation or empirical-analytic research would take too long. So the event broke down of its own accord.

Unlike the would-be team leader or the tool shed manager, this man did not use the opportunity to voice his interests. He acted his part according to the two main scripts he was familiar with. My pen and paper, questions and movement in the time and space frame of the company had made two other knowledge regimes feasible. He participated actively in the script of the health-and-safety regime, but he wanted no part in any productivity study. The conversation had proceeded on two levels: one was concrete and related to his job; the other was abstract and related to assumptions about different regimes of knowledge, which for me contextualized what I was doing in an entirely new way. Furthermore, I had gained a wealth of information about his job, and my emergent ideas about the gaps in the socio-technical system had been confirmed.

Reporting back

The next two weeks I organized and analyzed the data. Each conversation resulted in sheets of paper filled with verbatim notes of the replies to my questions. When an interviewee spoke too fast, I asked them to slow down, and when in doubt, I showed them what I had written. These sheets were to be the whole of the data set, and I intended to depersonalize the responses in order for others to have access to them. In addition to these sheets, I wrote extensive field notes every evening of my observations and reflections. From the data I generated a rough socio-technical map that indicated the main gaps in the system. The rich, non-verbal information I had in addition to the data from the interviews also allowed me to thematize the challenges of establishing a "self-learning organization", even if that had not been an explicit theme The fieldwork had revealed much about how the workers "learned to learn". Hierarchy, functional division and informal roles all reduced the possibility to gain and share knowledge in any type of self-reflective or self-learning way. I presented the main findings in a short report, which was refined and revised after discussions with my co-researcher. In the report I did not suggest what they should do to improve the system, I only mentioned that there were many suggestions, and that in the project we should aim to establish arenas and procedures in order to engage those with relevant experience and vested interests to work for changing that which needed change. Hence, the venture into empirical research was transformed into a contribution to the action research.

The report was sent to the project team members, and then presented at the next project team meeting. The company people launched directly into a discussion of its points, and by defining the situation in this manner we, the two researchers, became the audience. There were many exchanges, and I will only refer to one as an example. Toward the end of the discussion, the logistics manager claimed that as far as he could remember, none of his employees had come up with suggestions for improvement. He also claimed that it would be far too complicated to listen to every employee's opinion about their workstations and tasks, and then he concluded that inconsistencies and ambiguities could be solved by rewriting the work manuals. The plant manager did not agree, explaining, "Sometimes you have to place your hand on the machine to know what is wrong. You won't know that from some written manual." I did not know if he was talking about the report or the company's routines, and thought that it did not matter either way, the problematique was identical – abstractions on paper versus actual experience. Having started with a reference to his physical experience, the plant manager continued at a different level of abstraction: "Tacit knowledge is important, knowing how to do things. And we have to tap into this tacit knowledge in order to create a self-learning organization." He added that the idea of a self-learning organization had come from the other manager. That created a silence around the table, and my co-researcher used the opportunity to redefine the situation by suggesting that we now discuss what each of us should do as part of the next step in the project.

The meeting was a muddled affair, but at its core was dialogue, bringing to light critical contradictions, like the contradictions mentioned in the example above, between experiences and manuals, or between discussing in general terms or in terms of the practical actions of the people present, or between the interests of the workers and managers. Even though the aim of the research had been to identify logical and causal patterns in a form of inquiry that was detached and observational, its effect was to bring operative contradictions in the company out in public. Each time such a cross-road was reached, the conversation took one turn, only to return again to the same unresolved matter from a different angle. It was hard work, and no conclusions were reached, other than to schedule the next meeting. But some things did happen afterwards, and these led to small changes in the work and in the relations of power. A new gluing machine was purchased, and new automated workstations were installed. A team leader for the warehouse workers was assigned, and the team was to meet weekly, with the logistics manager present so that people would have the opportunity to talk with him.

The Second Research Situation – the Dialogue Conference

The research design of the R&D project was based on action research principles. There are different schools within action research, but at least three common dimensions were important in the project. One is that the purpose of the research is to contribute to change, emancipation or liberation, another is participatory inquiry, and the third is cycles of action followed by reflection in order to generate new and improved forms of action (Greenwood and Santos 1992; Bradbury and Reason 2001; Eikeland 2005, 2006; Greenwood and Levin 2007). This approach fitted well with the explicit aim of the project – to develop a self-learning organization.

The Democratic Dialogue Approach

In line with our approach, we had required that the project start with a two-day dialogue conference where all the employees at Electron participated. This is a critical feature of the action research approach on which we based the research, namely the "democratic dialogue". Democratic dialogue was used as a key communicative and theoretical concept in a Swedish research program, the LOM program in the 1980s, drawing on earlier research experiences (Gustavsen 1985, 1992). Through its direct influence on two Norwegian research programs, Enterprise Development 2000 (Gustavsen; Colbjørnsen and Pålshaugen 1997; Qvale and Pålshaugen 2000), and Value Creation 2010 (Fricke and Totterdill 2004), as well as on teachings in the Norwegian School of Management (BI), a number of University Colleges, and the work of the Worklife Institute in Sweden and the Work Research Institute in Norway, it has had a great impact on Scandinavian action research. The research methodology is based on action in the form of dialogue. Action research in the democratic dialogue approach has mainly been used to reshape the internal discourses of enterprises, and between enterprises (Pålshaugen 1998). Discourses in companies partly overlap and are partly disconnected, and the understanding of the part is far better than the understanding of the whole. With proper channels and arenas for sharing between the different discourses, an enterprise has a capacity for generating knowledge and learning. Such a capacity has been termed an "internal public sphere" in the enterprise (Pålshaugen 2001), a sphere where viewpoints, information and opinions may be exchanged and qualified, including those of the researchers. What the democratic dialogue approach does is to bring the different discourses of an enterprise together in an orderly fashion as a means of transformation.

The Dialogue Conference

The managers thought about the dialogue conference for weeks, and finally agreed. The site of the conference was one of the matters that had to be decided early on. After cost and logistical details were considered, the management decided on a nearby sports house. Location in itself is an important aspect of an event. In this case it was at a distance from the everyday surroundings of work, but in a location with which nearly all participants were well acquainted in their private lives. The house was the center of sports activities in the community where people had cheered their children, attended meetings or made coffee. It provided familiarity and imbued the proceedings with the familiarity of the everyday.

It was left to the researchers to make the scene ready for the event, and we did not have the locals' embodied knowledge of the place. What we had at our disposal were tables and chairs, flip boards, overheads, paper and pens, which we then arranged as props following our "script" of a dialogue conference. Tables and chairs for groups of 7-8 people filled most of the room, with paper and pens on the tables and flipcharts, overhead and screen a few meters in front of them. The tables were numbered, with the seating of the participants decided in advance. We also set up a table for ourselves to the side of the room, halfway between the other tables and the screen. Hence, the scenography of the room resembled a common conference set-up. The participants' "scripts" were placed on the tables in the form of a page with two rules (one, make sure everyone gets a chance to speak; two, you do not need to agree), a list stating which table they were to sit at during the first session of the conference, and an agenda. The agenda was three group sessions and three plenary sessions the first day, and two of each the next day, and approximate times were given. The topics for the sessions were not yet presented. On the first day they would first work on defining the present, then on visions and dreams about the future, and last concretizations of how to come from the first to the second. The groups were designed so that for the first session they were composed of people who worked together. In the second session they would be composed of a group of people from all functions and levels, with some consideration also of informal positions. For the third session we intended to draw out the main concerns from the first session and let people choose which topic they wanted to work on. The results of the group discussions would be briefly presented in plenary sessions so that all got the chance to be updated on the perspectives and concerns of the others. After dinner and for as long as necessary, the project team, strengthened with a few others, would plan the second day, based on the material produced.

We had just finished setting the stage when the participants started to arrive. All except the logistics and plant managers peeked into the room, but did not come in. The managers walked about the room and read the papers, and then came over to our table with an unexpected request – they were uncomfortable with the seating arrangements. They had discovered that they were going to be seated separately and be ordinary members of the work groups for that session. Now they claimed that the dialogues between the workers would be disturbed by their presence. It would be better if they could just listen in on the conversations. We had discussed precisely if there should be a separate management table when we planned the conference. The managers had then decided against it, as they said the three team leaders were not properly part of management, and a group of two was too small. (None of us knew then that the owner was going to participate, in fact we did not know until the same morning.) We reminded them of this, and also that the actual experience of dialogue was part of the event, and would be very different if experienced from the position of a spectator. Obviously uncomfortable, the managers consented.

This conference was a temporary disruption of the established social order. The shared understanding of the hierarchy thereby became public, as did the more limited perspectives defined by the different positions within it. The general definition of the situation was in the researchers' hands, and supported by props and dramaturgy more than by written and spoken words. Our instructions were very short and very practical. We researchers had, as far as we could, made it into an occasion for that type of reflection where knowledge and interests are one, and we did not contribute with our theoretical models or concepts; this was the responsibility of the participants. The first plenary sessions made it clear for all present that they shared the same problems. This resulted in some teasing between the logistics and the production workers. Each said they had thought the other one was the problem and was now confronted with the same accusation as they leveled at the other. The experiment of including the top managers with the workers had also gone well. As mentioned above, we had initially wanted them to work in a separate group because this would allow the relations of power to become clearer, but also an opportunity for mutual acknowledgement of the common nature of the problems.

At the end of the first day, the participants had jointly produced analyses of the situation in the company, worked on a vision and on a strategy, and had started to concretize the next steps.

Then we waited for the caterer to bring dinner, and my co-researcher walked into the middle of the room and announced that we had time for a summing-up session. He briefly retraced the events of the day, repeated the five main concerns that the participants had worked on last, and asked for input to each of them. One of the topics was the company's electronic workflow system. At first no one said anything. Then an engineer spoke up. He had invited himself to the conference on the grounds that he was working so closely with the production, and the managers had consented. What he gave us was a lecture on the quality of the workflow system in great technical detail. A worker interrupted him by saying quite loudly that the technology was probably fine, but still items disappeared from the lists or were registered in the wrong place and everything was not fine. Next, the plant manager interrupted him to talk at length about the workflow system, concluding that it was used in the wrong way. People at several tables protested loudly and simultaneously, some directed their frustration toward the engineer, others toward the plant manager and soon there were numerous debates and arguments across the tables.

We intervened and when some sort of order was restored, the assembly had divided into three groups. One was composed of the plant manager, the logistics manager and the engineer who now all stood in the middle of the room. The second group was all the people who were seated at the tables. The third was the researchers. My co-researcher had sat down again and for a while we just steered the flow of heated arguments. The workers were in unison that the system was unreliable, unpredictable and poorly attuned to their needs. The managers and engineers were equally certain that the workers were wrong, that they did not know the system well enough, and that their complaints were without foundation.

This situation was certainly not dialogical, but the outpouring of frustration washed away a lot of computer technology jargon, and occasionally they got down to actually talking about how the system worked. However, such brief exchanges were inevitably stopped by the engineer, who continued to talk about the merits of the technology. The communication followed a general overall pattern. First there was a challenge by someone, followed by outpouring of frustration, and finally more specific dialogue about more concrete experiences, which each time was stopped by a lecture on technology from one or the other of the managers. By the third round, the participants had started to repeat old arguments and claims and nothing new was emerging.

Our script required that we only deal with the form and not the content of the discussions. We could have followed this script by stopping the discussion and going on to the next topic, but on the other hand we were happy that the disparate viewpoints came out in a public setting created precisely for such a purpose. We could all learn more about what was going on, so I walked to the middle of the room and asked what the discussion was all about. Again the engineer began to describe the technology, so I cut him off as politely as I could and explained that I was trying to understand what they were really talking about. How much of the discussion concerned the technical details of the actual workflow system, and how much concerned other related issues, and what could these issues be? My question resulted in a very long silence. The audience appeared to be flabbergasted. The first response was a counter-question from a worker, and *I* was asked to explain what I could possibly mean. I said they seemed to talk about so many things at the same time, like work routines, division of labor, who shared and who did not share information, power to make decisions, inventories and so on. I gradually received more responses, but they were guarded and vague. The positioning of people in the room also changed. The managers and the engineer sat down again with the others, and now there were marked contrast between the company people and the researchers. In line with our script we did not want to interpret the situation or the workflow system, so in the end I asked if we could simply keep the matter open. The participants agreed. Again, like the muddled meeting when we discussed the first report, there had been instances of dialogue, and this time the operative contradictions had manifested themselves in a much more direct manner.

In the planning session after the dinner, there was another round about the workflow system. The plant manager suggested that we should drop it from the agenda and leave the problem to the engineers. The logistics managers disagreed, and the union representative was adamant that the topic be included, so it was. The next day we divided the participants into groups that closely resembled their everyday work groups and asked them to continue to work on the three topics that had emerged as the most concrete the day before (one of these was the workflow system). Several groups worked on the same topics, and the plenary sessions were productive for comparison and mutual adjustment. In the last session we asked them to make concrete action plans, beginning with the next day. We left the groups mainly as they were, except that we this time organized the five managers into one group. After all these were the ones with the power to make decisions: the symbolic effect, as the other groups addressed their requests for time, resources, personnel and equipment to start work with the identified development tasks, was not lost on anyone.

After the conference, we gathered all the sheets that the participants had produced and wrote them up. Then we used the next two weeks to analyze their content with the purpose of designing the project. In the final report we suggested alternative ways to organize the project, considering procedures, arenas, time frames, participation and resources. We did not discuss any of the content of this knowledge, but only attached copies of all the texts produced at the conference, page after page with suggestions for improvements. The next months were spent setting up work groups, writing mandates and aligning the activities of the project with the flow of activities in the company, which again reshaped both discourses and relations within the company, although not in as dramatic fashion as during the conference.

The changes that occurred after that were the work of the company people. Those who were not directly involved in the project became involved because of changes in the hierarchy, or because somebody started to do tasks differently or use new words. The new team leader in logistics and the new workstation for the production worker are two concrete examples. The concept of self-learning organization was trashed, and instead the energy was spent on realizing a team organization. The two research situations discussed above were the only direct interaction with many of the people working in the company. In the main part of the two years the project lasted, we were discussion partners at the project team meetings.

Discussion

Seeing research as performance allows for an identification of aspects of research methods that are not accessible from other perspectives. What the presentation of the two research situations has revealed is the fact that conventional social science methods and action research are not merely different in degree, they are different in kind. The most striking difference is in how the two types of performances arrange a social setting. Action research disrupts the flow of social interaction in a fundamental way. It positions participants in ways that are unfamiliar to them, and it thereby reveals the ways that are familiar. This happened when the two managers in Electron suddenly changed their mind and did not want to participate with the same social status as the workers – as ordinary participants. But not only does it reveal the patterns, it makes them work in alternative ways, thus generating experiences with possible new forms of interaction. Conventional social science methods on the other hand leave matters more as they are. In the research situation described here, that was particularly noticeable due to the initial aim of participant

115

observation. However, even an interview-based survey does not sustain the same kind of radical reorientation that follows from an action research approach. It removes interviewees one by one from their surroundings, but their fundamental workings are not disturbed.

Another striking difference is how the two types of performance affect the form of communication. In this instance, conventional science dominates any conversation by insisting on one specific language game in which the concepts and terms relevant for the script are given priority. If the content of the research concerns "self-learning organization" or "socio-technical systems", as was the case in the first research situation, then those determine what it is socially possible to talk about. Concerns, idioms or expressions that do not fit with the script do not gain the same legitimacy as those that do. For example, the invitation to engage in the language game of two other regimes of knowledge, those of the health-and-safety movement and the productivity movement, were refused. Action research on the other hand strives to not privilege one type of conception over another, and hence allow the flow of expressions that serve to constitute a social world to come forth, independent of the speaker's position in a hierarchy. This makes for less clear-cut logical or causal explanations forced on the dialogue by the definition of a hegemonic discourse. An example of the tension that creates is what happened at the conference when the Electron people attempted to diagnose their problems with the workflow system. But precisely by not forcing the issue into clear-cut causal terms, it served as a productive point of orientation for a number of otherwise disconnected discourses.

A third difference regards the effects on the content of knowledge. In conventional social science, the stage is rigged according to the content of a script, and it is the responsibility of the researcher to ensure that the game is played according to the rules of this script, in order to possibly improve the script. This means that the content of the knowledge is exported from the situation in which it emerged and imported into another social setting, the scientific community. Here it may very well serve to reorient the manner of work, whereas it does not have that effect on the source of the initial insights. Action research on the other hand does not have a script in the same manner, rather the script details the process, but there is no plot. The plot is generated by the actual interaction, and can then very well change as a result of reflection on that action. In this manner it can support change in the context where it emerges, because knowledge is not extracted without anything given in return, as is so often the case in conventional social science.

Action research aims to transform our ways of knowing, conventional social science to expand the boundaries of the known. However, despite the explicit concerns of the two approaches, there are some unintended consequences of the two approaches in the ways they affect the workings of the social world. Put very schematically, the two forms of inquiry had the greatest effect on the following types of change in the company.

	Impact of the research performance:		
	On work	On power	On language
Empirical-analytic/ historical-hermeneutic	Some	Little	Much
Systematic action	Some	Much	Little

Table 1. Degree of impact of the research performance

Although conventional science does not aim for immediate change, the result of the research was in some small ways immediately noticeable on the forms of work. A new gluing machine or more ergonomically correct workstations may not be much in the big picture, but it certainly meant much to the people using the equipment in their work. Action research does aim to have an impact on work, but in this case the impact was not direct, and was connected with the transformation in power. Also, the transformation was not fundamental. For example, the distinction between worker and manager was not overcome, but at least the experiences and concerns of the workers gained legitimacy through the new ways the teams operated, and this again changed the manner of work in small, but important ways.

The conventional social science research on the one hand had little influence on the relations of power. On the other hand it did have an effect on language. By asking the specific questions in specific terms, it made it possible for those asked to reflect on and discuss their experiences in new ways. The idea of a "socio-technical system", and the opportunity this allowed to explicate the relations between people and production, served this purpose. Another example is the import of concepts from social science, namely "team organization" and "self-learning organization". The first proved productive in the company, the other was next to meaningless in this context. In contrast, the action research approach did not contribute with new concepts, models and theories, in order to leave room for the existing ones and not risk dominating with alienating modes of language. (As demonstrated by the discussion with the would-be team leader, the alienating effect of the concept of self-learning organization is to be taken seriously if dialogue is the aim.)

In action research the medium (research methods) is also the form (truth, in the form of self-reflection). In social science they are separate. What the two research situations show, then, is that action research is more than only one research method among many in the ordinary toolkit of social science, as its epistemological foundations are so vastly different, and one method cannot be judged according to the principles of the other.

References

Arendt, H. (1989) [1958], *The Human Condition*. Chicago: University of Chicago Press.

Austin, J. (1975) [1959], *How to doTthings with Words? The William James lectures delivered at Harvard University in 1955*. Edited by J.O. Urmson and Marina Sbisà. Cambridge, Mass.: Harvard University Press.

Berg, B.L. (2007), *Qualitative Research Methods for the Social Sciences* (6th Edition). Boston: Pearson.

Bernhard, R. (2005), *Research Methods in Aanthropology. Qualitative and Quantitative Approaches*. AltaMira Press.

Connerton, P. (1989), *How Societies Remember*. Cambridge: Cambridge University Press.

Eikeland, O. (2005), "Pragmatisk vending – kunnskapsteoretisk møteplass?" In Fossestøl, K. (ed.) *Nytt arbeidsliv – nye former for kunnskapsproduksjon*. Vol. 12, Pp. 23-30. Oslo: Work Research Institute.

Eikeland, O. (2006), "The validity of Action Research – Validity in Action Research", Pp. 193-240 in Nielsen, K.Aa. and Svensson, L. (eds) *Action And Interactive Research – Beyond Theory and Practice*, Maastricht and Aachen: Shaker Publishing

Emery, F. and Thorsrud, E.; in co-operation with Engelstad, P.H., Gulowsen, J. and Qvale T.U. (1976), *Democracy at Work: the Report of the Norwegian Industrial Democracy Program*. Leiden: Martinus Nijhoff Social Sciences Division.

Evens, T.M.S. and Handelman, D. (eds) (2006), *The Manchester School. Practice and Ethnographic Praxis in Anthropology*. New York and Oxford: Berghahn Books.

Fricke, W. and Totterdill P. (eds) (2004), *Action Research in Workplace Innovation and Regional Development*. Amsterdam/ Philadelphia: John Benjamins.

Gluckman, M. (2006), "Ethnographic data in British Social Anthropology". In Evens, T.M.S. and Handelman, D. (eds) *The Manchester School. Practice and Ethnographic Praxis in Anthropology*: Pp. 13-22. New York and Oxford: Berghahn Books.

Henrick, J. (2002), "Decision Making, Cultural Transmission and Adaptation in Economic Anthropology". In Ensminger, J. (ed.) *Theory in Economic Anthropology*, Pp. 251-295. AltaMira Press.

Goffman, E. (1959), *The Presentation of Self in Everyday life*. Garden City, NY: Doubleday.

Greenwood, D.J. and Levin, M. (2007), *Introduction to Action Research:Social Research for Social Change*. Thousand Oaks, California: Sage Publications.

Greenwood, D.J. and Santos, J.L.G. (eds) (1992), *Industrial Democracy as Process: Participatory Action Research in the Fagor Cooperative Group of Mondragón*. Assen: Van Gorcum.

Gustavsen, B. (1985), "Workplace Reform and Democratic Dialogue", *Economic and Industrial Democracy* 6:461-479.

Gustavsen, B. (1992), *Dialogue and Development: Theory of Communication, Action Research and the Restructuring of Working Life*. Assen: Van Gorcum.

Gustavsen, B., Colbjørnsen, T. and Pålshaugen, Ø. (eds) (1997), *Development Coalitions in Working Life*. Amsterdam/ Philadelphia: John Benjamins.

Habermas, J. (2002) [1971], *Knowledge and Human Interests*. Boston: Beacon Press.

Habermas, J. (1984-1987), *The Theory of Communicative Action*. Boston, Mass.: Beacon Press.

Mitchell, J.C. (2006), "Case and Situation Analysis". In Evens, T.M.S. and Handelman, D. (eds) *The Manchester School. Practice and Ethnographic Praxis in Anthropology*, Pp. 23-44. New York and Oxford: Berghahn Books.

Pelto, P.J. and Pelto, G.H. (1978), *Anthropological Research: the Structure of Inquiry*. Cambridge: Cambridge University Press.

Pålshaugen, Ø. (1998), *The End of Organization Theory? Language as a Tool in Action Research and Organizational Development*. Amsterdam: John Benjamins.

Pålshaugen, Ø. (2001), "The Use of Words: Improving Enterprises by Improving their Conversations". In P. Reason and H. Bradbury (eds), *Handbook of Action Research: Participative inquiry and practice*, Pp. 200-209. London: SAGE.

Reason. P. and Bradbury, H. (eds), (2001), *Handbook of Action Research: Participative Inquiry and Practice*. London: Sage.

Trist, E. (1981), *The Evolution of Socio-technical Systems*. Occasional paper no 2. June 1981. Ontario Quality of Life Working Centre.

Qvale, T.U. (2002), "A Case of Slow Learning? Recent Trends in Social Partnership in Norway with Particular Emphasis on Workplace Democracy". *Concepts and Transformation* 7(1): 31-56.

Qvale, T.U. and Pålshaugen, Ø. (eds.) (2000), *Forskning og Bedriftsutvikling – nye samarbeidsforsøk*, Vol. 9. Oslo: Arbeidsforskningsinstituttet.

Winslow, D. (2002), "Space, Place and Economic Anthropology. Locating Potters in a Sri Lankan Landscape". In Ensminger, J. (ed.) *Theory in economic anthropology*, Pp. 155-181. AltaMira Press.

4 The Action Researcher as Change Agent: On Dialogue Facilitation and Network Collaboration[1]

Jarle Hildrum and Siw M. Fosstenløkken

Introduction

While literature about industrial action research (IAR) tends to highlight the effects of action research generated dialogues, such as increased organisational democracy and productivity, few contributions direct explicit attention to the relationship building efforts necessary to instigate and maintain the dialogues. Therefore, this chapter illuminates a previously neglected aspect of IAR by focusing on the ways in which the application of a specific set of AR methods affects relationship building in network collaboration. The aim is to improve our understanding of the action researcher as dialogue facilitator in IAR. We address this topic by drawing upon experiences from an action research (AR) project in a network of eight industrial companies in Norway.

Before we present these experiences, it is necessary to state where we are coming from, that is, to outline the specific AR tradition to which we belong, and the specific AR methods that we use in the project. Hence, this chapter is organised as follows. The next section addresses the perspective of IAR, along with its methods as applied at the Work Research Institute (WRI). Thereafter, the AR project is presented, followed by the empirical findings. Finally, we offer a concluding discussion in which we outline implications for IAR and provide suggestions for future research.

Industrial Action Research

Following Greenwood (1998:4), we define action research as 'social research carried out by a team encompassing professional action researchers and members of an organisation or community seeking to improve their situation'. Kurt Lewin, who reputedly first coined the term, describes AR as having the dual goal of examining social systems and bringing about positive changes in those systems (Lewin,

---

1 This chapter has been written as part of the strategic research programme (2003-2007) at the WRI, Oslo.

1946). An important aspect of this duality is the conviction that the best way to learn about and understand a social system is by trying to change it. Thus, AR is not simply a way to generate knowledge about how individuals interact and change their environments, it is also a change mechanism that helps people and organisations understand and transform their own environment (Reason & Bradbury, 2001).

In the course of the six decades which have passed since Lewin's article was published, AR has proliferated into a wide range of different perspectives, each constituting an approach in its own right. For instance, the approach of action science encourages researchers to study themselves in collaborative action with their research objects, thereby aspiring to transform the practice of social scientific research itself (Argyris et al., 1985). By contrast, industrial action research, which dates back to Lewin's influence on organisational psychology and organisation development, can be distinguished from other approaches on the basis of a strong emphasis on workplace democratisation, organisational improvement, and close collaboration between researchers and organisational members (Kemmis & McTaggart, 2000). This tradition is particularly strong in Scandinavia and emerged through a sequence of large IAR projects in this region from the mid-1960s and onwards (e.g. Emery & Thorsrud, 1969; Emery & Thorsud, 1976; Elden, 1983; Gustavsen, 1985, 1992; Emery & Emery, 1993; Pålshaugen, 1998; Eikeland, 2001). These projects took place in step with an evolving collaborative process between the main union and the main employers' federation on national strategies for the democratisation and improvement of working life (Pålshaugen, 1998).

IAR is specifically relevant for this current topic due to a strong objective of facilitating constructive and broad-based dialogues within and across organisations. Indeed, a key goal is to encourage a broad dialogue towards improving the organisation and to subsequently negotiate strategies to safeguard that the dialogue does not break down. Inspired by Ayas and Zeniuk (2001), the specific value and relevance of IAR lies in the fact that external action researchers might – through their independent roles and their application of methods for reflective practices – help organisational members acquire a broader perspective of their situation and see the systemic aspects of the problems they are experiencing. Drawing upon their respective project experiences in Fokker and Ford Motor Company, these authors suggest that by facilitating an iterative process that shifts between action and deep reflection, action researchers might help organisational members shift attention from individual preferences to collective preferences and joint action (Ayas & Zeniuk, 2001). Similarly, reporting from an AR project in four Norwegian industrial service firms, Hildrum and Strand (2006) conceive of industrial action researchers as 'inter-community brokers', mediating and translating between different organisational communities with disparate perspectives and agendas. Their study also points out a number of challenges associated with AR, such as barriers to entry in important communities and employees' scepticism towards external change agents. In order to facilitate constructive dialogues, then, industrial action researchers depend heavily on various methods, for example such as those developed at the Work Research Institute.

Methods of the Work Research Institute

Our approach to action research falls into the above mentioned category of IAR and is strongly informed by the research tradition of our current employer, the Work Research Institute. This tradition can be characterised in terms of three methodological building blocks:

The *first* building block is a strong emphasis on promoting democracy in working life: an important goal of AR is to change organisations in such a way that the employees are given greater opportunity to shape the future of their own workplace. Taking this emphasis as a starting point, WRI researchers typically seek to expand an organisation's development-oriented dialogues and continuously bring in new voices and perspectives (Pålshaugen, 1998). Pålshaugen (1998) argues that action researchers' job is to prevent a situation in which a minority of organisational members acquire a monopoly on defining organisational reality and the various measures that must be implemented to solve the organisation's problems. The action researcher should try to ensure that a broad variety of perspectives enter organisational dialogues (Pålshaugen, 1998). In the course of the last decade, increasing attention has been directed towards expanding the dialogues outside the borders of single companies and networks to encompass other agents in the local environment, such as policy makers, universities, research institutions, and various public agencies (Ennals & Gustavsen, 1999).

This inclination towards democratising organisational development processes is relevant in marking out differences between action researchers and other candidates to the change agent role, such as managers and business consultants. Since managers' primary task is to improve the organisation's economic performance, they are likely to direct their activities on a (limited) set of areas which evince the greatest potential for innovation. However, purposeful and persistent agency directed at a limited set of areas might 'backfire' in the sense that it erects learning barriers around interlinked groups in focus, while excluding others from offering their valuable perspectives to the organisation's development-oriented dialogues. Action researchers' activities are less likely to encourage such borders, since they start from the principal goal of facilitating democracy and preserving heterogeneity in the dialogues.

The *second* building block is a long-standing tradition of developing strategic partnerships with major labour market organisations. From the 1960s and onwards, WRI has nurtured a close collaborative relationship with the main Norwegian union and employers' association, centred on the shared objective of improving conditions in working life. This relationship is relevant because it paves the way for WRI researchers to access and gain legitimacy as change agents in Norwegian companies. Indeed, by negotiating access to companies through both employers associations and unions, WRI researchers have a good starting point for entering and gaining legitimacy in a broad range of organisations.

The *third* building block is a set of practical methods and strategies to facilitate broad organisational and cross-company dialogues. One frequently used dialogue method is the *search conference* (Emery & Purser, 1996; Emery 2003). A search conference is a participative event that enables a large group of diverse members to collectively create a plan that its members will implement themselves. Typically, 20 to 50 people from an organisation or a community work progressively for two or three days on creating plans and projects, alternating between small-group work sessions and large-group plenary sessions. During these dialogues, the conference participants draw heavily on joint features such as flip-charts with mutual ideas and concepts, project plans, and shared strategies. The outcomes of a search conference are various, ranging from innovation and new strategies for growth, to new alliances and organisations. Common to all outcomes is that they entail action (Emery, 2003). A related method which is also frequently used at WRI is the *dialogue conference*, in which the main goal is to visualise a multifaceted picture of organisational reality and empower organisational members to jointly improve that reality (Pålshaugen, 1998). In relation to these conferences, the role of the researchers is to work out a conference plan in collaboration with the management and union representatives, and to assist in organising, facilitating, and structuring the dialogues during the course of the conference.

Although action researchers have well-proven methods available to them, a one-off application of these is of course not sufficient to sustain constructive dialogues over time. At any point in time during an organisational AR project, critical events might occur that threaten to put a stop to whatever dialogues and organisational democratisation processes which were instigated in the conferences. Examples are organisational restructuring, inter-department conflict, market changes, the emergence of a serious competitor, or any other event that compels people to divert their attention from the dialogue to some other, more pressing issue. An important task of the action researcher is to respond swiftly and flexibly to such events, seeking to sustain valuable dialogues by assembling new sets of agents and refocusing the dialogues according to the change in context (Hildrum & Strand, 2006). Another strategy for sustaining development oriented dialogues, one which has been pursued by WRI researchers in recent years, is to educate a set of internal employees and managers in dialogue methods so that they can take responsibility for sustaining the dialogues after the action researchers have left the scene (Winther, 2007).

In the following empirical sections, we focus explicitly on the relationship building efforts necessary to commence and maintain such AR-generated dialogues through an examination of a specific AR project, as presented below.

The Action Research Project

This AR project is part of a national R&D programme called Value Creation 2010 (VC2010). VC2010 started in 2000 and is an action-oriented research programme organised by the main Norwegian labour market organisations, the Research Council of Norway, and Innovation Norway (the national agency for industrial development). Its institutional foundation rests upon an agreement from 1983 between the main union and the main employers' association. An important element in this agreement is to offer joint financial and research-based support to organisations wanting to improve their situation by means of extensive employee participation in development work. The programme organises a large number of AR projects in corporate settings spanning most of Norway's regions. The Work Research Institute is responsible for conducting VC2010 in the county of Telemark. The cornerstone in work life employment in Telemark is the chemical process industry in the Grenland region, which provides the empirical material in this study. Based on the above mentioned institutional arrangement, the WRI researchers negotiated access to the industry through the regional offices of the two major labour market organisations.

The industry consists of a network of eight firms, seven chemical process plants and one large company providing industrial property and infrastructure. The companies are located close to each other (within a 15 km radius) in the Grenland region, about 350 km southwest of Oslo. They constitute the largest concentration of advanced process industry in Scandinavia (approx. 5000 employees and an annual turnover of more than €2 billion). All the firms are owned by internationally leading corporations, rely heavily on export sales, and are exposed to fierce international competition. Together, the firms control large professional and technical resources and also have good transport facilities and fairly well developed infrastructure for this kind of industry. They enjoy a positive political and social environment for heavy industry, a good labour market with access to highly skilled workers, and strong industrial relations. In addition, the firms have local access to energy, deep water harbours, well-qualified suppliers/contractors, and adequate educational institutions (Qvale, 2008). For an overview of the firms, see Table 1 below.

Table 1: The network

Company	Business	Number of employees	Turnover in 2005 (mill. EUR)	Export share
1. Borealis	Plastics	500	412	90%
2. Eramet Comilog	Metal compounds	200	100	100%
3. Herøya Industripark	Industrial support infrastructure	1100	313	50%
4. Yara*	Fertilizers	410	500	90%
5. Hydro Polymers	PVC, caustic soda, polymers	350	375	30%
6. Norcem	Cement	225	113	15%
7. Noretyl	Ethylene and propylene	166	275	95%
*8. Norske Skog Union**	*Paper and pulp*	*340*	*100*	

* In 2003, a new plant, Yara, entered the network, increasing the total number of plants to eight. However, in early 2006, Norske Skog Union was closed down, so that the number of plants reverted to seven.

Empirical Material

The empirical findings presented in this section have been collected through participant observations in meetings and conferences attended by company representatives (Jacobs, 1974), and 24 semi-structured interviews with managers and employees in the participant firms. Between August 2001 and December 2006, WRI researchers organised a total of six dialogue conferences in the network, in which managers and employees from all levels of the companies were present. During the same period, the researchers regularly attended two formal committees which were responsible for organising collaborative activities within the network, and in which the companies' top managers and union leaders participated. During these conferences and meetings, the researchers made extensive notes which were circulated among the participants for comments and subsequently converted into reports and memos. The participants themselves also made notes and reports, which were compared and integrated with the researchers' notes. In addition to these observations, the empirical study draws upon records of correspondence taking place between the researchers and the field agents prior to and between the conferences and the meetings.

It is important to note that the authors of this paper joined the AR project in January 2005 and report their own experiences from that time onwards, involving two dialogue conferences, 21 meetings with managers and union representatives, and e-mail correspondence taking place in between these meetings. The paper's account of action research experiences from before 2005 derives from notes and reports written by five WRI researchers who were involved in this earlier stage of the project.[2] Informal interviews and talks with these researchers and with managers and employees provide additional information.

The study documents dialogues within and across the companies, as well as those expanding from within the network to constellations associated with political activity and economic development in Grenland and Telemark at large. The analysis examines the dialogues in relation to the activities of the action researchers and to a number of organisational changes which took place within the network in the course of the project.

Drawing upon this qualitative material, the next section demonstrates how the action researchers contributed to instigating and smoothing the progress of constructive cross-company dialogues in the network. To describe how the action researchers proceeded, it is useful to describe the project as it unfolded through the following three phases: (i) August 2001 – the network context upon the researchers' entry; (ii) August 2001-December 2006 – the researchers' collaboration with the field members; and (iii) January 2007 – the field context at the point of reporting. The collaboration is still ongoing, but the discussion in the paper concerns the activities up to 2007.

Empirical Findings: Dialogue Facilitation and Network Collaboration

August 2001: The Network Context upon the Researchers' Entry

Before the launch of the AR project in August 2001, the network companies were already collaborating through two regular discussion groups – one for the

---

2   These researchers are Thoralf Qvale (project manager), Øyvind Pålshaugen, Lars Klemsdal, Kathrine Holstad, and Iver Prestkvern.

top managers and one for the companies' union leaders. These groups had been in operation for several years, and constituted two distinct constellations in their own right. Beyond these top-level groups, there was little formalised collaboration across the firms. At this point, each of the firms encompassed its own unique practice centred on various areas of expertise, such as the operation of advanced laboratory equipment and monitoring and control of chemical processes. While many of the operations were linked to specific practices within single firms, like for instance the operation of specific chemical process equipment, others centred on more general functions which were common to all the firms, such as technical maintenance and HR. In spite of the fact that some of the companies' internal practices were overlapping, there was little interaction centred on concrete joint activities. One exception was in the case of crisis response (each firm had their own small group focusing on crisis handling in the plants related to fire, gas leakages, and explosions), in which there had been cross-company collaboration for several years. Moreover, since the firms recruited employees from the same local environment, and occasionally swapped employees, there were many informal social interactions and relationships across the organisations.

During the months preceding the establishment of the AR project, the firms experienced major financial problems. The change rate for Norwegian currency was high – as were wages and duties – whereas the prices on the world market were low (Qvale & Holstad, 2005). As the economic situation grew even worse during 2001, and the potential for cost-cutting within each firm was almost fully exploited, future opportunities for cost-cutting had to be found through collaboration and integration between firms in the network. At this point in time, action researchers from WRI came in contact with the firms' top managers and union leaders and presented the VC2010 programme. After a few initial meetings, the managers and union leaders became interested in the programme's principle of organisation development through broad participation and decided to launch an action research project. One manager explained this decision in the following way: '*Since we had been trying for a long time to create more extensive employee networks across the firms, the approach of the VC2010 programme was attractive to us. We realised that we have no chance of generating really successful collaborations across the companies unless we involved people at all levels of the organisations*'.

The fact that the researchers accessed the companies through both the top managers' group and the union leaders' group further opened up for access into several different levels of the companies. Following the wishes of the managers and the union leaders, the project's main objective was to extend existing cross-company collaborations to encompass not only managers and union leaders, but also employees at all levels and functions. The purpose was a broad search for opportunities to cut costs and strengthen competitiveness, and thereby reduce the risk of dismissals and downsizing. As a part of this deal, the directors of the regional branches of the main union and the main employers' organisation were assigned the task of supervising the project, while two researchers from WRI were assigned the task of instigating and sustaining broad cross-company development dialogues.

August 2001-December 2006:
The Researchers' Collaboration with the Field Members

As a first move towards reaching the project objective, the researchers suggested to organise a dialogue conference in which people from all levels of the firms as well as a number of external agents such as politicians, local researchers, and civil servants would participate. This suggestion was a direct implementation of the principle of broad participation in organisation development and the promotion of democracy in working life (Emery & Thorsrud, 1976). The motive behind involving external participants was to help the firms search for development opportunities beyond the network, and to discuss whether resources in the broader regional environment could be employed to mitigate the companies' economic challenges. The managers and union members accepted the idea of arranging the dialogue conference, but were sceptical towards bringing in external participants. At this point, the firms' sole motivation for collaborating was to reduce costs, and the managers and union representatives feared that external participants could draw attention away from that objective. The representatives from the regional labour market organisations shared this scepticism, fearing that the researchers were trying to introduce regional development strategies which would oust the labour market organisations' existing regional development activities. This scepticism illustrates a general challenge that any external agent might encounter when entering and trying to instigate broad-based dialogues in organisational environments in which they are newcomers and have little local knowledge.

To gain the trust and support of the local agents, and to gain legitimacy as cross-company facilitators, the researchers spent considerable time during the autumn of 2001 on collaborating closely with managers and union leaders accommodating their different viewpoints and creating a redefined conference plan. In this context, WRI's long-standing collaborative relationship with the labour market organisations was helpful in the sense that some of the managers and the union leaders were familiar with action research and the researchers' objective of facilitating democratic development processes.

An important part of the facilitating effort was to define a clear-cut and mutually agreed objective for the conference, and thereafter make sure that a broad group of managers, union representatives, and employees signed up to participate. This was challenging since different stakeholders had different objectives. While the plant managers were eager to search for short-term cost reductions, the representatives of the unions had more long-term objectives in terms of exploring opportunities for building a pipeline for transportation of natural gas from the North Sea to Grenland. In this process, the conference plan functioned as common ground between the researchers, managers, and union representatives, in the sense that the researchers e-mailed the conference plan back and forth between the agents and gradually incorporated different viewpoints and meanings. In between these e-mail exchanges, there were also several meetings in which the project plan was presented, discussed, and adjusted. These e-mail exchanges and meetings went on for several weeks until a mutually accepted project plan had been reached. This resonates with Hildrum and Strand (2006), who highlight the potential of project plans and other documents as vessels of negotiation.

Instigating Cross-company Dialogues

The first dialogue conference took place on January 7th and 8th, 2002, and involved 50 employees from all levels of the firms, as well as representatives from the regional labour market parties and researchers from local R&D institutions. The conference was organised along a sequence alternating between small group discussions and plenary meetings. During the first day, the participants were assigned to small, heterogeneous groups comprising representatives from different firms with different work tasks and rank. The groups were then asked to describe the networking companies' and the region's most desirable future, and to outline the areas in which the firms should collaborate amongst themselves and with the local environment in order to realise that desired future.

During the subsequent discussions, the groups wrote down their miscellaneous answers and comments on large sheets of paper. In some of the groups, certain members had difficulty understanding one another and interpreted the same concepts in different ways. For instance, there were different interpretations of the concept 'collaboration', especially regarding whether the collaborations should encompass only the firms in the network, a larger set of firms, or the whole region including the public sector. In some of the groups, the researchers intervened directly and translated between people who misinterpreted one another. As external agents, the researchers were able to take on the facilitator role without being suspected of trying to support one viewpoint or stakeholder over another. In this process, the large sheets of paper functioned as common ground in the sense that different group members wrote down their different, and sometimes diverging, interpretations and discussed these. Towards the end of the group session, the group members wrote down their answers on one large sheet of paper.

Afterwards, the participants gathered in a plenary meeting in which they presented the results from the small group meetings and discussed common challenges and opportunities facing the firms and the region. In this plenary meeting, the researchers chaired the dialogues and visualised the variety of perspectives and organisational realities expressed by the different groups by attaching the paper sheets on the wall. Here, the researchers did not try to force the group to agree to one specific interpretation, but rather helped clarify different viewpoints, avoid misunderstandings, and keep the dialogue going. At the end of the session, after having discussed these different perspectives and realities, the participants agreed on a set of technical and administrative areas in which the network of firms should collaborate in the future.

The second day of the conference, the participants were assigned to small, homogeneous groups comprising people from different firms but with similar position and work tasks. The groups were asked to discuss ways in which the companies could establish and successfully execute collaborative projects within the areas defined during the first day. Here, like in the previous group sessions, the group members wrote down their answers on large paper sheets, and the researchers occasionally intervened to help the participants tackle ambiguities and divergent interpretations. Finally, in the last plenary meeting of the conference, the participants presented the results from their group conversations and discussed mutual goals and future collaborative activities. Again, the researchers chaired the dialogue sessions marking out contrasts between different viewpoints and translating between people who misinterpreted one another. At the end of the day, the top managers and union leaders from all of the firms made a commitment for concrete collaboration within technical maintenance, logistics, and transport infrastructure, supply of energy and raw materials, HR, and information and lobbying activities.

The physical results of the conference was a large pile of paper sheets and transparency slides that the researchers transcribed, systematised, and converted into a preliminary conference report. The report was then e-mailed to the conference participants with a request for comments. After the researchers had received a broad set of comments from the various participants, they changed the report accordingly, resubmitted it, and asked for approval. Thus, once again, the action researchers translated between the participants using a shared document as a vessel of negotiation and communication. On the basis of the collectively approved conference report, the participants made a binding commitment to follow up on their goal of identifying and launching joint development projects.

While the conference in itself did not create new constellations or strongly interconnected constellations, it did function as a starting point for linking togeth-

131

er previously isolated groups through the activation of new cross-company dialogues. The researchers facilitated this process by carefully planning the conference according to established methodology, by supporting the group discussions, and managing all plenary sessions towards the integration of work into a common product, i.e. the conference report. After this initial conference, the researchers' main objective was to contribute to keeping the dialogues going and keeping communication channels open between the involved parties.

Keeping the Dialogues going in Development Projects across the Companies

Shortly after the conference, the managers and union leaders abided by their commitment to continue and extend the collaboration by establishing three joint projects: one focused on establishing a shared company for technical maintenance, another on logistics and transport systems, and the third on shared information and lobbying activities. In this period, the firms also decided to allocate more resources to the existing collaboration project on crisis handling, aspiring to create a joint crisis response unit. To ensure capable supervision of the projects and continued development, the firms institutionalised the collaboration through two formal committees: one broad steering group involving key actors from the firms in the network and the regional environment, and a smaller executive committee, involving managers and union representatives from each firm.

The committees, in which the researchers held a seat, were given the responsibility of supervising the projects and searching for opportunities to expand the collaboration in the future. The steering group convened about once every second month, while the executive committee met once every three weeks. From this point onwards, the researchers interacted regularly with the field members in the committee meetings and a number of informal gatherings taking place in between. Their main task in these meetings was to help organise new conferences, give advice as to how the network collaboration could be improved, and facilitate the project's execution. Here, as in the conference, the researchers operated as dialogue facilitators helping different agents, such as managers and union representatives, formulate common goals, strategies, and activities. In 2002, 2003, and 2004, three new conferences were organised: the first focused on opportunities to utilise the region's R&D resources, while the other two focused mainly on strengthening and widening existing cross-company and regional collaboration projects. In this period, the volume of collaboration across the firms increased as people engaged in repeated and profound discussions about their shared work practices.

During the same period, the network collaboration projects started to produce some concrete results. The most important among these emerged in 2002 in the form of a shared information and lobbying office and a joint crisis response unit. In the same year, the firms also merged together their corporate health care offices into a shared health centre. In the field of technical maintenance, there were close dialogues and collaboration across the organisations and the technicians soon discovered that there were considerable gains to be made by merging together maintenance of electromotors and large valves. As a result of these cross-company dialogues, two new collaborative projects were established, one for electromotors and one for valves.

2004-2006: Market Changes and Waning Dialogues

In early 2004, the market changed into a high international demand for the companies' products. As a result, times got better, production increased, and focus shifted. The new economic situation rendered the objective of cost-cutting less critical than in 2001. And, the cross-company dialogues and collaboration that centred on cost-cutting lost their previous thrust and became far less frequent and enthusiastic. Moreover, increased production also meant reduced time to spend on dialogue activities. Hence, at this point, there was a danger that a further continuation of the dialogue processes, nurtured and developed through the project, would end.

To cope with this critical event, the researchers suggested changing the focus of the dialogues in the committees and the conferences from 'cost-cutting within the network' into 'lobbying activities towards central political milieus for the purpose of developing the entire Grenland region'. The intention behind this change was to sustain valuable dialogues by refocusing the topic according to the change in context. Moreover, following the principle of broad participation, the researchers worked systematically to link up more external agents to the network, such as firms from other industries, regional policy makers, and research institutions, thereby converting the development strategy of the network into a regional development strategy. This inclination towards continually bringing in new perspectives into the firms' development dialogues represents a specific trait of action research at WRI (e.g. Pålshaugen, 1998).

This suggested strategic change was realised in a dialogue conference in June 2005. The conference encompassed participants from a wide spectrum of local firms, R&D institutions, and the public sector. In addition, national political leaders and national union leaders were also present. The conference had two themes: The first was to discuss a parliamentary proposal about Norwegian industrial policy. Here, the objective was to use this text document as a starting point for discussing what would be a favourable industrial policy for Grenland. The second theme was to discuss a proposed 'desirable vision for Grenland in 2010' developed by the regional labour market organisations. More specifically, the 'vision' was a multimedia presentation to be viewed on computer screens describing desirable developments in the Grenland region, such as improved transportation infrastructure and a new football stadium.

In this conference, 'the vision for Grenland in 2010' and a 'favourable industrial policy' functioned as vessels for debate in the sense that the participants had different opinions about what they should encompass, and used the conference to agree about shared interpretations and viewpoints. While some placed strong emphasis on education, others emphasised favourable conditions for certain forms of industry. It not only helped to forge coordinating links across the firms, but also facilitated new encounters between existing groups in the field. In these discussions, it appeared that there was less need for the researchers' activities since many participants by now had become very familiar with the dialogue conferences and several participants could take on the facilitator role themselves. This is precisely the end goal of a dialogue methodology, to enable the organisations to become self-going and continue their development projects on their own. In the aftermath of this conference, the network directed more emphasis on influencing regional and national industrial policy, using subsequent conferences and meetings to influence the government to develop favourable economic framework conditions and infrastructure for industry.

January 2007

It is now time to describe the field context at the point of reporting in January 2007, examining what role action research played in collaboration activities, project outcomes, and linkages within the network. Compared to the situation in 2001, in 2007 there is much more interaction and collaboration within and between the networking firms. The most important examples of cross-company collaboration are in the areas of crisis response and technical maintenance. At project initiation, each firm had its own independent crisis unit specialising in fire extinguishing and handling emergencies in the plant. During the project, crisis support personnel from the seven firms met regularly, sharing their experiences and ideas and, little by little, established a new company centred on shared practices.[3] Similarly, there is also collaboration across company employees working on the maintenance of valves and electrical engines. Although this embryonic collaboration has not re-

---

3   At the time of writing, this company, called Norward, is growing fast and delivers its
    services to a large number of customers in Norway and abroad.

sulted in major organisational change such as the creation of a new company, it has led to the creation of new maintenance solutions and new, shared collaborations with maintenance service suppliers. It is important to note that these cross-company collaborations extend beyond the network, reaching out to numerous other firms, political interest groups, public organisations, and unions within Grenland and Telemark at large.

Currently, the network has taken on the role of a lobby organisation to influence the government to develop favorable economic conditions and infrastructure for future industry. The prime mover in this large AR project, Thoralf Qvale (2008:143), summarises the story in these words:

As the feeling of crisis and corresponding necessity of working together in order to survive has been replaced by optimism and a struggle to manage expansion, find new workers and so on, one might say VC2010 has completed its mission in Telemark .

Concluding Discussion: Relating Cross-company Dialogues and Organisational Change to the Researchers' Practices

While past research has demonstrated the relevance of action research in commencing dialogues between people both within and across organisations, it has directed little attention to the particular ways in which the application of dialogue methods affects relationship building across companies in a network. This study contributes to IAR by addressing the relationship building efforts necessary to instigate and maintain the dialogues. This is done by providing an empirical example of a large AR project on how a set of dialogue facilitation methods affects cross-company dialogues and relationship building in network collaboration.

It seems reasonable to argue that considerable changes, learning, innovation, and collaboration processes have taken place in the network, as well as in the Grenland region and Telemark at large, since the start up of the AR project (see also Qvale, 2008). During this process, the action researchers performed many tasks and functions that clearly contributed to promoting cross-company relationship-building and network collaboration:

Initially, as shown in the empirical part, it was crucial to gain legitimacy in the network, with managers, unions, and employees. Legitimacy was built through interaction with people in the network as the researchers took on an active role in arranging meetings, establishing meeting places, and conducting dialogue conferences. In this manner, they were able to gain trust through the ways in which they gathered together people from previously disconnected divisions, levels, units, and organisations. As a result, people with complementary knowledge and experiences, as well as people working within the same professional area, but in different companies, started collaborating.

As dialogue facilitators, the researchers helped instigate constructive dialogues between various groups by using specific dialogue methods and conference methodology. The researchers contributed specifically selected themes for discussion with an aim to help different people in different parts of the network to formulate common goals and development strategies. As the dialogues unfolded, the researchers translated between participants who had difficulty understanding one another. In these processes, the researchers made active use of various vessels for communication, such as project plans, future scenarios, and concepts related to organisation development, allowing all participants to negotiate on equal terms about the meaning of these.

Over time, the dialogues became institutionalised through the establishment of several arenas of regular dialogue, such as project meetings and organisation development forums, and an annual conference. In addition, as the dialogue facilitation methodology grew familiar within the network, the organisational members themselves were able to sustain dialogues and collaboration on their own.

Taken together, the findings here confirm that action researchers can successfully operate as dialogue facilitators in network collaboration. Moreover, it seems clear that the cross-company dialogue process, common goals, and project implementation, as well as many learning effects, would not have been achieved without the active involvement of the researchers.

Further, directing attention to AR methods is justified because it helps delineate the specific role of action researchers in such a context, as compared to the roles of other agents, such as for example managers, experienced employees, and external consultants. In this respect, it seems that action researchers may have an advantage. The findings suggest that action researchers can take on the facilitator role without incurring the same kind of difficulties as those facing employees and managers. We suggest that, by virtue of coming from the outside with no high stakes in organisational politics, action researchers are likely to be perceived as impartial facilitators in the dialogue process. We are not denying the possibility that other external agents, such as business consultants, can also capably take on the dialogue facilitator role. But in the context of this network, it is important to note two advantages of the WRI action researchers: The first is a set of AR methods and strategies which have been specifically developed for facilitating and translating dialogues within and between industrial firms. The second is WRI's long-standing collaborative relationship with the Norwegian labour market organisations, which helped the researchers gain legitimacy as facilitators between managers and union leaders. It is conceivable that other external candidates to the facilitator role, with no formal link to the labour market organisations, would have experienced more difficulty in gaining this legitimacy.

These findings have implications for further research. Because existing research places much emphasis on the effects of cross-company dialogues, but little emphasis on the relationship building effort through which such dialogues are instigated, developed, and sustained, we suggest more detailed research into the concrete methods and practices dialogue facilitators rely on in their efforts to turn dialogues into useful vessels for organisational development.

References

Argyris, C., Putnam, R. & Smith, D. (1985), *Action Science: Concepts, methods and skills for research and intervention*. San Francisco: Jossey-Bass.

Ayas, K. and Zeniuk, N. (2001), 'Project-based learning: Building communities of reflective practitioners' *Management Learning* 32(1): 61-76.

Eikeland, O. (2001), 'Action Research as the Hidden Curriculum of the Western Tradition.' pp.145-155 in Reason, P. & Bradbury, H. (eds.): *Handbook of Action Research: Participative Inquiry and Practice*. London: Sage.

Elden, M. (1983), 'Participatory research at work.' *Journal of occupational behaviour* 4 (1): 21-34.

Emery, F.E. and Thorsrud, E. (1969), *Form and content in industrial democracy: Some experiences from Norway and other European countries*. London: Tavistock.

Emery, F.E. and Thorsrud, E. (1976), *Democracy at Work: The Report of the Norwegian Industrial Democracy Program*. Leiden: Martinus Nijhoff.

Emery, F. and Emery, M. (1993), 'Participative Design, Work and Community Life: 1974, 1975, 1985, 1992.' In Emery, M. (ed.) *Participative Design for Participative Democracy*. Centre for Continuing Education. The Australian National University.

Emery, M. and Purser, R.E. (1996), *The Search Conference: A powerful method for planning organizational change and community action*. San Francisco: Jossey-Bass.

Emery, M. (2003), 'Searching: The theory and practice of making cultural change.' In van Beinum, H., Ennals, R., Fricke, W. and Pålshaugen, Ø. (eds.) *Dialogues on Work and Innovation*. Amsterdam: John Benjamins.

Ennals, R. and Gustavsen, B. (1999), *Work Organization and Europe as a Development Coalition*. Amsterdam: John Benjamins.

Greenwood, D.J. and Levin, M. (1998), *Introduction to Action Research*. Thousand Oaks, CA: Sage.

Gustavsen, B. (1985), 'Technology and Collective Agreements: Some Recent Scandinavian Developments.' *Industrial Relations Journal*, 16(3): 34-42.

Gustavsen, B. (1992), *Dialogue and Development*. Assen: Van Gorcum.

Hildrum, J. & Strand, G. (2006), 'Overcoming challenges in writing about action research – the promise of the development story.' *Systemic Practice and Action Research* 20(1): 77-89.

Jacobs, J. (1974), 'Participant Observation in Prison.' Journal of Contemporary Ethnography 3, pp. 221-240.

Kemmis, S. and McTaggart, R. (2000), 'Participatory Action Research.' In Denzin, N.K. & Lincoln, Y.S. (eds.), *Handbook of Qualitative Research* (2nd edition), pp. 567-605. Thousand Oaks, CA: Sage.

Lewin, K. (1946), 'Action Research and Minority Problems.' *Journal of Social Issues* 2, pp. 34-64.

Pålshaugen, Ø. (1998), *The end of organization theory? Language as a tool in action research and organizational development*. Amsterdam: John Benjamins.

Qvale, T.U. (2008), 'Regional Strategies to Meet Globalizaton: How Single Plants Innovate together to Remain Viable and Secure Employment. The Grenland Industrial Cluster and Telemark.' *International Journal of Action Research* 4 (1+2): 114-154. Mering: Rainer Hampp.

Qvale, T. & Holstad, K. (2005), 'Collaborative Strategies for Industrial Renewal. An Action Research Approach in Grenland.' Paper prepared for the HSS05 conference, Tønsberg, Norway, June 1-3, 2005.

Reason, P. & Bradbury, H. (2001), 'Introduction: Inquiry and Participation in Search of a World Worthy of Human Aspiration.' In Reason, P. and Bradbury, H. (eds.) *Handbook of Action Research: Participatory Inquiry and Practice*. London: Sage.

Winther, F. (2007), *Large systems change: integrated leadership development and reflexive machineries*. Doctoral dissertation, Norwegian University of Science and Technology, Trondheim.

Section 2: Organizational development techniques and theorizing as practice

5 A Methodological Framework for Constructing Generic Knowledge with Intended Value both for Academia and Practice

Marie-José Avenier

"The true is precisely what is made."
[*"Verum esse ipsum factum."*]
Vico G., 1710, *De Antiquissima* (English transl., 1988, *Ancient Wisdom.*)

Introduction

Fieldwork reveals that members of organizations know a lot about management, strategy-making, organizational practices, and organizational commitment, to name but a few subjects. Most of this embodied knowledge (Lam 2000) can be considered as "unbeknownst" to those who have it. Indeed, most practitioners are unaware of what they know because they have never had the occasion or the motivation to think about it, let alone the time and/or the energy to try to *remind* it (Wittgenstein 1958) – which in itself is not an easy task.

Researchers in the field of management who are aware of this phenomenon may be eager to construct academic knowledge by drawing upon practitioners' experience and embodied practical knowledge. Despite the potential enrichment offered to both management theory and practice by such an approach, the specific issue of *developing knowledge relevant for practice from practitioner experience* that is also *considered academically valid* has not been directly dealt with in the literature, nor have the epistemological problems it poses been studied. As a consequence, management scholars seeking to adopt such an approach lack guiding frames of reference. This chapter aims to fill this methodological gap within a particular theory of knowledge, the radical constructivist epistemological paradigm (Glasersfeld 1984, 2001, 2005; Le Moigne 1995; Riegler 2001).

Our initial goal was to develop a methodological framework useable as a heuristic guide by researchers seeking to build knowledge in management sciences by drawing upon practitioner experience.[1] The resulting framework was constructed and implemented in different settings (Avenier & Albert 2005; Avenier & Albert 2006; Avenier 2008) and turned out to have broader implications than initially

---

1   Addressing specifically and in detail the complementary issue of how practitioners may draw upon researchers' theories is a complex issue whose study is beyond the scope of this already long chapter.

intended. Indeed, as further discussion will reveal, this methodological framework may be used as a guide for any collaborative research project with practitioners aiming to develop knowledge intended to be valuable both for scholars and practitioners.[2] Because a linear presentation needs to choose a particular entry point, the chapter presents this framework from the perspective of research projects aimed at constructing academic knowledge that captures practitioner knowledge.

The paper is organized into three parts. The first part begins with an overview of the epistemological paradigm in which this framework has been developed. After recalling the foundational assumptions of the radical constructivist epistemological paradigm, it focuses on the notion of epistemic work, which plays a core role in the process of knowledge legitimization in this paradigm. The notion of generic knowledge which offers ways of overcoming the issue of generalization in this paradigm is then introduced. The second part provides an overview of the framework set forth in this paper. The framework is presented from the standpoint of the researcher rather than from that of the practitioner. It focuses more on the way researchers work and elaborate knowledge in collaboration with practitioners, than on the work of practitioners during such collaborative projects. The third part offers a discussion organized around three main issues: first, a reflection on the convoluted process by which the methodological framework – presented in the second part in a fairly neatly packaged form – was progressively conceptualized in the course of doing collaborative research; second, a discussion of the differing roles of practitioners and researchers in the various processes involved in the framework; finally, the third issue addresses the position of the framework in the action research perspective.

Knowledge Generalization and Legitimization in the Radical Constructivist Epistemological Paradigm (RCEP)

This section begins with a presentation of the constructivist epistemological paradigm in which such a methodological framework is epistemologically defendable. It then successively examines what knowledge validation and generalization may mean in such a paradigm. This leads to the introduction of the notion of generic knowledge.

---

2   This framework, however, is not about designing knowledge that generates mechanisms within an organization so that they continue after the researchers have left the premises.

The positivist epistemological paradigm in which most sciences, particularly the sciences of nature, have developed over the last three hundred years, as well as the so-called "scientific method" (Rosenberg 1988) associated with that paradigm, appears to be particularly ill-suited to social sciences due to several factors.[3] These include human reflexivity, the inherently creative and purposeful nature of human action, and more generally, the perceived complexity of humans and organizations. Most organizational phenomena are shaped by the purposeful actions of human beings who are endowed with creative and reflective capabilities. These capabilities are not, however, unlimited. This often makes hypothesis testing unreliable in social sciences. Indeed, the human beings acting as subjects of a study are capable of inventing unexpected behaviors to reach their own goals, goals that might not have been imagined by the researchers who designed the test. Hence, the capability of social theories to predict (and therefore prescribe) a future course of action is not as strong as mechanists seem to think it is, although it is not entirely null (Tsoukas 2005).

A constructivist theory of knowledge seems, from my perspective, better suited to the construction of knowledge in the social sciences. However, under the "constructivist" label we find theories having very different scopes – fundamental theories of knowledge construction (Glasersfeld 1984, Guba & Lincoln 1989), theories of social construction of social phenomena (Berger & Luckman 1966), or even theories of social dynamics (Giddens 1984). These various theories are not necessarily consistent with each other, and thus it is crucial to specify which constructivist theory of knowledge I shall refer to in this chapter. The foundational assumptions of the chosen theory, the RCEP (Glasersfeld 1984, 2001, 2005; Le Moigne 1995, 2008; Riegler 2001), are listed below:

Phenomenological assumption A1: Humans cannot know such a thing as an independent, objective world that stands apart from their experience of it. The existence of an objective world populated by mind-independent entities – a "world-as-is" – is neither denied nor asserted. The "world-as-experienced" by a human being is knowable.

The world-as-is designates Kant's *noumene*, namely things as they are *in-themselves*, i.e. as they might be prior to being experienced. The world-as-experienced designates the phenomenal appearance of things.

Assumption A1 means that the RCEP is agnostic (Riegler 2001). More precisely, it considers that if a world-as-is exists, it is not known whether this world-as-is

---

3   See for instance Morgan and Smircich 1980; Le Moigne 1995; Mir and Watson 2000; Tsoukas 2005.

intrinsically resembles the perceptions it induces. Moreover, if the world-as-experienced by a subject happens to match a world-as-is, this subject is not able to be aware of it and is even less able to prove it. Hence, in this paradigm, making foundational ontological assumptions appears pointless.[4]

Assumption A2: A human being expresses his/her knowledge of his/her world-as-experienced as symbolic constructions called representations.

In the RCEP, representations are considered as interpretations of a subject's experience: it is impossible to know whether these representations match a hypothetical world-as-is. And if it happens that they do, there is no way to prove it. Hence, for radical constructivists, "'To know' is not to possess true representations of reality, but rather to possess ways and means of acting and thinking that allow one to attain the goals one happens to have chosen" (Glasersfeld 2001: 9). In other words, the role of knowledge elaboration shifts from constructing (supposedly) *true* representations to constructing *functionally fitted* representations.

Assumption A3: Knowledge is teleologically and recursively oriented by the deliberate cognitive action of building a representation of the phenomenon under study.

Assumption A3 means that radical constructivists consider that the knowledge constructed depends on both the purpose for which it is constructed and the context in which this construction takes place. In addition, if the purpose evolves, the representation and the knowledge constructed may evolve. Moreover, the knowledge constructed, in turn, may modify the prior knowledge that served to build it.

Consequently, in the RCEP knowledge, construction is portrayed as a process of intentional construction of representations based on experience. The teleological character of knowledge construction stated in assumption A3 is also recognized by Van de Ven and Johnson (2006: 814) when they state: "Any given theory is an incomplete abstraction that cannot describe all aspects of a phenomenon. Theories are fallible constructions that model a partial aspect of reality from a particular point of view with particular interests in mind."

When knowledge is considered context and goal-dependent as in the RCEP, generalization is a crucial issue. The next section offers a way to face this issue.

---

4   The radical constructivists' refusal to make foundational assumptions is not yet well accepted for reasons that Glasersfeld summarizes in the following way: "From my point of view, the trouble is that most critics seem to be unwilling to accept the explicit, programmatic statement that constructivism is a theory of knowing, not of being. That a model of the construction of knowledge could be designed without making ontological claims about what is known, is apparently difficult to accept." (Glasersfeld 2001: 10)

Because of knowledge's goal and context-dependence postulated in assumption A3, in the RCEP generalization cannot purport to establish supposedly universally applicable theories. Rather it will designate a process of upward extension in conceptual generality of substantive knowledge via a process of conceptualization and de-contextualization called genericization (Avenier 2009). Genericization aims to develop so-called *generic knowledge* (Avenier 2007a). The notion of generic knowledge extends that of generic proposition developed by the pragmatist philosopher Dewey (1938). Generic knowledge expresses knowledge about kinds of things and processes rather than about particular instances – episodes or events – or about statistical regularities. Generic knowledge can take the form of meta-models, frameworks of consistent generic propositions. It can also be expressed as "technological rules" (Van Aken 2004), and "knowledge artifacts" (Jarzabkowski & Wilson 2006) such as portfolio matrices or Porter's five forces and generic strategy models.

So in the RCEP, knowledge does not present itself in the form of normative universal principles or predictive theories. It aims to provide scholars and practitioners with heuristic guides which need to be contextualized so that idiosyncratic circumstances of particular settings can properly be taken into account. These guides have three roles: encouraging scholars and practitioners to be reflective (Schön 1983); offering them penetrating insights on their concerns; and/or stimulating their creative action by showing them plausible ways to attain their goals.

Generic knowledge permits a kind of knowledge accumulation to take place, an essential feature of the knowledge construction process in sciences. This can occur by relating new knowledge to existing knowledge and/or suggesting novel ways of differently reconstructing existing knowledge. The way in which knowledge accumulation can be legitimized in the RECP is just one aspect of the more general issue of knowledge legitimization in the RECP that is examined in the next section.

Epistemic Work: a Central Role in Knowledge Legitimization

The question of how to establish the validity of a theory has long been settled in positivist epistemologies: an assertion or a theory is considered valid as long as it has withstood all tests performed on it (Popper 1959). This question is still, however, under debate in constructivist epistemologies. Even though Piaget (1967) offers some fundamental ideas on knowledge legitimization in the constructivist epistemologies, discussions are still ongoing.

For Piaget, legitimization work relies on a process of *rigorous epistemological critique* carried out by researchers themselves. In fact, the spirit of what Piaget calls epistemological critique is captured by what is now referred to as reflexivity (Weick 1999; Tsoukas 2005; Yanow & Schwartz-Shea 2006). However, to retain Piaget's explicit reference to epistemological concerns, the phrase *epistemic work* will be used rather than the less precise term reflexivity. This has the advantage of emphasizing that legitimization in the RCEP rests on two legs, namely epistemic work and empirical work, which need to be recursively adapted to fit each other throughout the research project. In order to achieve this mutual adaptation process, there is ongoing integration of newly gathered information within the theorizing process. This integration occurs simultaneously with the adaptation of the current theorizing, thanks to the creation of new categories and properties to fit the newly gathered information as well as the previously collected information.

Epistemic work questions the consistency and the relevance of the successive decisions researchers make throughout the entire research process. For instance: Why adopt one particular root metaphor over another? Why take on certain theoretical references as opposed to other ones? Why abandon a current research track for another? Why choose this particular organization for fieldwork? Such a reflective approach in research is in line with Tsoukas' (2005) conception of researchers as reflective research practitioners.

Epistemic work amounts to engaging in an inquiry on the process of inquiry (Dewey 1938), or to subjecting the research process to inquiry (Mir & Watson 2000). These authors argue for transparency on *a priori* theoretical positions because theory, even default theory, influences the way research problems are defined. More precisely, all research is premised upon a variety of assumptions, which researchers need to make transparent in their work. The theoretical position held by a researcher not only guides their basic position, but also determines what gets construed as a research problem.

In order to empower epistemic work, researchers need to render explicit the information allowing them to track the cognitive process being followed, as well as the information that fuels this cognitive process. More precisely, researchers need to specify the foundational assumptions of the epistemological paradigm within which the research has been carried out and to provide a detailed report of the research. Such a report has to account for the (usually) convoluted progress of the research project. This includes elucidating the various iterations in the expression of the research question, the theoretical references that have been successively considered, as well as the empirical information gathered in the field and the continuous interplay between information gathering and processing (Strauss & Corbin 1998).

The report has to describe how the epistemic and the empirical work have been mutually adapted during the research project. It also has to give explanations for the inferences that led to the articulation of that knowledge, in particular and when relevant, the coding performed, the conceptual categories built, and the relations established between categories (Glaser & Strauss 1967). In addition, the consistency of these inferences with the assumptions of the underlying epistemological paradigm has to be shown.

Such a detailed description of how things have actually been done is usually deficient: generally, researchers completely write their presence out of the research in an attempt to give an objective character to their accounts. Readers rarely get a glimpse into the "messy" part of the research, the researchers' motivations, compromises that were made during the process, or details concerning the specific circumstances that drove the research in its unique directions (Mir & Watson 2000). Yet it is this information that permits the reader to judge and assess the scope of legitimacy of the knowledge being set forth.

Epistemic work is not simply concerned with the cognitive process. It also concerns the explicit knowledge being produced by questioning the deeper meaning of the involved notions, discussing theoretical foundations, and by showing how the new knowledge relates to the already published knowledge.

In this paradigm, knowledge is openly acknowledged as provisional. It has the status of *plausible hypothesis which fits experience*. Hence, research done within the RCEP can build upon knowledge generated within the positivist paradigm – but the converse does not hold.

Considering the crucial role of epistemic work in the methodological framework which is going to be presented, its different facets in the various processes involved in this framework will be highlighted and illustrated. To do so, I will use examples taken from a particular ongoing research project carried out using this framework as a guide.

A Methodological Framework for Constructing Generic Knowledge

Most articles and textbooks[5] on qualitative research in the social sciences depict the research process as comprising a number of successive phases or steps that are iterative and tightly linked to data (Eisenhardt 1989). The number of phases may vary from four to eight according to the level of detail chosen in defining the phases. The basic phases include: research design,[6] data collection, data analysis, and reporting (Yin 1984).

---

5   See for instance Yin 1984; Eisenhardt 1989; Huberman & Miles 1994; Denzin & Lincoln 2003.

6   Research design describes a flexible set of guidelines that connect the research question to theoretical notions, strategies of inquiry, and methods for collecting empirical materials.

Instead of representing the methodological framework set forth in this chapter in terms of a chronological sequence of *phases* or *steps*, it has been conceptualized from the standpoint of the *processes* involved. Five main processes are distinguished which, as shown in Diagram 1, can be carried out iteratively, namely:
- Conception of the research design
- Construction of local knowledge
- Construction of generic knowledge
- Communication of generic knowledge, and
- Activation of generic knowledge

Diagram 1: A Methodological Framework for Developing Generic Knowledge

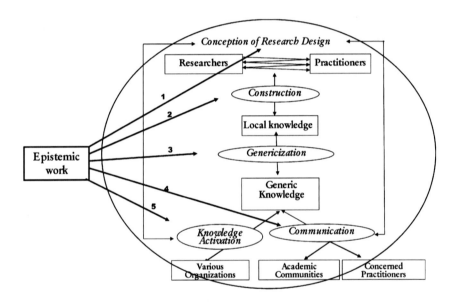

Legend:

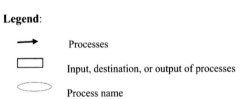

→   Processes

▭   Input, destination, or output of processes

◯   Process name

Each process involves a specific type of epistemic work. In the next sections, these five processes will be presented individually, in the order of the arrows symbolizing the specific epistemic work associated with each process in Diagram 1. However, before that, two important points have to be underscored.

First, as displayed in Diagram 1, the five processes are carried out interactively. Nonetheless, the process of conceiving the research design always comes first. Then, this process encompasses all the other four processes, in the sense that it both shapes the other processes and may evolve during the entire research project in relation to the actual unfolding of the other processes, which is a fairly common feature of action research (Eikeland 2006).

Second, the relationship between the five processes is circular, in the following sense: once the research design has been temporarily stabilized, a particular research project conceived within this framework can continue with any of the other four processes. For instance, the research project can aim at activating some available knowledge in an organization as an action research project. During this process, interaction between researchers and practitioners will enable the co-construction of further local knowledge, which can then serve to build further generic knowledge, and so on.

Conception of the Research Design

At the outset of any research project, even before starting to reflect on research design, the epistemological paradigm in which the research will be carried out needs to be specified – the RCEP in our case. The research design (see Exhibit 1 for an example) then comprises three main facets which are interrelated: 1) defining the general topic and clarifying the main research question that will be studied, 2) specifying the major theoretical references likely to be used, and 3) defining a strategy of inquiry (Denzin & Lincoln 2003) comprising the contemplated research method, the type of setting within which the empirical work will be carried out, and the tactics for collecting information.

Indeed, on the one hand, "*What* we know and *how* we know are recursively linked. (…) The kinds of research questions asked, the objects selected for study, and the criteria for evaluating knowledge claims are all intimately connected with the underlying assumptions of what is valid knowledge and how it may be obtained" (Tsoukas 2005: 6, 309).

Exhibit 1: Synopsis of the research design of the project used throughout this chapter for illustration purposes

☞ Epistemological paradigm: The radical constructivist epistemological paradigm.

☞ Central research question: The overall research project aims at developing knowledge about the design of strategic management systems based on complex thinking.

☞ Academic and practical interest: Globalization and the diffusion of new technologies contribute to increased world complexity. Considering that only complexity can help cope with complexity (Weick 1979), developing knowledge on complexly designed strategic management systems is increasingly relevant for practice and offers challenging issues for academia.

☞ Major theoretical references:
  o Complex thinking (Ashby 1960; Weick 1979; Morin 1992; Morin & Le Moigne 1999; Tsoukas 2005)
  o Strategy (Johnson et al. 2004; Mintzberg & Waters 1985)
  o Research methodology (Glaser & Strauss 1967; Yin 1984; Eisenhardt 1989; Huberman & Miles 1994; Denzin & Lincoln 2003)

☞ Strategies of inquiry:
  o A longitudinal case study: this is the most appropriate way to study processes, their design, their implementation and their evolution.
  o Organizational setting for field study: an international medium-size network service company in the international freight transportation industry named Beauvais International (BI).
  o Reason for this decision: as explained later in the discussion section, the BI CEO deliberately and explicitly redesigned the organizational and managerial systems of her company in reference to principles of complex thinking in 1996-1997.

Tactics of inquiry: Interviews (CEO, top and middle managers, salesmen and other staff members); observations of how work is getting done in various offices and cross-docking areas; as many BI internal documents as possible. The goal is to obtain as much information as possible on how the management systems have been designed and implemented, and why; as well as on how they have actually been operating, how they have evolved over the years, and why.

On the other hand, "The virtues of techniques and methods cannot be determined and categorized in the abstract, because their precise nature and significance is shaped within the context of the assumptions on which the social scientist acts.

Qualitative research stands for an approach rather than a particular set of techniques, and its appropriateness – like that of quantitative research – is contingent on the nature of the phenomena to be studied" (Morgan & Smircich 1980: 499).

Since they are recursively linked, the three topics involved in specifying the research design have to be handled jointly. The mutual consistency of the choices made in this specification needs to be justified. The identification of the three facets of research design obviously calls for epistemic work to be performed on the central research question in reference to the literature survey. Epistemic work corresponding to Arrow 1 (in Diagram 1) also involves examining the main available theoretical references relevant to the research question, as well as identifying the organization(s) in which the empirical work could take place.

Once the major theoretical references and the organization[7] for fieldwork have been identified, defining the modes of knowing that will do justice to the phenomenon under study (Burrell & Morgan 1979) calls for further epistemic work. This work is based on answering the following questions: Which particular methods of investigation (tools or techniques) are to be chosen, why, and how should they be implemented? Which practices are to be observed,[8] how, and why? Which practitioners are to be interviewed, in what order, how,[9] on the basis of which interview guidelines, and why? Which organizational documents should researchers try to obtain (such as minutes, meeting reports), and why?

Henceforth, the methodological framework will be presented in the particular case of a project aiming to construct knowledge by drawing upon practitioners' experience with regard to the research question studied. Throughout this chapter, it will be systematically illustrated on examples drawn from an ongoing research project which aims at developing generic knowledge on management systems' design (Avenier 2008).

Construction of Local Knowledge

The primary aim of the progressive gathering and processing of information – these being jointly carried out tasks – is to build local knowledge (see Exhibit 2 for an example). Here the term "local" (Geertz 1983) stresses the *situated* character of

---

7   For writing purposes, I speak of an organization and field of study in the singular, as if there were only one organization involved.
8   By "observations to be made", I mean observing what people actually do (Cook and Brown 1999), and listening to what they tell each other (Samra-Fredericks 2003).
9   Namely, will the interviews be semi-directive interviews, elicitation interviews (Vermersch 1999; Saucedo Ramos 2003) leading to narratives of practices, narratives of experience, etc.?

the knowledge built at this stage. Indeed, local knowledge's legitimization relies on the fact that it has been elaborated at some point in time on the basis of observations, internal documents, and practitioner knowledge and experience as narrated in interviews. Hence, local knowledge depends on the particular practitioners interviewed, their particular background and location in the organization (which itself operates in a particular context), and so forth.

Exhibit 2: Examples of local knowledge at BI

☞ While individual empowerment of operational managers generally promotes managers' individualism, the collective empowerment of each of BI's operational teams, together with the fact that these empowered teams were urged to behave as learning teams, fostered mutual aid between BI agents within and across teams.

☞ At BI, the abolition of "management by objectives" for salesmen and of any reference to the notion of local profit centers has enabled the emergence of a European commercial network within which salesmen actively collaborate.

The epistemic work associated with this process (Arrow 2) bears on studying theoretical references relative to notions encountered in fieldwork, and the specification of the empirical work performed and to be performed (see Exhibit 3 below). The latter is based on answering questions such as: How should the interview guidelines be progressively adapted? Are there any practitioners, other than those initially included, whom it would be relevant to interview for triangulation purposes? Does the research question resonate with the concerns and experience of the interviewed practitioners? Is the local knowledge being elaborated shared by all of the interviewees?

Exhibit 3: Example of epistemic work during the construction of local knowledge at BI

The fact that BI's management system was based on the notions of a "learning organization" (Senge 1992) and "empowerment" (Bowen & Lawler 1992; Argyris 1998), and that this system was dedicated to the implementation of a strategy of "customer intimacy" (Treacy & Wiersema 1993), led me to also study these references.

The interview guidelines were progressively adapted to include further questions on the current functioning of certain procedures. These questions emerged during the interview process and between the interviews. For instance, in the first interviews I discovered unexpected aspects of the system, such as a procedure for the management of the salesmen called "Quarterly Global Evaluation" (QGE, presented in the Appendix). When reflecting on these aspects, I found out that I needed to obtain further information. For instance, why did a particular salesman declare in his last QGE that certain matters were important learning goals for him for the coming quarter?

Another question systematically examined at this stage is whether there is enough information for triangulation purposes. Reflecting on this question made me aware of certain limitations of the case study carried out at BI in 2003 (which are brought up in the discussion section). For instance, along with a fellow researcher we had concentrated on interviewing top and middle managers and salespeople. Henceforth, I needed to interview more frontline employees.

Reflecting on the relevance of the research questions for BI managers made me realize that it was primarily the BI CEO who was interested in the research question. As brought up in the discussion, one of her main interests is to be urged to reflect upon a number of organizational routines that she would otherwise no longer think of questioning.

Construction of Generic Knowledge

The construction of generic knowledge is accomplished through conceptualization and de-contextualization of local substantive knowledge *via* the systematic study of multiple comparison groups, possibly taken from other case studies (Glaser &

Strauss 1967; Charmaz 2003). It proceeds by making inferences from the comparison groups being considered and, more generally, from fieldwork in relation to previously elaborated local knowledge and all sorts of other knowledge (academic, local, generic, etc.) available on the topic.

As already mentioned, generic knowledge can take various forms, such as that of meta-models, frameworks, and patterns. Patterns are built from regularities identified in the phenomenon under study. Because of the phenomenological assumption A1 above – which states that humans cannot know such a thing as an independent, objective world that stands apart from their experience of it – these regularities are not considered as the expression of permanent, ontological underlying mechanisms or law-like causal relationships (as in conventional research). Rather, they are considered as perceived temporary stable patterns, which, in management studies, may stem from recurrent behaviors associated with an organization's formal and informal systems.

Exhibit 4: Example of tentative generic knowledge relative to the design of managerial systems aimed at coping with contemporary business complexity

☞ Numerous managers feel that they are confronted by a multitude of bipolar phenomena such as short-term and long-term concerns, deliberate and emergent strategies, individual and collective matters, local and global concerns, empowerment and regulation, continuity and change.

☞ Handling and maintaining tension between opposite and complementary poles of bipolar phenomena can help managers better cope with business complexity.

☞ Processes facilitating the handling and maintaining of such tensions are not easy to design and implement, nor are they comfortable to operate. On the contrary, it is easy to drift towards the relative easiness of designing, implementing, or operating managerial processes attending to only one of the two opposite poles.

☞ Any top manager who is convinced of the relevance of implementing this kind of process in his/her firm, has to set up devices1 aimed at continually reminding himself/herself, and his/her staff as well, to continually operate in a dialogical process mode which has been designed for this purpose; and to not slip towards the relatively more comfortable position of focusing only on the easier or more pressing pole demanding attention.

The epistemic work associated with this process (Arrow 3) involves checking whether the chosen conceptual references permit the obtained information to be handled, or whether certain other references would be better suited. It also consists of clarifying the new notions introduced and of showing how they can be related to existing knowledge. This often calls for revisiting some of the literature initially studied, as well as for a further literature survey on notions that have emerged in the conceptualization process. For instance, I revisited Morin's (1992) principles of complex thinking (and in particular what he means by "dialogical" process[10]), Ashby's so-called "principle of requisite variety" (1960), and Weick's (1979) view derived from this principle, which states that "only complexity can cope with complexity". This also led me to study Bernard-Weil's (1988) contributions on ago-an-

---

10 In this chapter, the term "dialogical" is taken in the following sense: a dialogical process is a process which continually maintains a tension between two opposite and complementary notions or phenomena (Morin 1992), such as, for instance, attending jointly – and recursively – to short term and long term concerns. This can be viewed as an extended sense from its usual meaning of "pertaining to, or characterized by dialogue".

tagonistic phenomena (which are another way of referring to bipolar phenomena, see Exhibit 5), as well as Morgan's (1986) view on holographic organization. The congruence between the information gathered at BI and the conceptual references considered in the research project comes from the fact that epistemic work progressively addressed all the conceptual references that had been used at BI as guiding landmarks in the design and implementation of BI systems. Epistemic work also bears on legitimizing the inferences made to build the meta-model or the generic principles and propositional statements set forth.

In order to give an understandable account of the knitting together of epistemic work with empirical work that was accomplished during the construction of the generic knowledge shown in Exhibit 4, more information on BI activity and functioning would be needed than this chapter can provide. Instead, the reader will be referred to the presentation of the progressive conceptualization of the methodological framework in the discussion section. It provides an account of how epistemic work and empirical work were coupled in the conceptualization of the methodological framework.

The legitimacy of the constructed generic knowledge depends on the epistemic work that has been performed in producing it and relating it to pre-existing knowledge, as well as on its coupling with fieldwork, particularly *via* the local knowledge on which it is based. This legitimacy is not absolute, but contingent. Indeed, it depends on a number of circumstances, including the cognitive context in which it has been developed, namely the researchers' culture and the information obtained in the fieldwork, as well as the knowledge, experience, culture, and reflective behavior (Schön 1983) of the practitioners involved.

As further developed in the discussion section, conceptualization of generic knowledge and the epistemic work that goes with it are mainly and typically performed by the researchers involved in the project. Indeed, practitioners' regular organizational tasks do not generally leave them much time to do this work, even when they may have an interest in doing it. In fact, knowledge legitimization relying on rigorous epistemic work differentiates the generic knowledge elaborated in collaborative research from that usually developed by practitioners alone. This latter is usually based more on empirical experience than on relating the generic knowledge to diverse possible conceptual references through deep epistemic work.

There are two further ways of enhancing the legitimacy of generic knowledge: its activation in concrete settings and its communication to those scholars and practitioners potentially interested in the developed knowledge.

Communicating research findings to academic communities is a well-known requirement of scientific research. In the specific case of knowledge developed with the intention of being valuable for practice, communication to potentially interested practitioners actually helps legitimize this knowledge *via* its recognition by certain practitioners as potentially useful.

The design of communications for scholars and practitioners usually requires further epistemic work (Arrow 4) on the knowledge to be communicated, and on ways of communicating it in order to render it readily understandable for the audience (see Exhibits 4 and 5 for examples). Adequate contextualization of the knowledge and shaping of the message in relation to the specific context of the audience also often require further epistemic work. In the case of interactive communications, moreover, remarks, questions, or illustrations from the audience usually spawn further epistemic work – as illustrated in the discussion section – and quite often generate ideas for additional research projects. This is symbolized in Diagram 1 by the feedback arrow pointing towards the rectangle labeled "Conception of research design".

Exhibit 5: Example of a possible academic formulation of the generic knowledge exposed in Exhibit 4 essentially for a practitioner audience

According to Ashby's so-called "principle of requisite variety" (1960) and to the position that Weick (1999) derived from it, which states that "only complexity can cope with complexity", only complexly designed management systems can help firms cope with the perceived complexity of the current economic and business environments.

Morin's (1992) "dialogical principle" of complex thinking unites two ago-antagonistic notions or phenomena (Bernard-Weil 1988), i.e. opposite and complementary notions or phenomena which, at first glance, would seem to exclude one another as, for instance, empowerment and regulation.

The dialogical principle suggests that management processes be designed and implemented so that tension between the ago-antagonist poles of the numerous bipolar phenomena managers currently face be continually maintained. For instance, combining short and long term concerns instead of jumping from the most urgent concern to the next; devising reward systems which take into account both individual and collective performance; designing processes which help stimulate innovative ideas and actions, and then integrate the most promising perspectives into the firm's deliberate strategy (Mintzberg & Waters 1985).

Such dialogical processes are not easy to conceptualize and design. An empirical study gave evidence that they are not easy to operate either (Avenier 2008). This study reports on a CEO strongly convinced of the soundness of implementing such processes in her firm. However, certain crucial management processes had not been designed in a dialogical manner. Additionally, a process that had specifically been designed to be operated dialogically was in fact not operated in a dialogical mode. Some years later it became apparent that these oversights generated certain malfunctions in the firm, as illustrated in the Appendix.

These observations can be interpreted as suggesting that one can easily drift towards the relative easiness of designing, implementing and/or operating managerial processes attending to only one of the ago-antagonistic poles.

This research project has several managerial implications (see Exhibit 4 for examples of some of these implications).

Putting the elaborated knowledge into practical use is both a primary purpose of generic knowledge elaboration in this framework, and a means to enhance its legitimization *via* putting it to the test of actual experience in authentic settings. As a consequence of the assumptions of the RCEP recalled in the first part of the chapter, any available knowledge, when put into use, is to be considered as a heuristic guide whose goals are to arouse scholars' and practitioners' reflection, to provide them with a complementary understanding of the problem at hand, and/or to stimulate their creative action.

Putting knowledge into action requires its contextualization and interpretation according to the specifics of each setting. Considering the complexity of practice, contextualization cannot be treated as a mechanical process. So, instead of speaking of knowledge application, some authors speak of knowledge put to action (Jarzabkowski 2003) or knowledge put into use (Glaser & Strauss 1967). I prefer to speak of knowledge activation (Tenkasi et al. 2007), the term "activation" being more specific than the terms "use" and "action". Indeed, sometimes knowledge activation does not lead to any other action than the cognitive action of attempting to integrate it into one's thought processes.

To say that an individual activates some knowledge in a particular situation means that he/she takes that knowledge into consideration in his/her thinking about the situation. Taking knowledge into consideration means treating it as thought-provoking or as a means to illuminate a problematic situation. It does not mean treating it as a prescriptive rule for obtaining the desired outcome. Knowledge activation can permit the appropriation of this knowledge, i.e. the integration of this knowledge into the individual's prior knowledge. This operation can induce modifications not only to the individual's prior knowledge, but also to his/her initial interpretation of the activated knowledge. In other words, when activation occurs, this has an impact on both the individual and the knowledge: neither is left intact. "The person who applies theory becomes, in effect, a generator of theory, and in this instance the theory is clearly seen as process: an ever-developing entity" (Glaser & Strauss 1967: 242).

Trying to activate generic knowledge in a setting other than those settings in which it has been developed calls for further empirical work aimed at understanding the specific circumstances of the new setting. It jointly calls for further epistemic work (Arrow 6) aimed at clarifying the deeper meaning of the notions involved and investigating the legitimacy of activating this knowledge in that setting given its specific circumstances. Tenkasi et al. (2007) underscore that this contextualization benefits from being accomplished jointly by practitioners and researchers involved in the action research project. Furthermore, re-contextualization often involves reconstructing the corresponding knowledge in relation to the particular setting considered, which often generates new research questions to be studied. This is symbolized in Diagram 1 by the feedback arrow pointing towards the label "Conception of research design".

Discussion

The discussion will address three issues. First, it will offer a reflection on the process by which the previously presented methodological framework has been conceptualized. This process is directly related to research projects that I have carried out at BI since 1998. Then, the respective roles of practitioners and researchers in the construction of local and generic knowledge will be examined. Finally, the place of this framework in the action research perspective is discussed.

An "In Itinere"[11] Conceptualization of the Methodological Framework in Relation to Research Projects Conducted at BI

Since the conceptualization of this methodological framework cannot be dissociated from the various research projects that I have carried out at BI since 1998, I shall start with briefly narrating the story of these research projects.

1998-2002: Informal Interchanges in Order to Get Mutually Acquainted

My long-lasting relationship with BI began in February 1998 at a conference for top managers, titled "Management and Complexity". I was presenting a conceptualization of a generic strategy adapted to complex environments, labeled an "*in itinere* strategy"[12] (Avenier 1999). BI's CEO was presenting how she had designed and recently implemented a new management system for her company in reference to complex thinking (Morin 1992). This was the first time I had met a CEO

---

11 The Latin phrase "*in itinere*" qualifies a process whose course is adapted during its advancement according to the evolving circumstances it encounters as it unfolds. Hence, an "*in itinere* conceptualization" means that the idea of this conceptualization did not pre-exist the research project: it emerged as a result and by doing the research. In this chapter, I shall also speak of an "*in itinere* strategy" to refer to a specific mode of strategizing. In this mode, a strategy may evolve during its enactment in order both to adapt to the evolving circumstances which the organization encounters and to integrate certain new ideas which may emerge along the way.

12 The expression "*in itinere* strategy" (see previous footnote) is meant to translate the French expression "*stratégie chemin faisant*".

who autonomously held such views on management and complex thinking. I usually have to argue strongly in an attempt to convince CEO's of the soundness of complex thinking principles as guides in designing certain strategies or management processes for their firms.

After listening to each other's presentations, we immediately perceived mutual interest in the other's experiences and views. In our first interchange, she underscored that, in her company, she had recently abolished certain conventional management practices – such as salesmen management by objectives and systematically treating local units as profit centers. She was currently experimenting with various unconventional approaches, such as a strategy of customer intimacy and instituting operational teams as empowered learning teams. Furthermore, she stated that she would accept my studying her firm's management systems.

The only way that management sciences researchers can run *in vivo* experiments is within the action research framework. However, finding an organization whose top managers are ready to engage in action research with university researchers in the area of strategy is extremely difficult, because of the high stakes involved in strategy matters. Hence, meeting this CEO, who was ready to open her company's doors to let me observe *in vivo* experiments she was carrying out in the area of strategic management, appeared to me as a wonderful opportunity that was too good to pass up.

This is how my relationship with BI started in 1998. Between 1998 and 2002, I carried out a number of open-ended interviews with BI's CEO. The goal was to discover the company, its history since its creation in 1957 by the present CEO's father, its evolution and the newly implemented organization and managerial systems based on complex thinking and dedicated to the implementation of BI strategy. The BI CEO gave me a number of internal documents presenting her strategic vision. This included the customer intimacy strategy in which she had engaged her company in 1996, and which had progressively been adapted according to environmental evolutions and to new ideas which had emerged along the way. Hence, I realized that BI strategy was actually enacted as an "*in itinere* strategy" (Avenier 1999). These documents described the new organizational and managerial systems[13] internally designed and implemented since 1997, as well as the rationale underlying their design.

---

13 For instance, the form used for salesmen's quarterly evaluation is shown in the Exhibit 6 in the Appendix.

My first formal research project at BI started in 2003. The goal was to understand the genesis of current BI strategy and operating systems. I also wanted to do what I now call epistemic work on BI's strategic management core notions, namely "customer intimacy" (Treacy & Wiersema 1993), "learning organization" (Senge 1992), and "empowerment" (Bowen & Lawler 1992; Argyris 1998). The project was carried out with a fellow researcher, with whom I wrote a longitudinal strategy case covering the time period from BI's creation in 1957 until 2003 (Avenier & Pellegrin 2004).

In this research, my colleague and I jointly interviewed 17 different BI staff members[14] out of the 170 BI employees, conducted four formal interviews with the BI CEO, and maintained regular phone and e-mail contact with her during the entire research project. We examined a large number of internal documents, such as the written documents that were prepared for all the strategic meetings that had been organized since she became CEO in 1991. We obtained copies of actual sales offers and meeting reports, as well as completed salesmen's evaluation reports. I also participated in the 2002, 2003, and 2004 strategic meetings.

When this study was completed at the end of 2003, I was eager to launch another research project on the topic that had instantly interested me when I first met this CEO in 1998, namely to develop knowledge on the design of management systems in reference to complex thinking, based on BI members' experience.

BI's CEO agreed to engage in such a collaborative research project under the condition that I be the only researcher interacting with the BI staff. Indeed, she considered that it could be disturbing and destabilizing for the BI staff to be observed and interviewed by several different persons wandering around the company asking questions. In this project, which started in September 2004 – and is still ongoing – I have conducted in-depth interviews of the BI CEO and four top managers. Overall, between September 2004 and April 2008, I have had 17 face-to-face, four-hour interviews with the BI CEO, and two one-and-a-half-hour interviews with each of the four top managers. These five people have played the most determinant roles in the design, implementation, and evolution of BI's formal management systems. I also had 14 interviews in various departments (operations, sales, marketing and design, accounting, etc.), mostly with frontline staff, in order to update and deepen the information gathered prior to September 2004.

---

14 More precisely, we interviewed 15 of the 94 employees located at Beauvais, the main site in France. We also interviewed 2 of 11 salesmen, one from London and one from Lyon.

In addition to interviews with the BI CEO, I regularly receive copies of certain e-mails which she sends to BI staff concerning the proper use of existing procedures or the introduction of new procedures – my name being simply added to her e-mail list. In addition to this, we have regular e-mail exchanges with essentially three purposes. First, obtaining further information on a specific question on which I am doing epistemic work. In her reply, she generally illustrates her thoughts using actual examples based on completed BI forms that she attaches to her e-mail, such as sales meeting reports, salesmen wages' charts, or samples of outputs from the reporting system. The second purpose of these e-mails is to initiate collaborative reflection on generic knowledge I am conceptualizing. The third purpose is to ask her permission for the publication of texts in academic journals or in professional publications, stemming from research projects at BI, which mention the name of her company. So far, not only has she always given me her permission for publishing these texts without deleting a single word, but she usually also makes additional comments which further enrich the text and/or my knowledge of BI.

Since 2004: The Need for a Better Adapted Methodological Framework

When I started in-depth interviewing of the CEO of BI in 2004, I felt that the main methodological frameworks available for case study research (Yin 1984; Denzin & Lincoln 2003) did not provide me with adequate landmarks to carry out this research project. So, I started exploring more specific literature on interviewing techniques, such as elicitation interviewing (Vermersch 1994, 1999), and narratives of practices and working life experience (Saucedo Ramos 2003), and I immediately put these techniques to use as I was learning about them.

Another difficulty I encountered resulted from the radical constructivist epistemological positioning of my research since the mid 90s. Indeed, since 1985, I have been working closely with Le Moigne, a French scholar who since the beginning of the 80s has been highly involved in the "new" sciences[15] epistemological critique. He contributed, and still contributes (Le Moigne 1995, 2001, 2002, 2003, 2008), to the ascertainment of the conceptualization of the RCEP, with which I have been feeling much more at ease than with the positivist or realist paradigms since the mid 90s.

As mentioned in the first part of the chapter, because of this epistemological positioning, I could not view generalization as the construction of rules or laws which would hold universally, i.e. which would be valid in any place and at any

---

15 For instance, quantum physics, cognitive sciences, sciences of information, sciences of communication, management sciences, sciences of decision, scientific ecology, and so on.

time. I had the feeling, though, that it would be *both* important *and* epistemologically defendable to develop a certain kind of generalization from the locally situated knowledge developed in an idiographic type of research, for instance by developing general knowledge in the spirit of Glaser & Strauss' (1967) formal grounded theory, though not from within a positivist epistemological paradigm, but rather from within a constructivist epistemological paradigm. This aspiration for developing knowledge from practice with some level of generality led me to return to the pragmatist philosophers. As a result, in Dewey's writings (1938) I found the notion of "generic propositions" which seemed to correspond fairly well to what I was looking for.

Finally, to summarize, this framework was progressively conceptualized through the knitting together of epistemic work and empirical work carried out during this research project at BI. This knitting was done at two distinct but indissociable levels – another ago-antagonist pair. On the one hand, it was accomplished at the level of the knowledge to be elaborated on the topic of management systems' design on the basis of BI members' experience. On the other hand, it took place at the level of the *in itinere* conceptualization of the methodological framework. This conceptualization took place thanks to the interplay of my readings on research methodology and pragmatist philosophy, my personal experimentation with this framework via the empirical work I was doing at BI on management systems' design, and as a result of feedback from research projects carried out by PhD students in this framework.

No BI members directly participated in the conceptualization of the framework. In fact, none of them were particularly interested in the research method I was using, and even less so in reflecting on the conceptualization of the methodological framework which was guiding my research. Besides, only a few BI members are moderately interested in the local knowledge which was drawn from the BI experience, and only the CEO has some genuine interest in the generic knowledge.

In addition, epistemic work on the framework conceptualization was stimulated by feedback I was receiving from academic peers when presenting it in various publications (Avenier 2007a; Avenier & Schmitt 2007a, 2007b), as well as at various conferences (Avenier 2007b; Avenier & Albert 2006, 2007) and academic workshops.

For instance, the initial labeling of "putting knowledge to the test of experience" was changed to "knowledge activation in authentic settings". Initially, the goal was to underscore that the framework suggests the possibility of "testing" knowledge's relevance and effectiveness in various settings different from the ones where it was initially elaborated. At a particular workshop, a scholar pointed out that this labeling does not encompass what I had described as a crucial goal of the knowledge elaboration process, namely knowledge's potential use in actual settings. This made me aware that I needed to give this process a more encompassing label. After much hesitation between various possibilities, I chose the current one which, in my view, covers the two possible goals just mentioned, namely *putting knowledge to use* and *putting knowledge to the test of practical experience in authentic settings*.

The Differing Roles of Practitioners and Researchers in the Framework

As previously indicated, BI members did not play any direct role in the conceptualization of the methodological framework. It will now be argued that practitioners and researchers play differing roles and make different contributions in collaborative research projects carried out in this framework.

In my view, these differing roles mainly stem from the differences in their prime functions and of the related competence, experience and knowledge associated with these functions: a manager's prime function is to manage, while an academic researcher's prime function is to teach and do academic research. As a result, they have different goals, knowledge, experience, competencies, and constraints. As a matter of fact, in certain research projects carried out with consultants, some consultants took a more active part in the conceptualization of generic knowledge than organization managers usually do, probably because knowledge construction is more directly connected to consultants' prime professional activities.

These differences are precisely what fuel and enrich such collaborations within a research project. Both parties can find mutual interest and enrichment because collaboration facilitates the achievement of their respective professional goals and may bring practitioners a feeling of personal fulfillment associated with a public interest endeavor.

The next two sections successively examine the specific roles of researchers and practitioners during the two processes of local and generic knowledge elaboration.

Practitioners and Researchers' Differing Roles in the Elaboration of Local Knowledge

In my experience, during the elaboration of local knowledge most of the practitioners involved behave as co-researchers, in the sense that the questions addressed by researchers to practitioners on their experience and practices push practitioners first to build representations of their practices – in the sense of assumption A2 above – and then to reflect on these representations in unfamiliar ways, i.e. to do some kind of epistemic work on these representations. For instance, a number of BI members came to our meeting with prepared notes on what they thought was important to tell me about their work at BI: the various evolutions their jobs had gone through (some have been working at BI for as long as 37 years), the difficulties they have encountered throughout these evolutions and in performing the tasks assigned to them, their current practices, what is nice at BI, what is problematic, etc.

Local knowledge born of the interactions between practitioners and researchers is typically a co-construction between them. However, these two kinds of professionals do not play the same role in this co-construction. For instance, elements of local knowledge that are elaborated in a face-to-face interaction between practitioners and researchers are subsequently shaped and written down by researchers according to their perceptions and understanding of these interactions.

Another example lies in the difference between cognitive postures: researchers address questions to practitioners in a sort of Socratic searching and inquiring dialogue, whereas practitioners ask few questions. Rather, they narrate their experience and offer representations of their knowledge. In addition, while listening to practitioners, researchers strive to make sure the answers obtained are sufficiently precise to enable satisfactory ulterior epistemic work on the described experience. This continual questioning about empirical materials needed later to progress on the epistemic front is a concern mainly, but not exclusively,[16] for the researchers.

In this process, both practitioners and researchers do epistemic work, but the kinds of epistemic work they do are different and have different goals. Practitioners' epistemic work bears mainly on their own experience and aims at expressing it in words. Conversely, as described in the second part of the chapter, researchers' epistemic work has several facets. For instance, it involves clarifying notions used in the organization and relating them to knowledge already available. It also involves identifying what should be considered as local knowledge among all the ideas that have been expressed in the interviews and in the assembled internal documents, as well as adapting the empirical work to the knowledge that is progressively being generated.

---

16 For instance, one day, at the end of the interview, a BI staff member asked me who I had interviewed so far, and who I was planning to interview next. After I had answered him, he expressed his surprise that I had not planned to interview "so and so". He considered that without obtaining information from this person, I would miss important information on the BI system. So, I interviewed that person too, who did give me information which indeed enriched my understanding of BI functioning.

Based on my experience at BI, practitioners' and researchers' respective roles are even more different during the elaboration of generic knowledge. The conceptualization work described earlier corresponds more closely to researchers' main professional skills and duties than to those of practitioners. During this process, the collaborative interactions between them take essentially two forms: first, researchers who reconnect with practitioners to clarify some points that were not examined in a sufficiently precise manner, or not at all, during the elaboration of local knowledge; second, discussing successive versions of the generic knowledge being elaborated. In my experience, these discussions can enrich both parties, as the following example illustrates.

I recently prepared an academic text (Avenier 2008) drawing some lessons from the BI experience in designing, implementing, and operating BI management systems in reference to complex thinking. The first part presented BI systems in relation to principles of complex thinking. The second part presented and discussed some tentative generic knowledge on the design of management systems aimed at coping with current business complexity. It developed, among other things, the generic knowledge summarized in Exhibit 5 above. In early February 2008, I e-mailed the BI CEO that text for two reasons: first, to ask for her permission to publish it, since it explicitly mentions the name of her company; second, to ask her specific questions in the perspective of the reflection developed in the present chapter. These questions were: In what way(s) do you find our face-to-face meetings useful? Have you found any usefulness in reading the attached paper? If yes, how so? Do you consider the statements presented in what is labeled Exhibit 4 above as potentially useful knowledge for you? Do you consider that the knowledge expressed in these statements might be useful to certain top managers who are not from BI?

To briefly summarize her answers, she states that reading the text helped her step back from the multitude of tasks which can fully occupy her days, and to reflect on her company's experience with complexly designed management systems. Raising this question led her to give me further information on BI's past experience and desired future evolution, which enriched my knowledge and understanding of BI. Her answers also explain in which respects Exhibit 4's statements seem useful for her, and why it would probably not be considered as such by other top managers – an important insight for feeding further epistemic work on how to communicate this kind of knowledge to top managers.

In short, practitioners and researchers play differing and complementary roles throughout a project in this framework for collaborative research. Taking advantage of these differing and complementary roles is precisely what makes collaboration likely to enrich both parties. There remains, however, one final question to be discussed, namely the place of this framework for collaborative research in the action research perspective.

Where Does this Methodological
Framework Stand in the Action Research Perspective?

At first glance, as presented in this chapter, this methodological framework may not seem to lie explicitly in the action research perspective, since it is presented mainly from the standpoint of the researchers' struggle to elaborate knowledge by drawing upon practitioners' experience. However, it can be related to the action research perspective in two ways. First, it was underscored that if the conception of research design always comes first, then, once the research design has been temporarily stabilized, the research project can start with any of the other four processes. In particular, it can start with activating some existing knowledge in a concrete setting, which can be viewed as a form of action research localized between the WRI tradition and the master-apprentice approach presented by Eikeland (2006). The second argument is that, in this framework, *via* the various interactions between practitioners and researchers involved in the collaborative work, the research project may indirectly influence actions which practitioners launch in the organization, in the same way that peer reactions to my presentations of the framework, mentioned above, influenced the way I conceptualized it. An example illustrating this phenomenon is provided in the Appendix. This second argument leads to the question of the specific reflective arenas and procedures for collaborative work in each process of the framework.

In the conception of the research design, the collaborative reflective arenas are essentially meetings with the practitioners who are in charge of the research project in the organization. The initial meetings aim at identifying the general topic of the research project, knowing that the research question itself will be progressively clarified and adapted in a collaborative manner during the research process. These meetings also serve to clarify any restrictions the researchers may have in carrying out observations and interviews, and in obtaining information relevant to investigating the research question.

In the elaboration of local knowledge, the collaborative reflective arenas are primarily the meetings where face-to-face eliciting interviews are carried out and local knowledge in the process of being progressively built can be discussed. Even though this did not take place at BI, in some organizations there can also be collective presentations and discussions of the local knowledge with the practitioners who have participated in the project.

In the elaboration of generic knowledge, the collaborative reflective arenas are essentially meetings with the practitioners in charge of the research project in the organization, where successive drafts of generic knowledge are presented, discussed, reflected upon, and improved. At BI, this collaborative reflection takes place in a one-to-one relationship between the CEO[17] and me, on the basis of a written document which I prepare and e-mail to her. Then she communicates the thoughts it aroused, either in a face-to-face meeting, or, most often, via an e-mail interchange with several iterations – which sometimes ends up as a dialogue by phone.[18] For me, these e-mail interchanges have a tremendous advantage over oral interchanges as they "naturally" constitute lasting, high quality empirical material, in the form of electronic files containing the exact words that the CEO used in the interchange.

In order to support our reflective collaboration, I usually send the BI CEO papers which are not written as academic texts for an academic public, because as Plummer (2001) aptly stated: a consequence of this mode of writing is to render most such texts unreadable. Indeed, I strive to send her papers containing the essential message expressed in readily understandable language and relieved of all "ornaments" associated with usual academic conventions. Then, from a revised version of this paper integrating the fruits of our collaborative reflection, I try to develop two kinds of documents: academic ones and documents intended for practitioners, both of which express the same fundamental message, but in differing styles and words, as illustrated in Exhibits 4 and 5 above.

In the process of activating generic knowledge in a particular setting the collaborative reflective arenas are typically those of action research. In the communication process (academic or with practitioners), they are mainly meetings supported by PowerPoint presentations prepared by the researchers and intended to stimulate collaborative reflection and discussion.

Concluding Thoughts

Like generic knowledge developed in the RCEP, this methodological framework is intended to provide heuristic guidelines for a certain kind of research practice. These guidelines aim at fostering reflection, offering insights on how research-

---

17 The BI CEO has not incited other top managers at BI to reflect on the knowledge elaborated in this project because she considers that they have been too busy during the years 2007-2008, due to concerns which are far removed from the topics of the current research project.

18 The distance between our respective workplaces makes it inefficient to have more than three or four face-to-face meetings per year.

ers may proceed, and/or stimulating researchers' creative action by showing them plausible ways to achieve their aim of developing knowledge recognized as both academically valuable and as having captured practitioners' experience – which makes it more likely to be valuable for other practitioners.

The guidelines it offers cannot always been strictly adhered to in actual practice. For instance, at the beginning of the discussion section, I explained the reasons why I am doing this research at BI as a lone fieldworker, while I consider with Van de Ven and Johnson (2006) that collaborative research projects benefit from being carried out by a research team rather than by a sole researcher. Indeed, teamwork facilitates and enriches reflection and more generally epistemic work. Nevertheless, in my experience, a lone fieldworker can still do some collective epistemic work with fellow researchers from his/her research group within his/her research lab. This is particularly helpful for overcoming certain limits of individual introspection in the surfacing of researchers' implicit assumptions.

This framework originated from the desire to provide landmarks for researchers eager to develop academic knowledge attempting to capture practitioners' practical knowledge, which could be useful for other practitioners, within a radical constructivist theory of knowledge. While the legitimization of interactive and transformative research methods such as action research is problematic in a positivist or realist theory of knowledge, the radical constructivist theory of knowledge offers an explicitly-grounded epistemological paradigm which allows the legitimization of knowledge generated by interpreting and processing information obtained by means of any research method – provided that the fundamental conditions of rigor and transparency are satisfied (Le Moigne 1995).

Such a theory of knowledge raises vexing questions when it comes to defining what generalization can mean in this theory. A way to overcome this difficulty has been offered with the notion of generic knowledge, and it was argued that this constitutes a legitimate way of conceiving of generalization in this theory of knowledge.

In positivist epistemologies, knowledge construction and knowledge validation are treated as two separate consecutive processes: the first aims at building theories, while the second purports to validate them by testing hypotheses on empirical data which are different from the data used for building the theory in the first place. In constructivist epistemologies, instead of *ex post* validation, the legitimization of generic knowledge has to be developed jointly and simultaneously with its elaboration. Hence the processes of knowledge generation and legitimization are carried out as two inseparable processes: each inference needs to be justified at the moment it is made, and not *a posteriori*, on the basis of both epistemic and empirical grounds.

Nevertheless, in research conducted from the viewpoint of positivist epistemologies, one also encounters epistemic work performed in a more or less implicit manner – generally more than less! – during the course of the two processes of theory construction and theory validation. This epistemic work takes place during the literature survey, the comparison of available theoretical references, the construction of knowledge claims and of the hypotheses to be tested, as well as when controlling the tests' technical validity.

Hence, as with Weick's (1989) view that theory cannot be improved until we improve the theorizing process, and we cannot improve the theorizing process until we describe it more explicitly and operate it more self-consciously, I consider that epistemic work is at the core of the practice of scientific research no matter what the underlying epistemological paradigm. In fact, epistemic work and empirical work need to be closely knit: they can be viewed as the two engines of the practice of scientific research that need to be mutually – and hence recursively – adapted during any research project aiming to develop knowledge relevant both for practice and academia.

Finally, if BI practitioners did not directly participate in the reflection on the process of developing knowledge from their experience or in the conceptualization of the methodological framework, the research projects carried out at BI did, however, catalyze the emergence of this framework by practicing it while conceptualizing it – through the recursive loop of "conceptualizing for practicing and practicing for conceptualizing", which is in the spirit of pragmatist philosophy as well as Vico's more ancient view as found in the epigraph. Besides, practitioners' theories, models, concepts, and reflections about their practices contribute to shaping the generic knowledge that is developed in any research project carried out in this framework. This chapter examined the ways in which local and generic knowledge developed in research projects at BI has influenced the BI CEO's reflection and action. Identifying the way in which the collaborative work done with other BI members may have influenced their own reflection and practice is still a question that has been left for further research.

References

Argyris, C. (1993), *Knowledge for Action, a Guide to Overcoming Barriers to Organizational Change*. San Francisco: Jossey-Bass.
Argyris, C. (1998), "Empowerment: The Emperor's New Clothes". *Harvard Business Review* May-June: 98-105.
Ashby, W.R. (1960), *An Introduction to Cybernetics*. London: Chapman & Hall.

Avenier, M.J. (1999), "La Complexité Appelle une Stratégie Chemin Faisant". *Gestion 2000* (5 Sept-Oct): 13-44.

Avenier, M.J. (2007), "A Generic Methodological Framework for Constructing Generic Actionable Knowledge". Paper presented at the *2nd International Conference of The Academy of Management – Research Methods Division*, Lyon.

Avenier, M.J. (2008), "La Pensée Complexe pour Relever les Défis du Management Stratégique d'Entreprises ? Retours d'Expérience". *Chemins de Formation* 12: 157-166.

Avenier, M.J. (2009), "Genericization", in Mills, A.J., Durepos, G., and Wiebe, E. (eds.), *Encyclopedia of Case Study Research*, London: Sage (forthcoming).

Avenier, M.J., and Albert, M.N. (2005), "An Empirical Study of Organizational Commitment Based on Systemic Modeling and Complex Thinking", *The First Organization Studies Summer Workshop*. Santorini, Greece.

Avenier, M.J., and Albert, M.N. (2006), "The Multiple Uses of Narratives in Constructing Formal Knowledge from Experience". Paper presented at the *Second Organization Studies Summer Workshop*. Mykonos, Greece.

Avenier, M.J., and Albert, M.N. (2007), "Constructing Academically Valid Workable Knowledge in Management Research: A Methodological Framework". Paper presented at *The Third Organization Studies Summer Workshop*. Crete, Greece.

Avenier, M.J., and Pellegrin, C. (2004), *Beauvais International : L'Intimité Client*. Paris: Centrale des Cas et Médias Pédagogiques.

Avenier, M.J., and Schmitt, C. (2007a), "Elaborer des Savoirs Actionnables et les Communiquer à des Managers". *Revue Française de Gestion* 33(174): 25-42.

Avenier, M.J., and Schmitt, C. (2007b), *La Construction de Savoirs pour l'Action*. Paris: L'Harmattan.

Berger, P.L., and Luckmann, T. (1966), *The Social Construction of Reality: A Treatise in the Sociology of Knowledge*. New York: Doubleday.

Bernard-Weil, E. (1988), *Précis De Systémique Ago-Antagoniste*. Limonest: L'Interdisciplinaire.

Bowen, D., and Lawler III, E.E. (1992), "The Empowerment of Service Workers: What, Why, How and When". *Sloan Management Review*: 31-39.

Burrell, G., and Morgan, G. (1979), *Sociological Paradigms and Organisational Analysis*. London: Heinemann.

Charmaz, K. (2003), "Grounded Theory: Objectivist and Constructivist Methods", in Denzin, N.K. and Lincoln, Y.S. (eds.), *Collecting and Interpreting Qualitative Materials*, pp. 249-291. Thousand Oaks: Sage.

Cook, S., and Brown, J.S. (1999), "Bridging Epistemologies: The Generative Dance between Organizational Knowledge and Organizational Knowing". *Organization Science* 10(4): 381-400.

Denzin, N., and Lincoln, Y.S. (2003), *Strategies of Qualitative Inquiry*. London: Sage.

Dewey, J. (1938), *Logic, the Theory of Inquiry*. New York: Henry Holt and Co.

Eikeland, O. (2006), "The Validity of Action Research – Validity in Action Research", pp. 193-240 in Nielsen, K.Aa. and Svensson, L. (eds.) (2006): *Action And Interactive Research – Beyond Theory and Practice*, Maastricht and Aachen: Shaker Publishing

Eisenhardt, K.M. (1989), "Building Theories from Case Study Research". *Academy of Management Review* 14(4): 532-550.

Geertz, C. (1973), "Thick Description: Toward an Interpretive Theory of Culture", in *The Interpretation of Cultures: Selected Essays*, pp. 3-30. New York: Basic Books.

Geertz, C. (1983), *Local Knowledge. Further Essays in Interpretive Anthropology*. New York: Basic Books.

Giddens, A. (1984), *The Constitution of Society: Outline of the Theory of Structuration*. Berkeley: UC Press.

Glaser, B.G., and Strauss, A.S. (1967), *The Discovery of Grounded Theory*. London: Aldine.

Glasersfeld, E.v. (1984), "An Introduction to Radical Constructivism", in Watzlawick, P. (ed.), *The Invented Reality: How Do We Know What We Believe We Know*, pp. 17-40. New York: Norton.

Glasersfeld, E.v. (2001), "The Radical Constructivist View of Science". *Foundations of Science, special issue on Impact of Radical Constructivism on Science* 6(1-3): 31-43.

Glasersfeld, E.v. (2005), "Thirty Years Radical Constructivism". *Constructivist Foundations* 1(1): 9-12.

Guba, E.G., and Lincoln, Y.S. (1989), *Fourth Generation Evaluation*. London: Sage.

Huberman, A.M., and Miles, M.B. (1994), *Qualitative Data Analysis*. London: Sage.

Jarzabkowski, P. (2003), "Strategic Practices: An Activity Theory Perspective on Continuity and Change". *Journal of Management Studies* 40(1): 23-55.

Johnson, G., Scholes, R., and Whittington, R. (2004), *Exploring Corporate Strategy*. Harlow: Pearson.

Lam, A. (2000), "Tacit Knowledge, Organizational Learning and Societal Institutions: An Integrated Framework". *Organization Studies* 21(3): 487-513.

Le Moigne, J.L. (1995), *Les Epistemologies Constructivistes*. Paris: PUF.

Le Moigne, J.L. (2001-2002-2003), *Le Constructivisme, Tomes 1-2-3*. Paris: L'Harmattan.

Le Moigne, J.L. (2008), "Who Conceives of the Individual?" *Constructivist Foundations* 3(2): 69-71.

Mintzberg, H., and Waters, J.A. (1985), "Of Strategies, Deliberate and Emergent". *Strategic Management Journal* 6(3): 257-273.

Mir, R., and Watson, A. (2000), "Strategic Management and the Philosophy of Science: The Case for a Constructivist Epistemology". *Strategic Management Journal* 21: 941-953.

Morgan, G. (1986), *Images of Organization*. London: Sage.

Morgan, G., and Smircich, L. (1980), "The Case for Qualitative Research". *Academy of Management Review* 5(4): 491-500.

Morin, E. (1992), *Method. Towards a Study of Humankind, Vol. 1: The Nature of Nature*. New York: Peter Lang.

Morin, E., and Le Moigne, J.L. (1999), *L'Intelligence de la Complexité*. Paris: L'Harmattan.

Piaget, J. (1967), *Logique et Connaissance Scientifique*. Paris: Gallimard.

Plummer, K. (2001), *Documents of Life 2: An Invitation to a Critical Humanism*. London: Sage.

Popper, K.R. (1959), *The Logic of Scientific Discovery*. New York: Harper and Row.

Riegler, A. (2001), "Towards a Radical Constructivist Understanding of Science". *Foundations of Science, special issue on Impact of Radical Constructivism on Science* 6(1-3): 1-30.

Rosenberg, A. (1988), *Philosophy of Social Science*. Oxford: Clarendon.

Samra-Fredericks, D. (2003), "Strategizing as Lived Experience and Strategists' Everyday Efforts to Shape Strategic Direction". *Journal of Management Studies* 40(1): 141-174.

Saucedo Ramos, C.L. (2003), "Family Support for Individual Effort: The Experience of Schooling in Mexican Working-Class Families". *Ethos* 31(2): 307-327.

Schön, D.A. (1983), *The Reflective Practitioner*. New York: Basic Books.

Senge, P. (1992), *The Fifth Discipline*. London: Century Business.

Strauss, A.S., and Corbin, J. (1998), "Grounded Theory Methodology" in Denzin, N.K. and Lincoln, Y.S. (eds.), *Strategies of Qualitative Inquiry*, pp.158-183. London: Sage.

Tenkasi, R.V., Mohrman, S.A., and Mohrman Jr., A.M. (2007), "Making Knowledge Contextually Relevant: The Challenge of Connecting Academic Research with Practice". Paper presented at *The Third Organization Studies Summer Workshop*. Crete.

Treacy, M., and Wiersema, F. (1993), "Customer Intimacy and Other Value Disciplines". *Harvard Business Review* 71(1): 84-93.

Tsoukas, H. (2005), *Complex Knowledge*. Oxford: Oxford University Press.

Tsoukas, H., and Hatch, M.J. (2001), "Complex Thinking, Complex Practice: The Case for a Narrative Approach to Organizational Complexity". *Human Relations* 54(8): 979-1013.

Van de Ven, A.H., and Johnson, P.E. (2006), "Knowledge for Theory and Practice". *Academy of Management Review* 31(4): 802-821.

Vermersch, P. (1994), *L'Entretien d'Explicitation*. Issy-les Moulineaux: ESF éditeur.

Vermersch, P. (1999), "Introspection as Practice". *Journal of Consciousness Studies* 6(2-3): 17-42.

Weick, K.E. (1979), *The Social Psychology of Organizing*. Reading, Mass: Addison-Wesley.

Weick, K.E. (1989), "Theory Construction as Disciplined Imagination". *Academy of Management Review* 14(4): 516-531.

Weick, K.E. (1999), "Theory Construction as Disciplined Reflexivity: Tradeoffs in the 90s". *Academy of Management Review* 24(4): 797-806.

Wittgenstein, L. (1958), *Philosophical Investigations*. Oxford: Blackwell.

Yanow, D., and Schwartz-Shea, P. (2006), *Interpretation and Method. Empirical Research Methods and the Interpretive Turn*. London: M.E. Sharpe Inc.

Yin, R.K. (1984), *Case Study Research – Design and Methods*. London: Sage.

Appendix

Examples of the impact of the ongoing research project at BI on the BI CEO's reflection and actions

---

Exhibit 6: The six points to be addressed in BI Salesmen Quarterly Global Evaluation (QGE)

1. Aim: Whenever, after a meeting, you withdraw a prospect from the prospective client file, explain your decision: why, finally, is this company not a potential BI target?

2. Training: If you wish to enlarge your knowledge of industrial matters in order to better understand a certain prospect's activities, indicate the specific training you need.

3. Refused offer: For every offer refused by a prospect or a customer, indicate your understanding of the reasons for this refusal.

4. Accepted offer: Whenever an offer is accepted, indicate why and where the BI offer made the difference over a competitor's offer.

5. Learning satisfaction: Describe what you have learned during the past quarter; what has brought you increased professional knowledge and comfort.

6. Learning satisfaction goals: Write down your *learning satisfaction* objectives for the next quarter.

The current research project at BI reveals that despite the CEO's intent to design and implement dialogical procedures and to operate them dialogically, the salesmen management process via the QGE procedure set up in 1997 – shown in Exhibit 6 above – was not dialogical (Avenier 2008). Indeed, it was focused on learning and did not mention anything about performance. In the long run, this had generated some malfunctions in BI's commercial department, such as the fact that some salesmen were not as commercially active as they were supposed to be.

This research project also reveals that the new formal system set up at the beginning of 2007 for salesmen management is still not dialogical. Indeed, it is based on figures which are immediately available through the interconnection of the newly implemented sales software with BI's integrated operational software:

for instance, for each salesman information includes sales details and the daily numbers of calls and visits made to prospects and customers.

This can be interpreted as a swing from a focus on learning forgetful of performance, to a focus on performance forgetful of learning. This swing has been stimulated by the awareness of the malfunctioning generated by the previous formal procedure, and reinforced by the hitherto instant availability of information on salesmen's actual activity. The new formal system overcorrects, in a way, the deficiency of the previous system. In this formal system, specific attention is no longer paid to the salesmen's individual and collective learning. The fact that the new system is somehow forgetful of learning makes it non-dialogical with respect to the ago-antagonist pair performance/learning – while it is, nonetheless, dialogical with respect to the pair individual/collective learning. It has the additional drawback of being poorly adapted for achieving the more important goal of operating BI's commercial department as a learning network, as called for by the CEO.

When, in one research report (Avenier 2008), the CEO read this interpretation – concerning the non-dialogical character of the new system and the misfit between ignoring learning and the philosophy of a learning European commercial network – this stimulated her reflection. Indeed, in her reply, she wrote: *"This comment perplexes me. Why do you say that? Sales' arguments are still in the same philosophy. (...) Currently, we are trying to gather customers' objections to sale's offers, in order to share these possible objections in the commercial network and to point out to salesmen the variety of possible questions and answers in case of customers' objections. This is difficult to do because salesmen have trouble recalling an objection within its historical context... We have to insist on this matter, because there exists therein a source of learning as well as, more importantly, a commercial lever."* (M. Bloch-Dolande, e-mail extract, January 21, 2008)

In my reply, I answered that the complementary information she offered in her e-mail refers to tasks which do not correspond to any item of the QGE (see Exhibit 6). In addition, these tasks do not directly impact the salesmen's variable wages, so that salesmen might not show much involvement in their implementation. I added that in my view, as long as individuals are not specifically pushed to reflect on what they have learned progressively in their work as well as on what they would need to learn during training in order to improve their professional skills, there is a fair chance that they will not reflect on these matters spontaneously.

Later, the CEO informed me of her ongoing project to set up webcams for weekly international videoconferences between salesmen and BI's top managers. These videoconferences aim at experience sharing and collective learning within the commercial department together with the top management, on the topic of answering customers' objections – which the CEO views as currently being a strong lever to improve the sales process. Principles of the QGE procedure could be re-invigorated in the videoconferences. Actually, the idea of reviving the QGE procedure during these videoconferences came to her upon reading my report. She had forgotten about this procedure, which had been difficult to implement in 1997. At that time, the commercial department manager had to put pressure on salesmen to get them to comply with it. Since he left in early 2004 and was not replaced, had taken this task back, the QGE procedure had progressively become inoperative, and she had forgotten about it.

To summarize, the interpretations that were offered to her (see Avenier 2008) stimulated her thinking around the question: "What do we do nowadays at BI to stimulate individual and collective learning, not only within the commercial network but also more generally within BI as a whole?" These interpretations also led her to launch several actions. These included accelerating the installation of webcams at each of the ten BI sites, and reviving collective reflection and learning around items that were originally in the QGE procedure. Although the QGE procedure was no longer useable in the same way that it used to be, its items still provide useful landmarks for the development of BI's commercial department as a European learning network.

6 On the Axiology and Actionability of Knowledge Creation About Organizations In Management Science Research

Rickie Moore and Michel Peron

Introduction

The topic of knowledge creation in management science is one that has sparked and continues to spark much debate. With no universal consensus and several ideological paradigms about management sciences, the processes of knowledge creation in management sciences and the usefulness and the actionability of the research and its results are major subjects of contention among management science researchers, practitioners and firms. Within the academic community, there has been an abundance of normatization, inspired by the hard sciences approach, with regard to what constitutes knowledge, and the processes for creating it. In spite of the many prevalent and passionate debates, several constructs and definitions have been ideologically disparaged and extensively usurped, and as such, they have been deprived of the richness of their value and abridged in their commonly referred meaning. In addition, in most management sciences research the complexity of the reality of organizations (Savall and Zardet 2004) is often reduced to a simplified representation in the pursuit of isolating a single variable for investigation. This denaturing process, together with the excessive and at times inappropriate utilization of the traditional hard sciences approach to management, which is a human, "soft" and inexact science, raises a number of issues about the validity, pertinence, sense making and applicability of the knowledge produced. As a result, the contributions of the extensive research in management sciences, especially in terms of knowledge creation processes and the usefulness of the results produced from the research, are equally debatable. In short, the axiology (value) of the knowledge created is widely put into question.

In this chapter, we revisit and explain the axiology of epistemology, the ontology (components) of organizations and the actionability of the knowledge produced in management sciences research. Our contention is that we cannot continue to adamantly ignore the fact that the normative approach to the creation of knowledge in management sciences is often incomplete and insufficient in improving organizations. We argue for a sustained and more pluralistic approach to knowledge creation that draws on the various sources and approaches. We defend our contention by demonstrating that the axiology of the knowledge produced through an inappropriate or incomplete approach impacts the actionability of the knowledge, can induce errors in judgment and management, and consequently raises questions about the value of the knowledge that is produced. This dilemma requires that we pursue and adopt more relevant and appropriate methods and steps, and we support our arguments by highlighting the Qualimetrics approach – a balanced quantitative, qualitative and financial perspective, developed and practiced around the world by ISEOR, (Socio-Economic Institute of Firms and Organisations/ Institut de Socio-Economie des Entreprises et des Organisations, University of Jean Moulin-Lyon 3), a French institute that specializes in management sciences research, as a pertinent example of the pluralistic approach to the creation of knowledge in management sciences research (Boje and Rosile 2003; Buono 2003; Buono and Savall 2007; Savall and Zardet 2008).

Axiology of Epistemology – the Hard Science Posture and its Limitations

Having been created from the traditional sciences, management science sought to define and portray itself identically in the likeness of its antecedents. In adopting a "hard science / traditional science posture", management science – the *"new"* science – espoused numerous practices and influences from the traditional sciences in studying and defining organizational ontology (reality), notably e.g. the isolation of objects of research for analytical inquiry, the quest for definitive laws about entities and objects of research, and prediction of events and actions. In the pursuit of scientific recognition, numerous schools of thought and practice have been developed, and as such, the academic community has been relatively divided among the different philosophies (positivism, interpretivism, constructionism, quantitative approaches, qualitative approaches, inductive approaches, deductive approaches, objectivity, subjectivity, etc.).

While the adoption of this "traditional science" posture is understandable and served as a basis for the launch and early development of management as a science, the limitations of this posture are increasingly problematic and unavoidable because unlike physical matter, organizations are ontologically complex – they combine different individuals with different characteristics working together for sometimes the same goals, finance, strategy, environments, etc., and they portray emergent properties. Whereas physical matter in laboratories may have fixed and identically repetitive states, humans are biological entities and they evolve over time, respond differently to the same stimuli, and so forth.

Consequently, the limitations of the hard science posture are forcing us to revisit our approach to knowledge creation in management and social sciences, and to question its structure, its validity and the limits to the knowledge itself. Based on this traditional science approach, a certain "normativism" occurred both in what can be considered as theory, and what constitutes the basis on which knowledge can be created. With the limitations of the traditional scientific posture in management science research, the legitimacy of the normative approach is increasingly being challenged. While traditional scientific methods, tools and techniques might have worked for the traditional sciences, their indifferent application to the new and untraditional management science, even though its origins can be traced back to the traditional sciences, frequently failed to yield the same results, and in addition distorts, ignores and artificially reduces the complexity of the object, thus leading to erroneous and partial interpretations. The complexity of organizations far outweighs the complexity of the simpler matter under investigation in the physical sciences.

In addition, stakeholders in the knowledge community, especially firms and organizations, have been increasingly challenging the academics and researchers about both knowledge creation and knowledge application (actionable knowledge), and are increasingly seeking to hold academics legally responsible for the knowledge they provide and sell. We distinguish between academics and researchers because academic norms do not necessarily require scientific participative observation. By scientific participative observation (de Gerando[1], Malinowski[2]), we mean an *in situ* approach whereby the observer goes into the field and is involved in the evolution of the organization, and not just observes it from a distance (external to the object) and remains uninvolved in its evolution. Part of the challenge comes from the fact that a great portion of hard science-influenced academic research is produced *in vitro* and is largely contemplative – i.e. it does not integrate the interactivity and the complexity of the object. Much of this type of research thus remains "theoretical" and lacks an applied dimension. While this sort of approach may be useful and relevant to the academic community, its lack of application / applicability (actionability) is problematic for practitioners. Practitioners tend not to read academic journals because they consider that the knowledge imparted in the journals is often abstract, difficult to grasp, inactionable and inapplicable, since they consider it to have been produced in an "ivory tower" disconnected from reality.

Increasingly, the academic community is attempting to address this long outstanding issue – the relevance and pertinence of management science research for its non-academic stakeholders. Firms have consistently criticized management researchers for ignoring their concerns and needs in terms of effective solutions to their problems. A widely held opinion by firm executives is that researchers are

---

1 French anthropologist (1772-1842), creator of the "participative observation" concept. 1822.
2 Polish-born British anthropologist (1844-1942), who is known for the method of participant observation from his book *Argonauts of the Western Pacific* (1922).

more preoccupied with obtaining significant amounts of data about the repeatability, replicability and probability of given research variables when conducting their research projects. For these executives, researchers are primarily creating more and more knowledge for the academic community and themselves, and, are in effect, learning less and less about organizations and their realities (Remus, 1980).

Ontology of Organizations – Organizations as Complex Research Objects

Compared to other objects of research, organizations are highly complex because of their biological and behavioral dimensions. Firms employ individuals who are very different even though they may share identical competencies. These individuals live very different lives and have very different values, expectations, attitudes, etc. They also react differently to identical forms and sorts of stimuli. The multiplicity and variety of persons (actors) who play a role in the firm also contribute to this complexity inasmuch as their positions and stakes are different. In referring to an organization as a complex object, our objective is not to reduce it to a snap-shot photograph of the building, the machines and the work force, but rather to consider it as a comprehensive and integrative mechanism that transforms inputs into outputs and results. This inherent ontological complexity is also understandable as firms and organizations are also increasingly international and global, and have to tackle the many issues of interculturalism and multiculturalism, not to mention the variety of institutional, national and international regulations and specificities.

The use of the biological sciences metaphor may be somewhat strange and disconcerting at first, but its appropriateness and applicability are relevant. Using the physical sciences metaphor as an alternative would be a very limiting and constraining exercise, as it would not conjure up, capture or appropriately and sufficiently reflect the dynamic and kinetic diversities, varieties and instable character of organizations. The biological metaphor (Savall and Zardet 2004), also resists the excessive normalization attempts of the physical sciences approach, because given that organizations evolve over time, their evolution "movement" and change make the stability of the organization difficult to predict.

Linguistics and linguistic precision are also very important and are neither neutral nor void of significance and meaning. Language is a primary vehicle of communication. Intervener-researchers, as consultants are referred to at ISEOR, are, on the one hand, required to take into consideration the problems posed by communication due to the polysemic nature of the vocabulary used in the exchanges – the same word has different meanings and conveys different notions socio-linguistically and multiculturally at the various levels of the firm and for different people, depending on their backgrounds, motivations, purpose, objectives, etc. On the other hand, we cannot ignore the fact that company actors may use the same word differently, with or without a common objective in mind. Objectives may even contradict each other and reinforce problems. Hence, shared meaning, sense making and sense giving (common lexicologies, socio-linguistics, etc.) are highly valued and necessary for effective and efficient communication.

Added to this complexity are different technologies, processes and systems that the individuals use in the operation of firms and organizations. On the whole, and in terms of knowledge creation in particular, the role and application of process are indeed fundamental because processes are construed in order to attain a specific result. In fact, the process generally determines the results. Company actors (executives, management, employees, etc.) apply a variety of processes in their operations, and management science researchers need to fully understand and integrate the impact of organizational process on their research.

These observations lead us to wonder why, in spite of all that is known about the reality of organizations and complex social objects, so many management science researchers who aspire to better resolve the problems that are confronting the firms are still embarking on reductive scientific research instead of embracing more holistic ones.

Epistemological Context, Mathematical Knowledge and Empiricism

Epistemology, the science of knowledge, formalizes three key dimensions on the nature of knowledge – i.e. what is it (how is it recognized), how is it obtained (what mechanisms exist for providing and acquiring knowledge), and finally, what is known or not known (what is the scope, magnitude, qualities, etc., of that which is known). According to the Stanford Encyclopedia of Philosophy, epistemology "is about issues having to do with the creation and dissemination of knowledge in particular areas of inquiry". The debates and questions about knowledge in the academic community and are not new, and are never ending. Knowledge may be the result of a "spark" – a dialogue between two or more persons. It may be fleeting, volatile and very relativistic – i.e. it is dependent on and conditional to the situation and context at a specific point in time. Our particular conception of knowledge is that it is temporal-spatial in nature, that it has to be construed as a dedicated and contextual tool within a strategy and that it stems from the implementation of the cognitive interactivity principle (see below). For us, knowledge is a result of a construction-connection dynamic that links and associates information about a given object.

Fundamentally, epistemology serves as a mechanism that allows us to understand and to question the validity of the knowledge that has been developed.

Two conceptions of knowledge creation and construction that influence our approach are

1) Knowledge is the object of precise validation according to the contradictory subjectivity, cognitive interactivity and generic contingency principles (explained later on). This type of knowledge is transferred to the company actors with whom they have been co-produced so as to help ensure the survival of the firm.

2) Knowledge is academic-like and can be construed as an exercise in model building, construction and creation which can help reinforce the grounding of the research rationale based on the three types of hypothesis – descriptive, explicative and prescriptive.

In traditional science, scientists shared the belief that a number of laws governed the existence, organization and function of matter and sought to uncover these laws through experimentation. Objects in traditional sciences – "wholes", were considered as the sum of their parts and were broken down into isolated components in order to study their make-up and properties. Scientists were then able to successfully identify those components that possessed exact properties which were constant and recurring across identical and different objects. This exactness led to the expectation of a guaranteed repeatability and eventual prediction about the object based on its consistent conformity. With such a setting, it was easy to replicate observations about the objects and to hypothesize about the probability (mathematical) that the permutations of observations would adhere to and validate the pre-conceived assumptions and descriptions. Over numerous experiments, laws were defined and theories established about the object itself. With mathematics being widely acclaimed as a perfect and exact science, these laws and theories were considered facts as they were proven mathematically. Scientific knowledge was thus considered to have been produced if it had been obtained through mathematical methods applied to large, statistically significant amounts of data.

Having outlined the historical foundation of management science and the ontological foundations of organizations, knowledge about organizations – and more importantly, intervention in organizations – would need to integrate and address this complex reality. As previously mentioned, indiscriminately applying the tools, methods or approaches of traditional science in order to discover and create knowledge in management is problematical, as the tools, techniques, methods or approaches would be inappropriate in a number of management contexts. Hence, the knowledge produced would not necessarily be the most pertinent and appropriate. Consequently, the axiology of the knowledge produced, even though it might be tightly circumscribed, would be limited.

The supremacy of the mathematical approach to traditional science undoubtedly and significantly influenced management science research. As part of its legacy to management science researchers, traditional science also created a reliance on extensive mathematical modeling in order to statistically validate research findings. For quantitavists, therein lies the necessary and sufficient condition of scientific and irrefutable knowledge in a universal sense. For us, such an exclusive approach poses the problem about the gap between organizational realities and their numerical representation. What is the extent of the distortion or misrepresentation? What are the biases? How to handle discrepancies?

Management science researchers for the most part adopted the need for large data sets figuratively represented as $n=1000$, in order to scientifically and statistically validate their results. The data sample needed to be large enough to demonstrate conformity and repeatability, and to assure the probability of the findings. Management science researchers were thus transformed into number crunchers and statisticians obsessed with the mathematical validation of their findings. Large-size data samples became the rule of thumb and the de facto basis of empirical and epistemological research.

However, large-size sample studies have not single-handedly satisfied all inquiries in management research. The philosophy of numerous researchers that empirical research could only be based on such large-size samples led to the refutation that knowledge could be produced from independent case studies and one-sample ($N=1$) or small-size sample ($N=100$) data sets. For this category of researchers, large-size data samples were necessary in order to test the validity and randomly (objectively?) confirm the existence of the newly acquired insight and/or knowledge. While there has been formal recognition of the learning produced from an individual case study, the traditional preference for large data samples still remains the "normative" litmus test of validation and application for the defenders of large-size data samples. In their view, research findings based on single case studies and one-sample data sets are only just assertions unless their validation can be demonstrated through the utilization of a large data set, and $N=1$ research is not empirical research.

The irony is that epistemologically, both worlds are actively engaged in the practice of empiricism – i.e. the development of knowledge through observation and experience rather than just by logic or theory. Yet, this principal pursuit and common purpose seems to be forgotten in the protracted and ruthless battle over the size of N (sample size). Although we posit that there is no universality to logic, we nevertheless do not question the notion of logic as another pertinent approach, even if logic itself is person-dependent and subject to variation.

In essence, researchers are caught up in the consequences of the dichotomy and dialectic that is an integral part of the management science research. The debate of whether N=1 is less important than N=10,000, or whether N=10,000 is the minimum condition necessary to formulate knowledge or theory, depends on the purpose and use of the results and outcome more than discovery or recognition of the knowledge itself. In comparing the two samples, more is not better, and less is not insignificant, because the objectives of the two inquiries are different. However, such a posture runs counter-intuitively to normative reasoning that considers more as better, and because a greater number is involved, the results are more representative and thus acceptable – i.e. there is a certain guarantee and security in the larger number.

Data and Information as Ingredients for Knowledge

Within management sciences, knowledge is often considered as an organized body of information, or as specific information about a subject and this is often a subject of debate as information is often misleadingly equated to knowledge. The very existence of knowledge as an independent notion can also be put into question as it can be considered as an accumulation of dormant and inoperative data, not necessarily collected systematically but which can be accessed and manipulated immediately by a data processing system for any specific purpose. In fact, organizations themselves – much as the human body in medical studies – can be considered as a collection of untapped reservoirs of information unsystematically displayed. ISEOR consultants methodically extract information in their intervention-research, since they consider organizations as archaeological digs, with hidden costs and hidden performances among others, representing their buried objects. But such a comparison should not be drawn out too far, because it clashes with one pivotal concept in the socio-economic approach to companies and organizations, i.e. the representation of the firm as a living entity (cf. bio-management) since its main components are men and women.

Information, therefore, is not so much dug out of the premises as elicited in some sort of Socratic maieutic approach, through face-to-face interviews. Intervention-research requires that researchers possess expertise in knowledge elicitation strategy and negotiation savoir-faire aimed at obtaining relevant information in a complex unit of different actors. The message will not get across to company actors if intervener-researchers do not master the technique which leads to an efficient and effective presentation of the mirror effect – i.e. the presentation of the information (or black spots) gathered during the course of the interviews with all those concerned, so as to illustrate the dysfunctions through the very few words used by the interviewers.

In order to compile reliable data, one has to cross-reference interviews, documents and scientific and participative observations (triangulation). Discourses do not necessarily reflect the reality, and can often consist of an incomplete and incommensurate appreciation of present events – i.e. a mix of hypertrophied elements that are exaggerated and over-magnified, hypotrophied elements that are understated and minimized, remnants of the past – as if they were current today, and an anticipation of the future – when people try to send messages that are convenient and self comforting and auto reassuring.

Resorting to historical documentary digs is thus necessary. Important information does not necessarily present itself by itself – spontaneously on a platter and given out or away, it has to be unearthed. Interesting information is not immediately available on the surface of discourses and speeches. If we resort to the archaeological metaphor, it is because it embodies and illustrates the fact that teamwork is necessary to bring invariance into focus, to pinpoint and to unearth valuable and reliable information.

Three fundamental questions in management science research – What, How and Why – correspond to the three following stages, i.e. information gathering, knowledge creation and sense making. The ultimate outcome of management research is not to become acquainted with the firm as a complex object, but rather to better understand it in order to better describe it and intervene appropriately when necessary. Unfortunately, if understanding is said to encapsulate the ability to learn, judge and make decisions, it also points to one's personal opinion and interpretation. While understanding is clearly a subjective construct and result, knowledge (except with philosophers) can be considered as being distributed across the entire objective-subjective spectrum.

Our discipline also has to deal with the eternal debate between positivism and constructivism. Positivism – a term applied to any system that confines itself to the data obtained from experience and excludes a priori speculations – relates in fact to empiricism in its un-hijacked form. As early as the Renaissance, the empirical approach came to be contrasted with the scientific one. Empiricists limit themselves to observations and are suspicious of all attempts at providing theoretical explanation. They trust experience. What works is what has been proven in practice. For Teddy Ward (undated), empiricism can be more broadly and ambiguously defined as the theory that all knowledge stems from sense experience and "internal mental experience". The empiricist draws his rules of practice not from theory but from close observation and experiment, emphasizing inductive rather than deductive processes of thought. Empiricists claim that no one could have knowledge of the world unless he had experiences and could reason, but this does not mean that either experience or reason by themselves could provide a kind of absolute certainty about the world. Ward then wondered, "What can?"

Sources and Types of Valid Knowledge

Philosophically, the distinction between *a priori* knowledge (i.e. knowledge obtainable by reason) and *a posteriori* knowledge (such as provided by experience) raises the question as to whether there is any prevailing type of knowledge as far as validity is concerned. The scientific validation of knowledge is thus a case in point as one of its objectives being to reach if not universality (no one firm is exactly identical to another), then at least generalizability or reproducibility. This fact also embodies the most controversial issue of internal validity versus external validity of any management research outcome. This controversy juxtaposes the conflict between qualitativists and quantitativists. The former claims that knowledge should be contextualized, refined and fine-tuned to be rendered valid and to generate repeatable results, and the latter advocates that the larger the size of the sample, independent of the context, the more replicable and valid is the knowledge.

ISEOR integrates both dimensions. ISEOR-like deconstructivist / constructivist interventions are at the root of their actionable knowledge creation. ISEOR argues that external validity increases with the number of cases studied, and multiple and diverse research enables an extensive production of generic knowledge (decontextualized core) because each new case is fraught with contextual, contingent, specific knowledge, but also with generic knowledge. Pride of place is given to context, measurement and analysis. The ISEOR ambition is nevertheless to incorporate specific cases into statistical series. Unique contextual knowledge can move to the level of conceptual knowledge due to the relationship between contextualism and general laws.

While paradigms influence and guide the design and implementation of management science research, the validity of the knowledge produced is a subject of numerous debates. On the one hand, knowledge can be said to be validated if its epistemological approach has been verified. On the other hand, given that there is no universal definition, knowledge that is not epistemologically verified is not necessarily invalid and should be excluded.

Generic Contingency, Contradictory Intersubjectivity, Cognitive Interactivity Principles

We are convinced the real key to effective knowledge creation lies in the generic contingency, contradictory intersubjectivity and the cognitive interactivity principles developed by ISEOR, since management research has essentially to deal with interaction. Interaction is a vital learning process. In fact, knowledge is a social product and exchange is a prerequisite for its creation (context of the firm).

Knowledge produced by researchers tends to be specific, hence, contingent by nature, *but* it also brings to light fairly permanent features and invariance. Every intervention undertaken concomitantly produces specific, conditional and contextual knowledge on the one hand, and common knowledge on the other. We therefore use the generic contingency principle to designate the epistemological framework that encompasses all the results obtained from all intervention-research. When key ideas related to given specific company dysfunctions (contingent) are brought to light, they will be added to similar ones already collected from previous intervention-research and will thus constitute a databank of generic key ideas. At ISEOR, this principle has been developed based on an analysis of the extensive accumulation of intervention-research carried out in numerous companies around the world. Diversifying information sources is the solution advocated by the ISEOR research team when it comes to producing generic knowledge.

The contradictory intersubjectivity principle consists in confronting the relative and subjective points of view of every actor, which should lead to numerous interactions between the company actors. As it is extremely difficult, not to say impossible to attain objective knowledge, this principle allows at least researchers to better circumscribe the subjective element. Multiplying different images or perspectives on a company improves the quality and significance of the information collected. Hence the necessity to collect information from a diversified and multiple pools of informants, as was indicated above. Besides, the contradictory intersubjectivity principle helps the intervener-researcher track down the "unspoken", an important component to take into account when taking stock of both explicit and implicit findings.

The cognitive interactivity principle between the company actors and the intervention-research team on the other hand brings positive results for both, since the subsequent knowledge is co-produced and even co-created. On account of their newly acquired knowledge, company actors are progressively led to modify their representation of the research object, i.e. their company, more specifically in qualitative terms. Knowledge acquisition throughout the firm is structured both vertically and horizontally and thus enables company actors to alter their perception of such and such problems, such and such sectors and eventually the wholeness of the organization. The issuing representation is bound to modify the actor's viewpoint on the operation of the firm, as well as their social behavior in the workplace. The major task of the researcher is then to validate or invalidate the hypotheses he/she formulated when embarking on the intervention, and most probably to express new ones. Knowledge creation is decidedly a never-ending process since it is indisputably linked to change.

Actionability of Knowledge

Having outlined the various handicaps and dilemmas concerning the axiology of knowledge produced in management sciences research, the application and implementation of the knowledge within the firms and organizations are seldom straightforward and often very problematic. The partial nature of the knowledge produced represents not only a hindrance in terms of implementation but can create newer problems. Ultimately, the sustainability of the intervention is compromised right from the very outset. As previously mentioned, practitioners prefer to create their own knowledge rather than incorporate academic research which is often perceived as inaccessible – and lacking in applicability, though it might be scientifically sound and statistically grounded.

Thus, how should management science researchers respond to this challenge? On the one hand, the axiology of knowledge produced may be epistemologically recognized, but on the other, the axiology of the actionability would be either deficient or significantly diminished.

The potential of Qualimetrics

In the preceding paragraphs we have traced some of the contributions of the ISEOR research institute and its intervention-researchers. Henri Savall, founder of ISEOR, driven by his socio-economic philosophy and drawing on the extensive intervention-research conducted by the intervener-researchers within the institute, developed Qualimetrics – an integrative qualitative, quantitative and financial approach to management science research and interventions. In fact, the ultimate target of the ISEOR approach is to study phenomena linked to the production of economic value with firms and organizations. Boje and Rosile (2003) note that

> management science, while more open to triangulating qualitative and quantitative methods, has been less able to link these to financial methods. The ISEOR Qualimetrics methodology (Savall and Zardet, 2004), can be described as being located in the middle between qualitative, quantitative and financial methods, and its research paradigm is situated between the empiricist / constructivist spectrum and does not exclude or choose one or the other.

For Boje and Rosile, they have appropriately labeled their methodology Qualimetrics as it integrates and articulates the three sets of methods. Qualimetrics is a bridge from and to qualitative, quantitative and financial methodologies, and for ISEOR the three sets of methods are intertwined, interrelated and dynamic.

Boje and Rosile (2003) further note that

Qualimetrics is an analysis of how organizational members as well as intervener-researchers construct, use and interpret statistics, relative to their contexts. There are contexts involved in producing numbers for use in accounting and management reports. There is hegemonic reductionism, where individual stories are reduced to numerical displays. And the numbers mean different stories and experiences to different people. Qualimetrics seek to recover this loss through root cause analyses, a search for the intertextuality of attributed causes and effect facilitated by a combination of observation, interviews and document analysis.

For Savall and Zardet, information – whether qualitative, quantitative or financial – is always partial.

ISEOR's approach is to study not just the firm or organization itself, but also the various phenomena that are encompassed in their management. ISEOR does not only consider the tangible and permanent factors and aspects (budgets, sales, inventory management, etc.), but also the unstable and immaterial (intangible) ones such as staff training. The mixture of both tangible and intangible elements increases the complexity of the object (the organization).

Unlike other action-research approaches, however, the ISEOR methodology goes further since intervener-researchers seek to transform the object observed (the firm or the organization) by experimenting both *on* and *with* it so as to better understand the phenomenon observed. Intervener-researchers negotiate an extended long term *in situ* participative observation agreement with the firm being studied so as to comply with the three previously mentioned fundamental principles – generic contingency, contradictory intersubjectivity, cognitive interactivity principles – and in order for them to produce their effect. Within the ISEOR center, the results of many case studies provide for the implementation of the generic contingency model. The constructivist / deconstructivist approach to the interventions respects the methodological protocol and facilitates the acquisition of data and the design of case studies. Through repeated experiments and interventions, the ensuing knowledge is accumulated, structured and modeled both for its genericity and specificity.

Intervener-researchers thus position themselves in a decidedly transformative posture relative to the research object. Therefore it should be underlined that in spite of appearances, an intervention-research having a transformative vocation is somewhat different from research conducted through participative observation (a method often used in the sociology of organizations and of labor). Indeed, one of the major principles of the intervention-research method consists in the scientific exploitation of the interaction between the researcher and his field experiment. Intervener-researchers adopt a constructivist posture and should not in any way be considered as surrogate managers. We should bear in mind that intervention-research is an ongoing process of strategy construction for producing, collecting and processing qualitatively controlled information. In short, intervention-research may be best defined and comprehended as a transformative and energizing process of interaction and intervention, as opposed to a contemplative or participative process of observation. The epistemological challenge therefore is to find a way to create knowledge about an object that is endowed with such characteristics. Traditional management documents do not feature immaterial investments and their amortization. We have never seen the discounted presented value of immaterial investments in any report whatsoever.

Through Qualimetrics, management science researchers are thus sensitized to the socio-economic impacts and context of the measurement and the dysfunctional outcomes of the way numbers are produced, analyzed and interpreted. Qualimetrics therefore recontextualizes data by exploring the subjectivity of their construction, the selectivity of operations applied and abandoned, and the ways in which some content is quantified and included while others are ignored.

The Qualimetrics approach is underpinned by the three principles of generic contingency, contradictory intersubjectivity and cognitive interactivity. Qualimetrics cuts across disciplines, contexts and circumstances. Its interdisciplinary, intertextual and integrative approach lays the foundation for a new approach to epistemology and the research methodology. In sum, Qualimetrics and the qualimetric modelization of the information obtained facilitate the restoration of the intrinsic richness and diversity of the complex object studied in management sciences. It provides meaning, reduces subjectivity and facilitates the aggregation and comparison of the elements of the object studies.

As we have shown, the topic of knowledge creation in management sciences is quite an intricate subject. Given the peculiarities and characteristics of the science, we are challenged to exercise due diligence in terms of our scientific intent, epistemology and empiricism. As we embark on the journeys of knowledge creation about organizations that are ontologically complex entities, it is important to recall that the axiological valuation of the knowledge produced will be determined not only by the users of the knowledge, but also by the rigor and appropriateness of the processes used in creating the knowledge. In terms of the actionability of the knowledge produced, we are challenged to integrate and to respond to the social demands of our objects of study for the useful, relevant and actionable work.

Given the numerous considerations that have to be taken into account and the various schools of thought that influence our work, we are also challenged to address the issue of representation of the object, the appropriateness of models, and the likely distortion and discrepancies that can occur. Wacheux (1996) notes that the management science researcher most often access not so much reality itself which is pre-existent to the research project, but rather the individual representations of reality built and fashioned from the individual's perceptions. For Quivy and Van Campenhout (1998), authenticity in research is thus a quest for truth – not absolute truth, rather truth that continually questions itself.

References

Boje, D. and Rosile, G.A. (2003), "Comparison of Socio-economic and other Transorganizational Development Methods". *Journal of Organizational Change Management,* 16(1): 10-20.

Buono, A.F. (2003), "SEAM-less-post-merger Integration Strategies: A Case for Concern". *Journal of Organizational Change Management,* 16(1): 90-98.

Buono, A.F. and Savall, H. (eds.) (2007), *Socio-economic Intervention in Organizations. The Intervener-researcher and the SEAM Aapproach to Organizational Analysis.* Charlotte, NC: Information Age Publishing.

Gerandó, J.M.de (1822-1823). *Histoire comparée des systèmes de philosophie : considérés relativement aux principes des connaissances humaines.* Paris: Alexis Eymery

Malinowski, B. (1922), *Argonauts of the Western Pacific: an account of native enterprise and adventure in the archipelagoes of Melanesian New Guinea /* with a preface by Sir James George Frazer. London: Kegan Paul

Moore, R., Savall, H., et al., (2001). A system-wide integrated methodology for intervening in organizations : the ISEOR approach. *Current Trends in Management Consulting, Research in Management Consulting Series.* Charlotte, NC: Information Age Publishing.

Moore, R., & Peron, M., (2007), SEAM, Change and Organizational Performance: The Importance of Incorporating Quantitative and Qualitative Assessment, *Socio-Economic Interventions in Organizations, Research in Management Consulting Series,* Charlotte, NC: Information Age Publishing.

Quivy, R. and van Campenhout, L. (1998), *Manuel de recherche en sciences sociales.* Paris: Dunod

Remus, W. (1980), "Why Academic Journals are Unreadable: The Referees' Crucial Note", *Revue Interfaces,* Vol. 10, No. 2, 1980, 4 p.

Savall, H. (2003), "An updated presentation of the socio-economic management model". *Journal of Organizational Change Management,* 16(1): 33-48.

Savall, H. (2003), "International dissemination of the socio-economic method". *Journal of Organizational Change Management,* 16(1): 107-115.

Savall, H. & Zardet, V. (2004*), Recherche en Sciences de Gestion, Approche Qualimétrique, observer l'objet complexe,* Paris: Economica.

Savall, H. and Zardet, V. (2008), *Mastering Hidden Costs. Socio-economic Performance*. Charlotte, NC: Information Age Publishing.

Wacheu, F. (ed.) (1996), *Méthodes Qualitatives et Recherche en Gestion*, Paris: Economica.

Ward, T. (undated), *Empiricism*. http://personal.ecu.edu/mccartyr/american/leap/empirici.htm

7 Creating Practical and Operational Knowledge from Action Inquiry Technologies

Lucia Alcántara

Introduction

Effective managers and consultants strive to sustain and enhance their skills through understandings of emerging concepts and strategies. Even with conferences and literature to assist, these practitioners are challenged with identifying appropriate venues to access practical, research-driven resources to sustain their level of expertise. Action inquiry technologies, often referred to as action technologies (AT), are a group of inquiry-based research methods which can be used to increase productivity through workplace learning projects (Marsick & Gephart, 2003). This chapter engages comparative case study methods to explore what opportunities are available to capitalize from these action-oriented research methods as a means for increasing practitioner competence. Two inquiries are presented which include descriptions of processes, outcomes, and implications for practice.

Action technologies (Brooks & Watkins, 1994) are a group of multi-purpose research and learning strategies which include action research, action learning, participatory action research, collaborative inquiry, and popular education. Action technologies share four primary key elements: participants are centric to the context being addressed; the intention is to construct new understandings of existing conditions; data are collected and used systematically; and outcomes focus on change (Marsick & Gephart, 2003). With the exception of popular education, the research aims of the other methods focus, to varying degrees, on stimulating organizational knowledge and either formal or informal individual knowledge (Brooks & Watkins, 1994).

One goal of this chapter is to expand current understanding of cutting-edge strategies for creating practical and readily applicable knowledge through the use of inquiry-based research methods such as those found in the AT family. The similarities among purpose, focus, and methods of the action technologies support this intention. This chapter draws upon existing literature to provide detailed information describing the inquiry-based process, and background. I then engage case study methods to provide insight into the practices and results of two inquiries; a systematic cooperative inquiry into leadership by social change agents, and an action inquiry into praxis by adult education practitioners. I was active as a co-facilitator in the systematic cooperative inquiry and a participant in the action inquiry.

Data obtained through interviews and direct observations inform the methods and outcomes in both cases. Documentation derived from current research and existing literature is utilized to present the implications for practice. Strategies to support the launching of successful action technology projects are also presented.

Action technologies (AT) offer practitioners opportunities to learn about their respective practice by engaging in inquiry and reflection on their experiences and existing knowledge. Their practical experiences can be readily transitioned into operational knowledge. Action technologies provide a salient methodology which managers and consultants can be employed to gather and interpret industry-specific data, capitalize on the expertise of peers, engage in dialogical practice, and optimize opportunities for real-time testing of new strategies.

Inquirers in both groups were able to expand their understandings of themselves and their respective practices and/or roles. The first case is a systematic cooperative inquiry, organized by an external, overarching organization. Participants in this group were able to maximize their learning opportunities, and gained integral understandings of the practice of cooperative inquiry. The second case is comprised of adult education practitioners engaged in an action inquiry into individual praxis. Their learning focused on personal development and professional practice as a tool for understanding and maximizing leadership characteristics. Instrumental learning grew out of respective understandings of their leadership profiles and application of suggested strategies and techniques. The action inquiry framework is described in greater detail in the section on practical applications.

Participants in both groups engaged in collective subjective reflection, testing of assumptions, and meaning-making. The respondents discussed how they learned in the moment, and reported learning about themselves and their practice. The social change agents learned about their own professional practices and cooperative inquiry through exploring closely held assumptions on social change organizing. They acquired new information by engaging in cycles of action and reflection and meaning-making from their lived experiences. Additional learning focused on the practice of inquiry-based research.

The social change agents experienced cooperative inquiry and engaged with techniques which they then used in their respective practices. They indicated that storytelling, use of metaphors, and reflective practices such as journaling were key aspects of their learning within the systematic cooperative inquiry group. Some of the co-inquirers went on to apply these methods in their respective practices in support of their cycles of action and reflection. The outcomes were overwhelmingly positive. The participants reported initially feeling apprehensive about testing their newly acquired techniques. While they were met with some resistance from co-workers, they forged ahead, and in the end, were met with unexpected and rewarding outcomes.

The adult education practitioners in the second group engaged action inquiry to explore new conceptualizations of self by collectively engaging in subjective critical reflection and in examining deeply held beliefs, values, and behaviors. Reflexive practices included journaling and deconstruction of professional practices and experiences. This action inquiry led to lifting up tacit knowledge and learning about themselves personally, their roles as leaders, and their influence on others. The action inquiry group reported changes in professional practice, and transformation of meaning schemes resulting from testing their assumptions and engaging in deep collective reflection amongst peers.

Action technologies are experience-based research methodologies, of which collaborative inquiry is but one, that offer opportunities for collective meaning-making through action-oriented processes to effectuate change in the given environment (Brooks & Watkins, 1994). The operating principles of cooperative inquiry are sufficiently aligned to those of the action technologies to negate the need to distinguish between them. Given the shared philosophical positioning, interdependence, prevailing literature, and research, the term action technologies will be used to expand current understanding and appreciation of the cooperative inquiry methods applied herein. While the distinction seems unnecessary, divergent features of the two methodologies will be highlighted whenever necessary to augment the readers' understanding.

Process

Action technologies have often been used as a viable method for workplace learning projects, they have been documented as effective in building an organization's capacity for learning (Bray, Lee, Smith, & Yorks, 2000) and their capacity to learn about how they learn and change (Marsick and Gephart, 2003). Action technologies have also been found useful as tools for collaborative problem solving (Coghlan & Brannick, 2001; Marsick & Gephart, 2003). Similar to other action inquiry technologies, cooperative inquiry groups are formed around a question of mutually compelling interest (Bray, Lee, Smith, & Yorks, 2000; Reason, 1998, 1994, 1999). Inquiry-based research methods function as an operative means for adult learning and for the creation of new understandings from experience (Reason, 1988; Bray, Lee, Smith, & Yorks, 2000).

The formation of inquiry groups is spontaneously generated (Reason, 1988; Yorks & Kasl, 2002). Spontaneous groups are those generally initiated, designed and directed by the participants themselves. Groups can also be organized systematically within more formally construed paradigms. Systematic inquiry groups are groups that have been generated and/or formally organized under the aegis of organizations and/or institutions which retain a vested interest in the outcome and the resulting products.

I make a distinction between the spontaneous groups and systematic groups, those managed and supported by an external, overarching institution. The latter differ from spontaneous groups in that the parent organization is an ongoing stakeholder in the inquiry process and outcomes. The investment of resources and vested interest introduced by external producers has an impact on the inquiry groups' dynamics and creates a tension not evident in spontaneous inquiries. Systematically generated groups can also be self-directed and range in levels of support and management provided by the overarching organization.

Action technology groups form around a mutually compelling question or problem. AT projects anchored in organizations are directed by overarching needs and focus on problem solving through change-oriented strategies (Brooks & Watkins, 1994; Marsick & Gephart, 2003). The initiation of an AT project begins by identifying a problem and forming a group interested in finding a solution. Once the group has been organized, co-inquirers take time to establish group norms, rules, location, length, and frequency of meetings (Reason, 1988; Yorks & Kasl, 2002).

Action technologies are driven by cycles of action and reflection (Reason, 1988). The cyclical process provides opportunities for participants to test assumptions and explore previously held understandings (see Figure 1). The process actively engages the participants in critical thinking, individual and collective subjective reflection, and exploration of their assumptions about meaning, intentions, actions, and activities in their respective practices. New understandings begin to evolve from this process.

The cycles of action and reflection support meaning-making and emergent understandings. The action and reflection process can give rise to deeper appreciation and new understandings derived from practice and what is known. In doing so, the newly forged knowledge is practical and operational because it is drawn from the participants' lived experiences, is directly related to their practice, has been identified as a relevant issue, and is anchored in real time. The emergent outcomes of action technologies provide opportunities for learning since the outcomes are directly influenced by the interests, needs, experiences, and existing conditions of the participants.

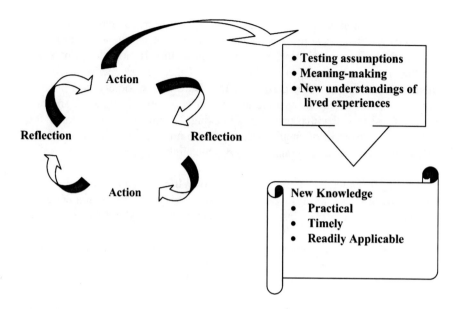

Figure 1. Inquiry Cycle

Background

Major research and existing literature discuss the benefit of individual learning and learning from action inquiry technologies. A review of literature utilizing education and social sciences search engines, including ProQuest, Wilson Web, ERIC, Education Full Text, and EBSCO Host, yielded very few documents describing how managers and consultants can capitalize on these methods to enhance learning about professional practice, and how they themselves learn about their learning. This chapter attempts to fill the gap in the prevailing literature.

The cycles of action and reflection can lead to deeper, more revealing forms of first, second, and third-person inquiry. The process of gathering data about oneself, through personal, interpersonal, and external sources is known, respectively, as first, second, and third-person research. Bill Torbert advances the use of first, second, and third-level action inquiries in group and organizational platforms to stimulate change in individual practice and in organizations. Torbert and Associates describe action inquiry as "*a disciplined leadership practice that increases the wider effectiveness of our actions*" (2004, p. 1).

First-person inquiry addresses the individual's development of a purposeful practice of inquiry into one's subjective experiences in order to achieve greater

199

awareness and ability to make conscious, cogent choices. In first-person inquiry, the focus of attention is to explore one's subjective perspective and bring it to the forefront of consciousness. Second-person inquiry is the practice of engaging *"with others in a face-to-face group to enhance our respective first-person inquiries"* (Reason & Torbert, 2001, p. 15). Third-person inquiry incorporates a broad perspective that engages the inquirer in visioning, strategizing, and other behaviors associated with propositional thinking. The practice of engaging in first, and second-person action inquiries positions the practitioner to achieve a deeper understanding of the underpinning factors which influence their thinking, choices, and practices.

Making meaning from the events in one's own life offers an opportunity for the emergence of new learnings (Alcántara, Kovari, & Yorks, 2005). In a collaboration between an academic institution and community-based practitioners, inquiry-based research methods drawing on lived experiences were used to explore techniques to increase strategic, conceptual, and creative thinking (Kovari, Hicks, Ferlazzo, McGarvey, Ochs, Alcántara, & Yorks, 2005), and issues of leadership development (Altvater, Godsoe, James, Miller, Ospina, Samuels, Shaylor, Simon, & Valdez, 2006).

Reflective practice is at the core of an individual's engagement in action research methods. The lived experiences of practitioners hold meaning and implications for their work product within a larger context. These implications are important to our understanding of research processes within the action technologies context. Discursive processes have been used as a means for merging reflective practice and action research in public sector reforms in the United Kingdom (Weil, 1998). The Critically Reflexive Action Research (CRAR) project is the basis for an analysis of reflexivity in action research. The more salient points of this study include the identification of differences in epistemologies as being critical to the organization's ability to change from positivist to post-positivist perspectives, as well as the deconstruction of practices as a means for creating space for emerging practices.

Weil focuses on engaging in multi-level reflection within the action research process. The facilitator engaged the group on simultaneously reflecting on individual dilemmas, while in the process of identifying a collective dilemma to focus the project. Both the individual and group dilemmas are used to produce learning. The facilitator draws upon data solicited through individual and group engagement. Using CRAR, Weil strives to enact a fuller model of action research, one which is reflexive, critical, and collaborative.

Weil asserts that reflexivity in the process of conducting research about an organization enables managers to function more effectively. The process teaches managers how to minimize defensive routines and become more familiar at handling ambiguous situations. Critical to Weil's findings are that practice with ambiguity within the action research process increases tolerance and provides opportunity for enabling alternative choices, responsible choices, and dimensions of interaction (p. 58). Weil's assertions suggest that reflexive practices can lead to opportunities for learning and for creating new knowledge within organizational structures

Coghlan and Brannick (2001) assert that in any action research project there are two parallel action research cycles in operation. They refer to this as meta-learning. One cycle is focused on the process of the research cycle, while the second concerns itself with reflection on the action research cycle. In essence, there is an action research cycle based on the action research process. In another document (Alcántara, in print) I contend that explicit engagement with the second, meta-reflection cycle would provide organizations an opportunity to increase their learning. Marsick and Gephart (2003) support the use of action technologies as a resource for organizations to learn about how they learn in the process of expanding the effectiveness of workplace learning. Characteristics of environments that can enhance learning and personal growth include opportunities for challenging perspectives and actively seeking and accepting dissenting opinions.

Organizational context influences the establishment of conditions for learning in formal settings. The inception of liberating spaces is an effective means to support the creation of new knowledge and meaning-making (Yorks, 2005). Yorks draws upon research conducted as part of a collaborative action inquiry in a Veteran's Administration Hospital in the United States. Liberating spaces as described are not grounded in physical reality. They are environmental conditions that allow for the organic emergence of new ideas and alternative approaches to existing organizational challenges. Similar operant conditions have been referred to as liberating structures (Torbert, 1991). Liberating structures optimally facilitate the individuals' feeling empowered and support new ways of thinking and of questioning assumptions.

As agents of an academic research driven institution in Spain, Villasante and Garcia (2001) advance concepts related to conditions for constructing knowledge in a Master's degree program. The authors serve as both faculty and managers of the academic program where they support students in required Participatory Action Research Groups (PARG). Their reflective analysis is based upon their practice, which is grounded in a program that focuses on facilitating social change and supporting the successful integration of their graduates as social change experts in government and public service organizations. Their contribution is contextualized in an environment where there is a demand for, and expectation of, deliverables and applicable outcomes. Villasante and Garcia succinctly describe the processes as being effective as a tool for learning within the academic environment as well as in the community.

Villasante and Garcia cite four key aspects of their successful pedagogical framework. The schematic includes participants who are interested in learning for purposes beyond degree acquisition, team learning focused on interactive engagement replete with workshops, discussion groups and interviewing, as well as the questioning of existing social science theories and methods. Their findings include the need for time, of which they assert there is never enough.

Their practice breaks with traditional academic methods by supporting collective subjective reflection within teams and allowing for consideration of innovative, untested methods. Description of the unorthodox practice of jointly engaging the PARG and faculty in reflection on action and critically subjective critique of the learning experience were also documented. The authors acknowledge the existence of institutional and contextual pressures to produce results within superimposed time lines and schedules that may not be in keeping with the PARG's development or research agenda.

At the participant level, enactment of specific strategies is necessary to ensure full participation in a reflective practice (McMorland & Piggot-Irvine, 2000). Included in their outline are methods for holding space for reviewing unexamined cultural norms, habits, and frames of reference, all of which are very similar to the activities found in action technology projects. McMorland and Piggot-Irvine advocate for holding the known in abeyance as a means of providing an opening for the unknown to emerge. This moment, they contend, is perilously fragile and a prime opportunity for authentic inquiry to emerge. The authors refer to the opening as white space and the process as productive enabling.

Understanding the actors, processes, and environmental conditions helps illuminate the functional aspects essential to comprehend the intricacies of inquiry-based research. In doing so, we create space for alternative discussions, which can contribute to practical applications that enhance learning from and about action inquiry technologies. These ingenious, yet straightforward research methodologies must become transparent so as to highlight their simplicity and potential as viable tools for research and knowledge creation.

Practical Applications

In this comparative case study I explore the experiences and learnings generated from two distinct inquiries: a systematically mediated cooperative inquiry managed by a research center, and an action inquiry self-managed by a group of practitioners. The first case is comprised of social change agents inquiring into aspects of their leadership, the co-facilitators, and the staff members from the research center. Their experiences and outcomes are then compared with those of the second case, a spontaneously generated action inquiry of adult education practices by practitioners from a doctoral program. As co-facilitator in the first case and co-inquirer in the second case, I offer an integral understanding of the differences and similarities into the architecture of the inquiry, processes, and outcomes. Insights into methods, practices, learnings and outcomes for both cases are also provided.

I conducted semi-structured interviews with participants from both projects. In the first case, interviews were conducted approximately 1 year after the project had been completed with three of five co-inquirers using the telephone. Four staff members from the supporting research center and my co-facilitator were interviewed in person. In the second case, four of the original nine participants were interviewed in person one year into the action inquiry group's duration, but before its conclusion.

The first inquiry concluded approximately 14 months before the interviews were conducted. It offers greater amounts of details because of the larger sample. Completion of the inquiry contributes to a wider breadth of experiences for the respondents to draw upon, as well as the existence of outcomes and products. The volume of findings should not detract from the relevance or significance of the findings drawn from the second inquiry.

Case 1 – Inquiry into Leadership by Social Change Agents:
A Systematic Cooperative Inquiry

The inquiry group in this case is comprised of five social change agents, staff members from the research center sponsoring the project, and the co-facilitators. The social change agents were selected to participate in a two-year national leadership development program in the United States funded by a large international philanthropic institution. A participant in the leadership development program organized a group of selected people to explore the question, "How can we teach people to be more strategic, conceptual, and creative in their thinking?"

As part of their commitment to the leadership development project the social change agents were required to participate in one of three qualitative research methods, ethnography, narrative inquiries, or cooperative inquiries. Participants had little, if any, previous knowledge or exposure to cooperative inquiry. Nor did they have full understanding of what the process would entail. The social change leaders saw opportunity to meet in varied locations across the country, and to work with people they had perceived as being interesting individuals. Once introduced to cooperative inquiry methods, the participants became motivated to engage in the inquiry process as a way of increasing their understanding of their practice as leaders in social change organizations. The social change agents felt that their respective practices as leaders had become stale, and that constituent actions were neither effectively sustaining nor advancing the goals of their organizations.

The cooperative inquiry group consisted of five social change agents and two co-facilitators, of which I was one. The social change agents were engaged in the group inquiry process as co-inquirers into their leadership practice. In this systematic cooperative inquiry, two external facilitators were assigned by the research center to facilitate and support the evolution of the inquiry process. Our group was diverse in gender, race, and ethnicity. We entered the cooperative inquiry with no overt expectations of the process or outcomes, and were initially, and remained, open to the experience of collaborative exploration through the cooperative inquiry process.

The social change agents (co-inquirers) were selected through a national award process for significant work in local communities that had been successful in improving conditions for disenfranchised and marginalized populations. The co-inquirers were anchored in a broader social context where issues of power, control of resources, equality, and social justice represent tangible real-time challenges. To be considered for the award, individuals and/or their organizations were nominated by colleagues or constituents. The philanthropy then engaged in collecting references and interviewing the nominees. Each year for five successive years (2001-2006), 15-20 leaders were selected to participate in the two-year leadership development program.

The multinational philanthropy selected a research center to support and manage the cooperative inquiry process. The research center was embedded in a graduate school public policy program situated in a large research-driven academic institution. The research center was committed to cross-sector critical dialogue that explores the complexities of leadership in the public sector and creative solutions for ongoing practice. Logistical support, including expenses and co-facilitators, were provided by the research center as part of their role as research managers. In total, the group held six meetings and requested additional time to complete their findings. Each meeting represented a cycle of action and reflection. Meetings lasted approximately 1½ days, during which the co-inquirers participated in discursive practices as a vehicle for meaning-making from lived experiences.

The meetings included identifying and questioning assumptions, the introduction of new concepts, and thoughts informed by media, literature, and daily life. As co-facilitators, Bruce and I worked with the co-inquirers' contributions to stimulate reflection and critical thinking. We drew upon adult learning practices and presented information that informed their thinking on how adults learned, explained, and modeled processes of identifying deeply held assumptions and critical thinking. We also engaged in subjective reframing (Mezirow, 2000) as a means for exploring assumptions about experiences, feelings, systems, or organizations. At the midpoint of the systematic cooperative inquiry process, the co-inquirers experienced a perspective transformation. They came to a collective awareness that only through subjective awareness and intentionality could they lead and support others in becoming more strategic, conceptual, and creative. In order to teach others how to think more strategically, conceptually, and creatively, they themselves would have to become more strategic, conceptual, and creative in their thinking and practice.

All of the co-inquirers reported learning and transforming their ongoing practice as leaders and social change agents. They changed their approach to professional practices by using their collectively created knowledge, and techniques in; training models, lesson plans, organizing meetings, and even sermons. Their transformations were supported through discourse and practices that culminated in collective and subjective meaning-making.

The responding co-inquirers reported that the inquiry process itself was the key to their learning. Critical reflection, storytelling, and use of metaphors were central to the emergence of this systematic cooperative inquiry. Jean, one of the co-inquirers, indicated that the inquiry process motivated her to take risks with her constituents and community partners. She reported using critical reflection in statewide meetings with constituents and stakeholders as well as in staff meetings. Through critical reflection, her organization was able to change its strategic approach to a long-term transportation planning campaign for a major urban city. Jean describes how she was motivated to utilize her experience within the systematic cooperative inquiry group in her daily practice,

So provocative just, well, it forced me to go back and do some exercises, you know, and I guess "risky" would be the other, you know, word I would use. Intensely reflective, provocative, and risky because you had to take risks if you were going to do these exercises, and people would roll their eyes at you or they'll say, "Wow, that's really cool",– or just miss the whole thing! [laughs] It was a risky thing in that respect. You know, just doing things differently than you had done them before. Jean, Co-inquirer

In the end, the co-inquirers learned about the practice of cooperative inquiry, their professional practices, and emerged having transformed their frames of reference and habits of mind (Mezirow, 2000), by borrowing from their lived experiences to engage in critical subjectivity and cycles of action/reflection (Reason & Torbert, 2001). This systematic cooperative inquiry group produced a final document of their learnings and techniques entitled "Don't just do something, sit there: Helping others become more strategic, conceptual, and creative" (Kovari, Hicks, LaFerlazzo, McGarvey, Ochs, Alcántara, & Yorks, 2005). Moreover, the learning was not limited to the co-inquirers: the co-facilitators and research sponsor staff also learned in the process of managing and/or supporting systematic cooperative inquiries. It is at this boundary that one finds a dearth of literature. Literature or research-based documentation that describes opportunities for meta-learning is extremely limited.

As co-facilitators, we gained perspective, increased understanding about social change practices in the United States, and increased our own understanding of facilitation. We valued learning about leadership, and were exposed to previously unbeknownst aspects of community organizing. Our appreciation of the diversity in perspectives between the social change agents and our respective world views grew as the inquiry unfolded. In addition to the other learnings cited, we emerged with a deeper understanding of our respective practices and ourselves as practitioners. Learning about our respective facilitation practices emerged from interactions with peers, co-inquirers, and research sponsor staff. Bruce, my co-facilitator, described learning about the practice of cooperative inquiry as follows:

I was learning a lot about CI itself. For example, even what I just said in this interview I wouldn't have said prior to this experience, that people come to the CI because they find the question engaging, but also because they want to be in the conversation with the people involved. And also because of the resource. Those were conclusions that came out of the sort of way that people talked about the CI. I learned a lot about the internal rhythms of CI and how you really need several meetings to get your traction going. So I learned a lot about the CI process. I also learned the different ways of sort of timing with each of the groups is very different. And I learned a lot about the question itself. Bruce, Co-facilitator

The research center supporting the systematic cooperative inquiry project is the offspring of a large well-known school of public policy situated in a prestigious research-driven university in the northeastern United States. As an emerging entity, the research center was at the time of the leadership development program in the process of establishing its prominence. They continue to strive for collaboration with social change agents and to inform leadership practices in the international not-for-profit sector. The research center functioned as sponsors of this systematic cooperative inquiry. The research center staff reported having gained a greater understanding about the practice of cooperative inquiry facilitation. They also indicated they had emerged with practical knowledge relative to management of an inquiry-based research methodology that serves as a tool for learning. Of the three sets of respondents in this case (research center staff, co-inquirers, and co-facilitators), the research sponsor staff were the most organized in their approach to learning. The research center staff appears to have been strategic in gathering feedback and data on their roles, practices, and subsequent impact upon the leadership development program. They solicited information on management practices informally and formally during small group sessions, large systemwide meetings, and one-on-one interaction with program participants.

The structured feedback process of gathering and pooling information led to changes in management practices ranging from the question selection process to identification of communication misalignment. In the early stages of the systematic cooperative inquiry project, tensions emerged between the research center staff, co-facilitators, and co-inquirers. The research center staff experienced challenges with communication. They were able to identify issues associated with how they conveyed their intended messages, and how the communication was perceived. Dawn, a research sponsor staff member, had first-hand experience with this communication challenge. When asked to talk about her experiences with the cooperative inquiry project, she reported learning and being challenged in the process:

> ... it took a long time to feel understood in the group, particularly vis-à-vis the awardees or a set of them. So for me, it is a very frustrating experience when you have one set of intentions and commitments. In this case, the intention to try to cause a shift in the power dynamic of how traditional research is done, to do something that's worthwhile to other people, to be of service, right? And to learn, to engage people to learn for your own benefit as well as for their benefit. And to be received as if your intentions were to do everything opposite of how you had hoped to do it is very frustrating and to not feel I mean, I felt in the beginning that people really didn't have an open mind about what we might want to do. Some people did, but some did not and they were the most vocal. Dawn, Research Center Staff

Case 2 – Inquiry into Praxis by Adult Education Practitioners: An Action Inquiry

The second case focuses on the experiences of seven adult education practitioners from different fields engaged in an ongoing action inquiry. At the time, we were all enrolled in an adult education doctoral program at a prominent academic institution in the United States. We came together, drawn to participate by a shared interest to interact with each other as colleagues and learners. After participating in an intensive two-day transformative leadership seminar, a core group of four participants invited four other attendees to engage in an inquiry into praxis, drawing upon *Action Inquiry: The Secret of Timely and Transforming Leadership* (Torbert & Associates, 2001) as the common text.

Some of the group members were interested in understanding and learning about inquiry as a process, others were captivated by the synergy that was present when we gathered. We shared an appreciation of exploring and understanding our respective frameworks and leadership characteristics in a common context. We were not committed to developing a specific question or a specific inquiry method. We were committed to exploration, critical thinking, co-creation, and emergence

207

of a collective and mutually enriching learning experience. Shared facilitation was perceived as both a challenge and an incentive.

Participants stated that they were particularly attracted to the idea of engaging in meaningful discourse, the intellectual repartee, and opportunity for individual reflection in a supportive and safe environment. In March 2006, the inquiry group was launched with nine practitioners diverse in racial, ethnic, and gender composition. We committed to coming together regularly. We succeeded in meeting approximately every 6-8 weeks in varied locations, initially in meeting spaces on-campus. Gradually we began to meet at each other's homes. Group facilitation, decision-making, agenda setting, and responsibilities for meeting logistics were shared.

During the early stages of the inquiry group's evolution, we became fascinated by the idea of delving into our self-awareness as leaders and learners in a group context. As adult educators, we were familiar with systems theory and the concept of single, double, and triple-loop learning. Individual knowledge and experiences as facilitators and consultants were shared and augmented with new information that served as the foundation for the co-creation of new understanding. To varying degrees, group members engaged with different techniques and strategies.

Early on in the inquiry, the four parts of speech as presented by Torbert and Associates (2001), namely framing, advocating, illustrating and inquiring, were a core theme that informed communicative practices for some co-inquirers. Co-inquirers were comfortable discussing the themes, and some actively applied the framework in the discourse. The environment that was co-created offered opportunities to broaden respective practices. Subjective critical thinking, reflection, and reflexivity were enhanced by discursive practices that regularly challenged thinking and assumptions.

All co-inquirers engaged in reflection. Actions however, were somewhat diffused as the group had not developed a question. The actions varied in scope and consistency. As co-inquirers, we appeared to be engaged in a collaborative and supportive gathering of individual inquiries. Some were exploring personal concepts, others explored professional issues. Not all group members engaged in actions, and those who did, did so asynchronously.

The discourse was deeply personal and revealing and gave rise to emotional, intellectual, and psycho-social conceptualizations of the action logics (profiles of leadership/management styles) described by Torbert and Associates. Inquiry meetings were at times affirming, validating our beliefs and practical knowledge. At other times, I found them to be emotionally and psychologically challenging. Twelve months after the inquiry was convened, I engaged in a convenience sampling during a break in the academic semester and surveyed several of my peers to explore the effects, if any, of action inquiry on individual practice.

Four of the original nine co-inquirers participated. The respondents all indicated that they entered the process without any expectations. They were attracted to the process by the people who were involved in assembling the group, feeling comfortable enough to be open, but challenged enough to generate personal and professional movement. They indicated having been attracted to the foundational content and opportunity to practice the different strategies of the action inquiry process to support the evolution of their leadership styles. Also appealing was the opportunity to engage in discourse as a tool for personal and professional growth.

All of the respondents reported experiencing either growth or change in their practice or personal way of being. There were two dominant outcomes: personal growth and changes in professional practice. The respondents categorized change as being related to their interpersonal engagement. They reported lifting up tacit knowledge and identified their learning as being subjective. The action inquiry framework purports that individuals can increase their sphere of influence and impact as leaders by developing our capacity to see others and ourselves in dynamic inter-relational contexts. Change and growth in this model incorporate multiple conditions and stem from an increased capacity for, and active practice in, learning and communication strategies that are proscribed by the model. The model does not offer a timeframe for change but does suggest that change is gradual, throughout an individual's life course, emergent and static. In other words, movement into more sophisticated competencies can also carry forth traits from more basic action logics.

The action inquirers described personal growth as having unearthed issues that related to their way of being in the world. Other action inquirers described changes in professional practice and/or interactive behaviors resulting from having engaged with the action inquiry process. There is evidence of instrumental and communicative learning having occurred. The more overt changes included the addition of new, highly specific communication strategies, greater understanding of their role, and management of their influence on others in a learning situation. Other outcomes included becoming a more reflective practitioner, increased confidence, heightened awareness of one's presence in practice settings, development of perspective, and greater appreciation of the mutually transformative power of love.

The co-inquirers reported engaging with issues related to self-perception and self-authoring. Most of the respondents agreed that their practice and respective organizations would benefit either directly or indirectly. One respondent cited change in perspective, but did not expect these changes would be manifest in the organizational context. Based on the interviews conducted, it is difficult to assess which specific aspects of the inquiry are directly related to the outcomes or co-inquirers' learnings. Eighteen months after being initiated the remaining six co-inquirers co-authored a conference paper depicting their experiences with developmental perspectives and diversity within the action inquiry process. Their outcomes and written product were closely aligned to some of what the group found to be most rewarding, namely developmental diversity and its' implications on transformative learning.

The action inquiry group was an emergent process dedicated to collaborative engagement with individual practice. It appears that the process, as applied in this case, functioned as a collection of individual inquiries dedicated to supporting the growth of the co-inquirers' respective practices through meaning-making, collective and subjective reflection as precursors to development of new understanding, and knowledge creation. Detailed future analysis would provide greater understanding of any correlations between individual in-group behaviors and impact on professional practice and personal development.

Conclusions and Implications

Action technologies offer opportunity for practitioners to enhance professional growth through discursive processes, reflection on experiences, critical subjectivity, meaning-making, and the development of new understandings. There also exist opportunities to test assumptions and experiment with new techniques and strategies. Collectively these processes support the creation of new knowledge that is grounded in the lived experiences of the practitioners. Readily applicable understandings can be created through use of real-life situations as a means for exploring issues that the inquiry participants consider interesting. The highly relevant and timely nature of these new understandings has the potential to develop into readily operational knowledge the moment they are applied in practice or personal domains.

Distinct points of convergence and divergence can be identified in the experiences of the inquirers in both cases. Group formation and engagement processes were similar and consistent with experiences documented in the existing literature. The inquiries cited in this chapter outline several key components in the development of practical and operational knowledge, amongst them are reflective practice and openness to engagement with the AT method. Both cases indicate benefits of reflective practice for practitioner learning and professional development. The practitioners reported suspending expectations of the research methods, exercising tolerance for ambiguity, and flexibility in applying the AT methods as being central to the outcomes. Flexibility and creativity in application are a recurring theme in both cases documented in this chapter.

Inquirers in both cases were employed in disparate organizations that had limited, if any, relationship and no access to the inquiry processes in which they participated. It is important to acknowledge that the launching of AT warrants attention to conditions in the organizational environment. Care must be taken to cultivate spaces that support non-traditional strategies that may push against positivist practices. I draw upon Yorks (2005) and Torbert (1991) to support the use of action technologies as a resource for organizations to learn about *how* they learn in the process of expanding the effectiveness of workplace learning. Characteristics of environments that can enhance learning and personal growth include opportunities for challenging perspectives and actively seeking and accepting dissenting opinions. Both of these inquiries took place in locations that were removed from the participants' employers, and their organizations did not have any influence over the groups' determination, outcomes, or products.

Outcomes for both groups were somewhat divergent. The outcomes may have been affected by exogenous factors such as time considerations and proscribed goals. Outcomes from the systematic cooperative inquiry group may have been expedited by the suggestion of outcomes introduced by the supporting research center. The process was driven by an inquiry question which had been decided upon during the first inquiry meeting. Expectations about the anticipated number of meetings and a proscribed time span were established prior to the groups' formation. The social change co-inquirers in the first case acknowledge that without resources to support their inquiry, their group may not have transpired. All of the co-inquirers lived in different cities, in some instances on opposite ends of the country over 3,000 miles apart.

By contrast, the action inquiry group was not obligated to produce any outcomes, nor did they have any pre-conceived expectations of their collective engagement. This group functioned with complete autonomy from any overarching institution. We were free to explore and engage in our preferred selections for as long as we felt it was necessary to do so. During the initial 10 months of the action inquiry group, no explicit decisions were made on process or outcomes. We shared literature in support of the discourse and successfully created an open and nurturing environment suitable for individual inquiry in a collective context.

The systematic cooperative inquiry group generated outcomes directly related to the agreed-upon question. Conversely, the action inquiry group did not have a question. Moreover, the outcomes of the action inquiry group encompassed personal and professional dimensions, held meaning for ongoing productivity, and reflected the intentionality of subjective exploration. In both groups, the knowledge produced was relevant, practical, and readily operationalized into the participants' life-world.

The systematic cooperative inquiry group was supported in producing a collaborative product documenting their learning and collective experiences. The support provided by the research center played a critical role in facilitating opportunities for the systematic cooperative inquiry group to document and collaborate on a written document that reflected the collective knowledge. The action inquiry group produced significant outcomes relevant to individual practice and personal growth and co-authored a conference paper on diversity in perspectives. The difference in presentation and/or packaging of the outcomes did not diminish the validity of their experiences or of the knowledge created by either group. Most significant is that both groups were able to create and operationalize practical meaningful outcomes customized to respective self-identified needs in support of personal and/or professional practice.

The two inquiry groups were similar in that they were drawn to the opportunity to engage with peers on mutually compelling topics relevant to ongoing real-time practice. The cooperative inquiry group reported being attracted by four conditions: the credibility of the convener proposing the question; the relevance of the topic to the situations they were experiencing in their work; the other individuals who would be around the table; and the resources that would create and sustain a productive working space. Participants in the action inquiry group were attracted by all but the final condition. Resources to create and sustain the meetings were not a consideration since the action inquiry group was completely self-sufficient.

Practitioners interested in changing their organizations can begin the process through personal transformation. Transformation theory postulates that learning is an emancipatory experience that leads to individual transformation (Freire, 2000; Mezirow, 2000). Mezirow asserts that change in the individual ultimately leads to change in her/his social environment. Practitioners are encouraged to be courageous, to explore and challenge existing assumptions about their respective practices as part of the quest for excellence. The literature suggests that practitioners must first go within in order to change external conditions.

There is an extensive menu of inquiry-based qualitative research methods. These methods can be explicitly engaged to harness individual and collective learning as a means for knowledge creation. Examples of successful application of two action technologies have been provided. Action technologies have been used successfully in communities, academic institutions, as well as public and private organizations. Advancement of the action technologies can enhance organizational learning practices and serve to benefit practitioners, researchers, and adult educators in a multitude of environments. Emphasis should be placed on the co-creation of products amongst co-inquirers, co-facilitators, and the research center that describe collaborative practices and knowledge products. Documentation of the practice of action technologies gives an opportunity to enhance learning about the process of managing and supporting research projects. Demystification of the processes associated with the creation of practical and operational knowledge can serve to mediate alignment of the participants' experiences and organizational expectations. Increased understanding of the conditions that facilitate or inhibit the processes may serve to sustain propagation and enhance confidence and support for action technology projects.

References

Alcántara, L. (in print), "Expanding Effectiveness of Workplace Learning Projects through Multi-level Application of Action Technologies". In Poell, R. & Van Woerkom, M. (eds.), *Supporting Workplace Learning: Towards Evidence Based Practice*, Routledge Studies in Human Resources Development.

Alcántara, L. (2007), [Research Proposal for *Not just talk: Individual and institutional critical factors affecting knowledge creation from Cooperative Inquiry groups*]. Unpublished manuscript, New York: Columbia University.

Alcántara, L., Kovari, V., & Yorks, L. (2005), "Cooperative inquiry as a tool for transformative learning: stories from community organizers who transformed their practice". In D. Vlosak, Kielbaso, G., & Radford, J. (eds.), *Appreciating the best of what is: Envisioning what could be*, proceedings of The Sixth International Conference on Transformational Learning (pp. 5-8). Michigan State University and Grand Rapids Community College.

Altvater, D., Godsoe, B., James, L., Miller, B., Ospina, S., Samuels, T., Shaylor, C., Simon, L., & Valdez, M. (2005), *A dance that creates equals*. New York: Research Center for Leadership in Action, Robert F. Wagner School for Public Affairs, New York University.

Bray, J. N., Lee, J., Smith, L. L., & Yorks, L. (2000), *Collaborative Inquiry in practice*. Thousand Oaks: Sage.

Brooks, A., & Watkins, K. E. (eds.) (1994), "The emerging power of action inquiry technologies". *New Directions for Adult and Continuing Education*, 63: 5-16.

Coghlan, D., & Brannick, T. (2001), *Doing action research in your own organization*. London: Sage.

Freire, P. (2000), *Pedagogy of the oppressed* (30th anniversary edition). New York: Continuum International Publishing Group.

Kovari, V., Hicks, T., LaFerlazzo, L., McGarvey, C., Ochs, M., Alcántara, L., & Yorks, L. (2005), *Don't just do something, sit there: Helping others become more strategic, conceptual, and creative. A Cooperative Inquiry.* New York: Research Center for Leadership in Action, Robert F. Wagner School for Public Affairs, New York University.

Lincoln, Y. (ed.), (1985), *Organizational theory and inquiry: The paradigm revolution*. Newbury Park: Sage.

Marsick, V., & Gephart, M. (2003), "Action research: Building the capacity for learning and change". *HR: Human Resource Planning*, 26(2), 4-14.

McMorland, J., & Piggot-Irvine, E., (2000), Facilitation as midwifery: Facilitation and praxis in group learning. *Systemic Practice and Action Research*, 13(2), 121-138.

Mezirow, J., & Associates (2000), *Learning as transformation*. San Francisco: Jossey-Bass.

Reason, P. (ed.), (1988), *Human inquiry in action: Developments in new paradigm research*. London: Sage.

Reason, P. (ed.), (1994), *Participation in human inquiry*, London: Sage.

Reason, P. (1999), "Integrating action and reflection through co-operative inquiry". *Management Learning Special Issue: The action dimension in management: Diverse approaches to research, teaching and development*, 30(2), 207-227.

Reason, P., & Torbert, W. (2001), "The Action Turn: Toward a transformational social science". *Concepts and Transformation* 6:1, 1-37, retrieved on April 28, 2004 from http://www2.bc.edu/~torbert/Action%20Turn,%20final%20 C&T.doc. (Now available at http://escholarship.bc.edu/william_torbert/12/)

Torbert, W. R. (1991), *The power of balance: Transforming self, society and scientific inquiry*. San Francisco: Sage.

Torbert, W. J., & Associates (2004), *Action inquiry: The secret of timely and transforming leadership*. San Francisco: Berrett-Koehler.

Villasante, T. R., & Garrido Garcia, F. J. (2001), "Methodologies for the participant construction of knowledge". *Systemic Practice and Action Research*, 14(4), 483-493.

Weil, S. (1998), "Rhetorics and realities in public service organizations: Systemic practice and organizational learning as critically reflexive action research (CRAR)". *Systemic Practice and Action Research*, 11(1), 37-62.

Wenger, E. (1998), *Communities of Practice*. Cambridge: Cambridge University Press.

Yorks, L. (2005), "Adult learning and the generation of new knowledge and meaning: Creating liberating spaces for fostering adult learning through practitioner-based collaborative action inquiry". *Teachers College Record*, 107(6), 1217-1244.

Yorks, L., & Kasl, E., (2002), "Toward a theory and practice for whole-person learning: Reconceptualizing experience and the role of affect". *Adult Education Quarterly*, 52(3), 176-192.

Section 3: On the rationality of theories – critical perspectives

8 Creating Value for Scholars and Practitioners: Lessons from Organisation Development through Action Research and the Processual Approach

David Coghlan and Aoife McDermott[1]

Introduction

In 2001 in a leading article in the *Academy of Management Journal*, Pettigrew, Woodman and Cameron commented on the state of the field of researching organisational change. They noted the fragmentation of approaches and some of the difficulties in capturing the dynamism that change involves. They called for a new pluralism in the study of organisational change and presented partnership between scholars and practitioners as a key challenge.

This chapter explores approaches to researching change which create value for both practitioners and academics through having an impact on academic knowledge and making academic research actionable. The two approaches explored have philosophically different underpinnings; however, valuable lessons can be derived from both organisation development/action research and the processual approach. Discussion as to what actionable knowledge means tends to diverge rather than to converge. Argyris (2003) conceives of actionable knowledge as that which allows organisational actors to implement their intentions. This is integrally linked to double loop learning. David and Hatchuel (2008) see Argyris' definition as restrictive and present actionable knowledge as when 'a pioneering company invents – consciously or not – a new management model' (p. 36). In their view, actionable knowledge has to be contextualised and universal definitions cannot be used ex ante to decide whether a given proposition is actionable knowledge or not. In this chapter, we are taking actionable knowledge to mean that the knowledge generated is useful to both scholars and practitioners (Adler and Shani, 2005). However, the two approaches presented differ in their interpretation of this. In the processual approach, actionable knowledge can refer to findings from in-depth longitudinal cases; however, reflecting the increased marketisation of academic research (Ferlie and McNulty, 1997), actionable knowledge from within this ap-

---

1 Funding from the Irish Research Council for the Humanities and Social Sciences is acknowledged.

proach increasingly refers to generalisable findings drawn from large-scale comparative studies (Pettigrew, 1990; Dawson, 2003).

In fact, organisation development/action research explicitly contests the description of the guidelines produced from processual research as actionable knowledge. We, in line with other researchers who use the organisation development/action research approach, explicitly contest the description of the guidelines produced from the processual approach as 'actionable knowledge'.

Partnership between academics and practitioners has been the subject of considerable reflection in recent years (Bartunek and Louis, 1996; Amabile et al., 2001; Rynes, Bartunek and Daft, 2001; Adler, Shani and Styhre, 2004; Bartunek, 2007). More lately, Shani et al. (2008) have produced a handbook that explores the nature of collaborative management research between academic and practitioners in considerable depth. This handbook specifically considers how such collaborative management research seeks to create actionable knowledge, i.e. knowledge that meets the needs and requirements of both the academic and practitioner communities of practice, who collaborate as a community of inquiry. In this same volume, Bartunek (2008) notes that academic and practitioner roles are socially constructed and that clarity between them is not always simple. In a similar vein, Coghlan and Shani (2008), also in the same volume, point out that academic researchers/practitioners/insiders/outsiders are mixed roles and that insiders or outsiders may be practitioners and/or academics who bring their perspective on theory and action to the community of inquiry

Thus, the primary focus of this chapter is the relationship between, and the advocacy of, collaborative partnership between scholars and practitioners. Collaborative research, involving insiders and outsiders and practitioners and scholars in multiple configurations, brings the values of theory and practice together in a way that the gap between theory and practice may be bridged (Adler et al., 2004; Shani et al., 2008). Communities of practice are formed within and between organisations, where complex issues are subjected to practical analysis and combined with scientific inquiry that seeks to build on the practical knowing and to understand it in order to generate new knowledge. Collaborative research, at the most basic level, attempts to refine the relationship between academic researchers and organisational actors from research *on* or *for* people to research *with* people. In doing so, it attempts to integrate knowledge creation with problem solving and 'inquiry from the inside' with 'inquiry from the outside' (Evered and Louis, 1981). As such, collaborative research is viewed as partnership among a variety of individuals forming a 'community of inquiry' within communities of practice (Coghlan and Shani, 2008). Collaborative research is typically constructed out of the interactions between practitioners' and scholars' perceptions of key issues and out of key themes that emerge when issues are jointly explored and analysed.

Organisation Development through Action Research

In this chapter we are discussing the organisation development tradition through action research. Organisation development (OD) is a particularly appropriate field within which to open this review of the two approaches: action research (AR) and the processual approach. Austin and Bartunek (2003) have reflected on how over the years, OD has aimed to link theory and practice, but, in fact, there have been many disconnections between practitioners' and scholars' approaches to contributing to new knowledge. They noted, following Bennis' (1966) distinction between theories of change and theories of changing, that scholars tend to focus on the former while practitioners focus on the latter. We need to note at the outset that both OD and AR have independent characteristics. There is a great deal of OD research that is not action research, and there is a whole world of action research that exists outside of the context of OD (McArdle and Reason, 2008). The OD tradition of action research occurs within organisations and aims to help organisations change and at the same time generate knowledge. Shani and Pasmore's definition of action research parallels many definitions of OD:

> Action research may be defined as an emergent inquiry process in which applied behavioural science knowledge is integrated with existing organizational knowledge and applied to solve real organizational problems. It is simultaneously concerned with bringing about change in organizations, in developing self-help competencies in organizational members and in adding to scientific knowledge. Finally, it is an evolving process that is undertaken in a spirit of collaboration and co-inquiry (1985: 439).

Action research is one of the distinctive features of OD and one of its core origins. Schein (1989) argues that the tap root of OD was Lewin's seminal work. Lewin was able to combine the methodology of experimentation with solid theory and a concern for action around important social concerns. For Lewin, it was not enough to try to explain things; one also had to try to change them. It was clear to Lewin and others that working at changing human systems often involved variables that could not be controlled by traditional research methods, developed in the physical sciences. These insights led to the development of action research and the powerful notion that human systems could only be understood and changed if one involved the members of the system in the inquiry process itself. So the tradition of involving the members of an organisation in the change process, something that is the hallmark of OD, originated in a scientific premise that this is the way a) to get better data and b) to effect change. So action research is not only a methodology and a set of tools, but is also a theory of social science (Peters and Robinson, 1984). The roots of OD are in science, and Lewin built a cadre of colleagues and students whose work in group dynamics and organisational research

219

became the foundation for what emerged later as OD. In Schein's view, OD was a 'quiet revolution'.

Action research repudiates the research-action split inherent in positivism and enacts dialogue between theory and practice with the aim of creating actionable knowledge. It does not impose expert knowledge, but rather creates collaborative environments where research experts and local stakeholders share and work with different kinds of knowledge and share the intellectual property. The collaborative process between researchers and local stakeholders involves shared question formulation, data collection, data analysis and testing in action. It demands reflective practice on the strengths and weaknesses of our own practice. The world does not deliver social problems in neat disciplinary packages. Because it is holistic, action research gives researchers the capability to study complex, dynamic difficult problems. Schön (1995) contrasts how researchers can view practice from the high ground, where they can study issues from a distance, with how they can be immersed in 'swampy lowlands', where problems are messy and confusing and the provision of a single technical solution does not work. He notes that unimportant issues may be studied from the high ground according to predetermined standards and rigour, while the critically important ones can only be confronted by being immersed in the swampy lowlands. His conclusion is that we need a new epistemology. Organisation development and action research belong to the world of the swampy lowlands where OD practitioners as action researchers are immersed and they develop a closeness to the people and to the formal and informal dynamics of an organisation (Coghlan and Rashford, 2006).

Shani and Pasmore (1985) argue that a complete theory of the action research comprises four factors: the context in which the action research takes place, the quality of relationships between members and researchers, the quality of the action research process itself and the outcomes. These factors provide the grounds on which OD/AR can be located within the challenge presented by Pettigrew, Woodman and Cameron. The focus on context is common, as is the emphasis on relationship between researchers and practitioners.

The Processual Approach

The definition of organisations from the open-system perspective, which emphasises context and process rather than structure, mirrors the development of themes in work conducted at the Centre for Corporate Strategy and Change at the University of Warwick. A mirroring of these themes is specifically evident in Pettigrew's (1985) articulation of the founding premise of the processual approach.

As long as we continue to conduct research on change which is ahistorical, acontextual and aprocessual, which continues to treat the change programme as the unit of analysis and regard change as an episode divorced from the immediate and more distant context in which it is embedded, then we will continue to develop inadequate and descriptive theories of change which are ill-composed guides for action. Indeed, as I have implied already, there is still a dearth of studies which can make statements about the how and why of change, about the processual dynamics of change, in short, which go beyond the analysis of change and begin to theorise about changing. (Pettigrew, 1985: 15)

Like action research, the Warwick tradition of processual research, offers 'the prospect that both theory and practice can be "bridged" and that engaged academic scholarship can make a difference' (Pettigrew, 2001: 66). To address the 'ahistorical, aprocessual and acontextual' (Pettigrew, Ferlie and McKee, 1992: 6) nature of much work on organisational change, the approach is based on the premise that change is a result of the interplay between the (1) content or *what* of change in terms of its objectives, purpose and goals; (2) the process or *how* of change implementation and (3) the organisational context of change in terms of the internal and external environment (National Co-ordinating Centre for NHS Service Delivery and Organisation R&D, 2001). As a result, in a similar vein to OD through AR, the approach is premised on getting close to the political and context-embedded messiness of organisational reality, and taking account of both formal and informal dynamics in organisational life. Similarly to AR, the processual approach attempts to move beyond studying change, towards changing.

Hence, like action research, processual research aims to contribute to both theory and action, albeit within different time-scales and with different emphases. Within this approach, the aim is to provide both practical and theoretically relevant knowledge. However, unlike AR, it does not aim to guide real-time action in the organisation under study, but rather focuses on generating mid-level theory and recommendations for the future. It does so through the description, analysis and explanation of the complex links between processes and outcomes in change (Pettigrew, 1997). Linking findings to outcomes has been used to provide pragmatic guidelines to managers (e.g. Pettigrew and Whipp, 1991). This focus has emerged from Pettigrew's conception of what the approach should achieve, but in spite of his role as among the founding authors of the approach, it is not universally accepted. Dawson (1997, 2003) is critical of attempts to introduce this positivistic orientation, with an associated desire to adopt participant observation rather than interviews, as a method of data collection in the approach. However, Dawson (2003) recognises that due to time and other constraints among researchers, interviews are increasingly utilised. As a result, researchers tend to adopt the role of outsider-observer, and do not take an active role as agents or actors of change. Thus, the processual approach differs markedly from action research in terms of the researcher's level of engagement, and the influence of the researcher's values on the research output. Nonetheless, concern for knowledge diffusion and implementation has increased with higher levels of external funding, meaning that the action-orientation of processual research findings, if not the level of engagement during the research process, has increased. In their discussion of changes in the organisation of process research, Ferlie and McNulty (1997) note 'an increasing emphasis on purchaser led criteria of output, "deliverables" and target realisation. There is pressure for greater researcher involvement in the policy process, and for shorter term, more action oriented research governed through contract.' This can take the form of joint researcher and practitioner 'action-planning' on the basis of research findings (Fitzgerald et al., 2006). In spite of a historic and increasing focus on producing actionable knowledge within processual research, researchers tend to be positioned as *external observers*, while they are presented as *engaged actors*, within action research.

Implications of Research by OD through Action Research and the Processual Approach for Scholar-Practitioner Collaboration

In moving to consider the implications of OD through action research and the processual approach for partnership between scholars and practitioners, the nuances of the researcher-practitioner relationship are central to our consideration. In the research process, the relationship spectrum is related to the method of data collection and can be considered to run from a one-way relationship premised on interviews, to a limited two-way relationship under participant observation, to a cohesive partnership premised on immediate problem solving in OD. In OD through action research, the researchers are engaged in an active and constructive partnership, engendered through a shared focus on achieving an immediate organisational goal. In processual research, the researcher-practitioner relationship can be premised on either a one-way relationship through observation or interviews, or on a two-way relationship through participant observation. Developing a collaborative relationship in the processual approach may be more difficult as there is no imminent benefit evident for the organisation or practitioner. However, the desire to guide future action (e.g. through the production of recommendations for future action) may be advantageous in this regard.

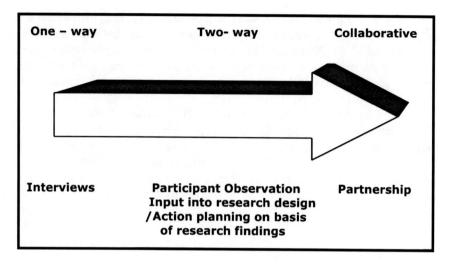

One – way	Two- way	Collaborative

Interviews	Participant Observation Input into research design /Action planning on basis of research findings	Partnership

Figure 1: The Relationship Spectrum

The nature of the relationship, as portrayed by Figure 1, reflects a value judgement about the nature of research. At one extreme, observation reflects an approach that can be expressed as doing research *on* people. At the other extreme, partnership between researchers and practitioners at the most basic level attempts to refine the relationship between scholar researchers and organisational or inter-organisational actors from research *on* or *for* to doing research *with* people. In doing so, it integrates knowledge creation with problem solving and 'inquiry from the inside' with 'inquiry from the outside' (Bartunek and Louis, 1996). Shani, David and Willson (2004) emphasise qualitative elements: true partnership between insiders and outsiders encompassing the dynamics and equality of integrated collaboration, emergent and systematic inquiry through systematic and reflective inquiry and actionable scientific knowledge, whereby the knowledge generated is both scientific and actionable. Bartunek and Louis (1996) emphasise that building up the research project also includes attention to the development of the collaborative research team. Working relationships have to be built and both parties need to be explicit about their respective goals. The questions which drive the inquiry and the action need to be developed together. The design of data collection processes, the collection processes themselves and the design and implementation of action need to draw on both sets of expertise. Similarly, the analysis and interpretation of data need to be done together. In short, all the stages of the research require collaborative action which draws on both perspectives and skills. Attention to content, process and cultural issues are critical to working with the task and relational challenges that arise within the partnership between researchers and practitioners (Coghlan and Rashford, 2006; Coghlan and Shani, 2008). As Coghlan and Shani point out, the collaboration extends to the writing and dissemination stages, so that writing is not left to the outsider academics, nor is the presentation of findings to senior management left to the insider practitioners.

While Dawson (2003) advocates partnership between scholars and practitioners in the processual approach, through participant observation, this is not only failing to move towards collaboration as advocated within OD through action research, but it is also declining within the approach. This is linked to the increasing orientation towards gaining understanding and building mid-level theory, to the end of guiding future action. Crucially, however, Dawson (2003) is critical of this trend, which is being encouraged by Pettigrew's (1997) emphasis on linking to outcomes. This focus on outcomes has led to the adoption of comparative case studies, which make structured cross-cultural and international comparison more feasible than within action research. For Dawson, however, this scaling-up away from the single case study, in conjunction with a shift away from participant observation, is leading to the neglect of detail which was the initial foundation of the approach. Nonetheless, by observing rather than directing or participating in the change, the processual research can be more uniformly applied than action research. This emphasises an ongoing tension within the approach between the depth of the data, the nature of the research approach and the generalisability of the data. This shift towards the researcher as external observer, engaged in the generation of mid-level theory through a positivistic research orientation, is not solely driven by the outcomes desired by researchers and/or their desire for publication. It is also driven by practitioners' desire for guidelines regarding future action. Thus, the scholar-practitioner relationship has implications for the research process in a number of manners. It is naïve to consider that relationships need only be cultivated during the research process itself. This can begin at the outset of the research, and certainly from negotiating the terms of entry.

Pettigrew, Woodman and Cameron's (2001) call for partnership therefore requires reflexivity from researchers' regarding the nature and purpose of the research endeavour and the underlying relationship with the participants. While both approaches provide insight into moving the research relationship away from research *on* towards research *for* and in partnership *with* practitioners, OD through action research is particularly valuable in outlining how this might be achieved.

Creating Value

At a time when change-related research is fragmented as a field, and has clearly delineated areas in need of further development, the aim in this context is to consider two approaches which address some of the critiques of change-related research raised by Pettigrew et al. (2001), specifically that of creating value for scholars and practitioners.

More specifically, both approaches implicitly address context at a variety of levels of analysis. They also inherently include time and history within their analyses, being methodologically focused around processes and action. The actions derived from both approaches aim to address organisational issues, normally with the intention of accruing positive benefits to organisational functioning and performance. In addition, both have a high concern with, and AR has a literature on, the partnership between researchers and practitioners. In fact, as per Figure 1, AR moves the approach towards collaboration. We now provide an example of each approach in order to illustrate how academic-practitioner partnership is exercised differently within each approach.

Due to its foundations in rich context-specific data, AR is not typically associated with structured comparative research. Although comparisons can be drawn between projects, this is typically not done in a manner which aims to derive theory. However, one example of this is evident in the collaborative CO-IMPROVE project (Coghlan and Coughlan, 2005; Coghlan and Coughlan, 2008). This is a case of action research in an inter-organisational setting, rather than the more typical intra-organisational setting. The objectives of CO-IMPROVE were to develop a business model to support the design, implementation and ongoing development of collaborative improvement between partners in Extended Manufacturing Enterprises (EMEs). It comprised collaboration across nine countries involved in the project, three EMEs (collaboration between buyers and suppliers with previous commercial and collaborative histories), four academic institutions and between business and academic participants. The objectives of this European Union-funded project included the facilitation of collaborative improvement of operations practice and performance in the EME through collaborative action research among both managers and academics. Implicit in the objectives of this project was an intention to contribute to actionable knowledge, that is, knowledge that can serve simultaneously the needs of a practitioner organisation and the scientific community. The participants explored collaborative management research in and by an inter-organisational network. They described and reflected on the process by which, and the setting within which, managers and academics collaborated as researchers across boundaries – including discipline and institutional boundaries, as well as those between academia and industry – to develop learning in collaborative improvement in the supply chain.

The OD approach through action research was enacted around cycles of action and reflection. Each EME submitted progress reports in advance of meetings of the entire research group and these were discussed and reflected on at the meetings and next steps were planned and then implemented in the next cycle of action. The data gathered, documented and reflected on by the researchers were fed to the various teams, who kept an overall watching brief of the progress of their area of responsibility. Academics wrote reflection papers which aired assumptions and inferences and which were tested in meetings of both academics and system integrator managers. In this way, there was continuous exposure of the events across the entire project, and their interpretation was made open to public reflection and analysis which then led to further action. The content of the academics' reflection notes were fed back to the group overseeing the development and application of the technology and acted as a driving force for the work of that group and the initiatives it took across the project. CO-IMPROVE can point to several significant contributions to collaborative research across boundaries and borders and to the development of inter-organisational collaboration in the EME and among academic researchers: the quality of the relationships between researchers and between researchers and the participating managers; the quality of the inquiry-in-action; and the outcomes in the context of increasing commercial pressures for continuous improvement in the EME.

A recently completed example of a processual project researching the roles, relationships and facilitating factors in the implementation of change in Irish hospitals is evident in McDermott (2006). The methods used in this project partially replicate those used in a prior project in the NHS (Fitzgerald et al., 2006). The aim of the project was to identify who takes responsibility for initiating, leading and implementing change within hospitals, the contextual factors at role, organisation and environment level which constrain and enable them, and how they may be supported. The objective was to develop a model to support the future implementation of government policy and internally driven service-improvement in Irish hospitals. The study involved case studies of three hospitals, across the public, non-profit and private sectors. Data were collected through interviews, non-participant observation and secondary data analysis. Explicit in the objectives of the project was the intention to contribute to actionable knowledge, which would simultaneously serve the needs of a practitioner, policy and research community. From the processual perspective, actionable knowledge was taken to refer to the production of guidelines for action in future policy making and implementation. Through an informal steering group, representatives of the policy and practice communities were engaged as partners in the research design process, influencing the research design, specifically the choice of sites and appropriate research participants. They also led to the expansion of the focus of the project, from considering the hospitals in isolation, to taking account of the influence of inter-organisational networks on the capacity and climate for service-improvement. While the level of two-way engagement with practitioners declined through the data collection phase, with participants acting as respondents rather than co-investigators or collaborators, throughout and after the completion of the data analysis respondents were fed back findings for verification and the collaborative generation of action plans and guidelines on the basis of the findings. Hence, there was limited two-way engage-ment with practitioners at the outset of the research process, a one-way relation-ship through data gathering and analysis, and a return to a two-way and even col-laborative relationship in the action-planning stages. This structure of engagement was agreed with each organisation prior to data collection.

Interestingly, the international comparative component attracted research sites, and a further push towards a large-scale multi-site, multi-case model emerged from the research sites themselves. This occurred during the access-negotiation period. Specifically, the organisations noted their increased willingness to participate in a multi-site research design, due to the perception of more robust and generalis-able findings that would be of value into the future. This was of concern as the research was not of immediate benefit to them, unlike in AR. Within the defined funding allocation for the research project, the adoption of a large-case multi-site design has had significant repercussions for the research methodology, which is premised upon confined periods of observation, interviews and secondary data, with collaboration via participant observation no longer feasible in practice. This example raises the fact that the nature of the research relationship need not be stat-ic throughout the process, and that even within constraints, practitioners actively engage, and can be engaged, in shaping the research process and outcomes.

The contrast between the two approaches to partnership points to how the notion and exercise of academic-practitioner partnership differs. In the OD/AR example, the practitioners were collaborators all through the research initiative. They attended all the research meetings, read and discussed the working papers that acted as reflection documents and were active participants in the discussions on both the progress of the action and of the development of theory (Coghlan and Coughlan, 2008). In the processual case, practitioners contributed to the research design and its progress in the initial stages, acted as respondents in the middle stage and as partners/collaborators in the final stages. Although both approaches make claims to 'actionable knowledge', the example draws attention to the differ-ent type of knowledge produced in each, the underlying differences in the research process, and in the degree of engagement with practitioners. Crucially, both can create value for scholars and practitioners.

Conclusions

Change is a key area of concern for scholars and practitioners alike, leading to Pettigrew, Woodman and Cameron's call for partnership between the two. However, moving towards such a partnership is complicated by the diversity of the literature on change and the multiple approaches to its research. This chapter has drawn upon two approaches which address this concern to developing partnership between scholars and practitioners. It has indicated that in moving to address these issues, researchers must engage reflexively with the purpose of the research process and the nature of the relationship underlying it. In particular, the two approaches outlined provide insight into moving towards partnership between scholars and practitioners, to create value for both. The nature of the relationship and the engagement of the researcher vary in each, and are associated with the form and time frame of the 'actionable-knowledge' desired.

References

Adler, N. and Shani, A.B. (Rami) (2001), 'In search of an alternative framework for the creation of actionable knowledge: Table-tennis research at Ericsson', in Pasmore, W.A. and Woodman, R.W. (eds.), *Research in Organizational Change and Development*, Vol. 13 pp. 43-79. Greenwich, CT: JAI.

Adler, N., Shani, A.B. (Rami) and Styhre, A. (2004), *Collaborative Research in Organizations*. Thousand Oaks, CA: Sage.

Amabile, T., Patterson, C., Mueller, J., Wojcik, T., Odomirok, P., March, M. and Kramer, S. (2001), 'Academic-Practitioner Collaboration in Management Research: A Case of Cross-Profession Collaboration'. *Academy of Management Journal*, 44 (2): 418-431.

Argyris, C. (2003), 'Actionable Knowledge', in Tsoukas, T. and Knudson, C. (eds.), *The Oxford Handbook of Organization Theory*, pp. 423-52. Oxford: Oxford University Press.

Austin, J.R. and Bartunek, J.M. (2003), 'Theories and Practices of Organizational Development', in Borman, W., Ilgen, D. and Klimoski, R. (eds.), *Handbook of Psychology: Vol. 12 Industrial and Organizational Psychology*, pp. 309-332. New York: Wiley.

Bartunek, J.M. (2007), 'Academic-Practitioner Collaboration Need Not Require Joint or Relevant Research: Toward a Relational Scholarship of Integration'. *Academy of Management Journal*, 50 (4): 1323-1333.

Bartunek, J.M. (2008), 'Insider/Outsider Team Research: The Development of the Approach and its Meanings', in Shani, A.B. (Rami), Mohrman, S., Pasmore,

W.A., Stymne, B. and Adler, N. (eds.), *The Handbook of Collaborative Management Research*, pp. 73-92. Sage: Thousand, Oaks, CA.

Bartunek, J.M. and Louis, M.R. (1996), *Insider/Outsider Team Research*. Thousand Oaks, CA: Sage.

Bennis, W. (1966), *Changing Organizations*. New York: McGraw-Hill.

Buchanan, D. and Boddy, D. (1992), *The Expertise of the Change Agent*. London: Prentice-Hall.

Caldwell, R. (2006), *Agency and Change*. Abingdon, Oxon: Routledge.

Coghlan, D. and Coughlan, P. (2005), 'Collaborative Research across Borders and Boundaries: Action Research Insights from the CO-IMPROVE Project', in Woodman, R.W. and Pasmore, W.A. (eds.), *Research in Organizational Change and Development*, Vol. 15, pp. 277-297. Oxford: Elsevier.

Coghlan, D. and Coughlan, P. (2008), 'Collaborative Research in and by an Inter-Organizational Network', in Shani, A.B. (Rami), Mohrman, S., Pasmore, W.A., Stymne, B. and Adler, N. (eds.), *The Handbook of Collaborative Management Research*, pp. 443-460. Sage: Thousand, Oaks, CA.

Coghlan, D. and Rashford, N.S. (2006), *Organizational Change and Strategy: An Interlevel Dynamics Approach*. Abingdon, Oxon: Routledge.

Coghlan, D. and Shani, A.B. (Rami) (2008), 'Collaborative Management Research through Communities of Inquiry: Challenges and Skills', in Shani, A.B. (Rami), Mohrman, S., Pasmore, W.A., Stymne, B. and Adler, N. (eds.), *The Handbook of Collaborative Management Research*, pp. 601-614. Thousand Oaks, CA: Sage.

Collins, D. (1998), *Organizational Change: Sociological Perspectives*. London: Routledge.

David, A. and Hatchuel, A. (2008), 'From Actionable Knowledge to Universal Theory in Management Research', in Shani, A.B. (Rami), Mohrman, S., Pasmore, W.A., Stymne, B. and Adler, N. (eds.), *The Handbook of Collaborative Management Research*, pp. 33-47. Sage: Thousand, Oaks, CA.

Dawson, P. (1994), *Organizational Change: A Processual Approach*. London: Paul Chapman Publishing.

Dawson, P. (1997), 'In at the Deep End: Conducting Processual Research on Organizational Change', *Scandinavian Journal of Management*, 13, (4): 389-405.

Dawson, P. (2003), *Reshaping Change: A Processual Perspective*. London: Routledge.

Evered, R., and Louis, M. R. (1981), 'Alternative Perspectives in the Organizational Sciences: "Inquiry from the Inside" and "Inquiry from the Outside"', *Academy of Management Review*, 6, 385-395.

Ferlie, E. and McNulty, T. (1997), '"Going to Market": Changing Patterns in the Organization and Character of Process Research'. *Scandinavian Journal of Management*, 13, (4): 367-387.

Fitzgerald, L., Lilley, C., Ferlie, E., Addicott, R., McGivern, G. and Buchanan, D. (2006), 'Managing Change and Role Enactment in the Professionalised Organization'. *Report to the National Co-ordinating Centre for NHS Service Delivery and Organization R&D*. London: NCCSDO.

McArdle, K. and Reason, P. (2008), 'Action Research and Organization Development', in Cummings, T.G. (ed.), *Handbook of Organization Development*, pp. 123-136. Thousand Oaks, CA: Sage.

McDermott, A. (2006), 'Effective approaches to change? Exploring roles in service improvement in Irish hospitals'. *Irish Academy of Management Annual Conference*. University College Cork: Ireland.

National Co-Ordinating Centre for NHS Service Delivery and Organization R&D (2001), *Managing Change in the NHS. Making Informed Decisions on Change: Key Points for Health Care Managers and Professionals*. London, NCCSDO.

Peters, M. and Robinson, V. (1984), 'The Origins and Status of Action Research'. *Journal of Applied Behavioural Science*, 20, 113-124.

Pettigrew, A. M. (1997), 'What is a Processual Analysis?' *Scandinavian Journal of Management*, 13 (4): 337-348.

Pettigrew, A. M., Ferlie, E., et al. (1992), *Shaping Strategic Change. Making Change in Large Organizations: The Case of the National Health Service.* London, Sage.

Pettigrew, A. M. and Whipp, R. (1991), *Managing Change for Competitive Success*. Oxford: Blackwell.

Pettigrew, A, Woodman, R. and Cameron, K. (2001), 'Studying Organizational Change and Development', *Academy of Management Journal*, 44(4): 697-713.

Rynes, S., Bartunek, J. and Daft, R. (2001), 'Across the Great Divide: Knowledge Creation and Transfer between Practitioners and Academics', *Academy of Management Journal*, 44 (2): 340-355.

Schein, E.H. (1989), 'Organization Development: Science, Technology or Philosophy?' *MIT Sloan School of Management Working Paper*, 3065-89-BPS.

Schön, D.A. (1995), 'Knowing-in-Action: The New Scholarship Requires a New Epistemology', *Change*, November/December, 27-34.

Shani, A.B. (Rami), Mohrman, S., Pasmore, W.A., Stymne, B. and Adler, N., (2008), *Handbook of Collaborative Management Research*. Thousand Oaks, CA: Sage.

Shani, A.B. (Rami), David, A. and Willson, C. (2004), 'Collaborative Research: Alternative Roadmaps', in Adler, N., Shani, A.B. (Rami) and Styhre, A. (eds.),

Collaborative Research in Organizations, pp. 83-100. Thousand Oaks, CA: Sage.

Shani, A.B. and Pasmore, W. (1985), 'Organization Inquiry: Towards a New Model of the Action Research Process', in Warrick, D.D. (ed.), *Contemporary Organization Development: Current Thinking and Applications,* pp. 438-448. Glenview, IL: Scott Foresman.

Watson, M. (2004), 'Change and the Nature of Context: What Contribution can the Processual Change Literature Make to our Understanding of Change in Closed Institutions in the Prison Service?' *Irish Academy of Management Conference,* University of Dublin, Trinity College, Ireland.

9 The Stalemate of Organization Theory: Ever New Frameworks, Never New Methods – May Actor-Network Theory provide an Exception to this Rule?[1]

Øyvind Pålshaugen

Introduction

In the wake of Habermas' works, what is termed respectively *theoretical discourse* and *practical discourse* have been conceptualised and defined in a number of ways (Habermas 1994; Benhabib 1992; Elliot 2005). Inspired by this discussion, I have suggested a very simple, pragmatic way of describing the main distinction between theoretical and practical discourse. To have theoretical knowledge of something means to *understand* it. To make practical changes of something means to *do* something with it. On this simple basis the distinction between theoretical discourse and practical discourse may be presented in one simple formulation: a *theoretical discourse is undertaken in order to understand* something, while a *practical discourse is undertaken in order to do* something. On the basis of this distinction, I have tried to show that the split in the discourse on organisations (organisation theory), between a theoretical and practical discourse, has had a few unintended and unnoticed consequences concerning the style of writing organisation theory (Pålshaugen 2004, 2006).

Because this splitting of the discourse on organisations into a practical and a theoretical discourse is largely unacknowledged, a certain style of writing has emerged, where organisation theory is written as if the addressee is *both* some general actor *and* other organisation theories (or theorists). On the basis of this presumption of a "double addressee", the predominant belief has also emerged that a comprehensive theory of organisation is inherently actionable. The connected belief that working out comprehensive theoretical frameworks is a necessary condition for undertaking organisation studies is not limited to the field of organisational research. It is predominant in most fields of research.

My concern is that this style of writing has produced a discourse on organisations that is very rich in general perspectives and concepts. It nevertheless remains too poor in content. Viewed from the experiences and perspectives of action re-

---

1 This chapter has been written as part of the strategic research programme (2003-2007) at the WRI, Oslo.

search, this paucity seems to be due to the restricted scope of methods applied in organisation studies, and the "thin" and small amount of data that result from it. Thus, to the question of how knowledge and experience from action research may contribute to the improvement of organisation theory, my conclusion has been this: for the time being, the most important contributions from action research to the discourse on organisations will be to make organisation theory become subject of a criticism that may provoke changes in the style of writing organisation theory. The critical question to be posed is this: Maybe the theoretical framework of organisation theory works to situate organisational research "outside" the real dynamic of organisations?

As a matter of fact, this question is a recurrent one within the discourse on organisation theory, albeit in a slightly different way. Usually, the question is raised in a way that does not question theoretical frameworks as such. Rather, the theoretical frameworks that are known *hitherto* are questioned or accused of missing essential parts of the real complexity of organisations, for not being able to grasp them or discover them at all, etc. This questioning of the theoretical frameworks available within the discourse of organisation theory is usually part of launching some *new* theoretical framework. Pointing at the shortcomings of the existing frameworks also means pointing at the relevance and legitimacy of a *coming* framework, namely the new one that oneself takes part in advocating.

Nevertheless, some frameworks are no doubt better than others. And it is not possible – or even wise – to say in advance that any new theoretical framework in organisation theory will have to be marked by the kind of problematic features I have outlined above. Perhaps I just happen to have read too much outdated organisation theory? Or, to turn the coin, perhaps I'm not sufficiently updated on new developments in organisation theory? In fact, my main thesis is that the shortcomings I have diagnosed concerning contemporary organisation theory are due to the limitations in methods rather than the proliferation of theories. Nevertheless, it might of course happen that some new theoretical framework can pave the way – or even require – methods that are more successful in bringing the real events and dynamic of organisational life into the discourse of organisation theory. For these reasons it may be appropriate to consider a few examples of organisation studies undertaken on the basis of one of the recently emerging approaches within organisation theory.

A good choice may be an approach explicitly developed in order to cope better with the real complexity of organisations than most established approaches, namely the so-called actor-network theory.[2] I have picked an anthology entitled

---

2   Another choice might have been the "complexity theory" developed by P. Stacey (cf. Stacey 2007). I have chosen the actor-network theory because that framework appears to be a more broadly applied approach than the "school" of Stacey.

Actor-network theory and organizing (Czarniawska & Hernes 2005a), containing empirical studies of organisations. According to the back cover presentation, this is a book in which

> European and American scholars apply actor-network theory in the study of various aspects of organization, including technology, organisational change, routines, virtual organization, strategy, power, market mechanisms, consumer behaviour public administration and knowledge management.

I have selected three articles quite different in aim and scope, but whose main focus is at the *organisational* level. The authors apply the framework of actor-network theory in order to better grasp and understand dynamic and complex processes within and across organisations. By examining three different studies, it may be possible to judge more specifically the editors' claim (on the back cover) about the benefits of actor-network theory as a framework for organisation studies: "Actor-network theory (ANT) is rapidly making its mark as a practical, challenging and intriguing tool for studying organization. Its unique approach to connecting people, artifacts, institutions and organizations enables it to shed light on complexities that so far have escaped works in organisation theory." An approach that aims to catch what has hitherto escaped organisation studies is exactly what we need. To find out whether this promise is kept, and in what way, we have to look into the texts. But since I cannot presume that all readers are well acquainted with actor-network theory, I will very briefly present some key perspectives and key terms, before taking a closer look at the articles I have chosen as examples of applying actor-network theory as an approach to organisation theory.

The perhaps most original – and no doubt one of the most attractive – features of the actor-network theory is that networks are not regarded as something which exist only among subjects or social entities. Even objects of any kind, be they tangible like machines or non-tangible like the content of documents, may be enrolled as part of a network. Thus the term "heterogeneous network" – networks may be made up by subjects, tangible objects and virtual objects alike. The conventional distinction between social and technical entities is deconstructed. Thus, also, the term "quasi-object": subjects and symbolic and virtual phenomena are usually not termed "objects". But with actor-network theory the static, ontological question of what something *is* has been replaced (or complemented) by the more dynamic question of how something works, functions or is used. The term quasi-object is coined to express that the phenomenon in question is *real* and thus has an objective existence, without necessarily being an object in the traditional sense of this term.

This short sketch of the anti-ontological ontology of actor-network theory might also ease the understanding of a third key term in actor-network theory: actant(s). Due to the relative novelty of action-network theory, both in time and

235

in perspective, its vocabulary has not yet been assimilated within the community of organisation theory. The vocabulary still bears sign of a certain tribal language. Thus, the term "actant" is briefly explained in the introduction to the anthology. It will be even briefer here.

In their introduction to the book, the editors quote the French semiologist Greimas, who coined the term in a different context as part of his structural analyses of literary works and narratives in general. According to Greimas, an actant is "that which accomplishes or undergoes an act" throughout a narrative. Greimas' project was to analyse the structural constituents of narratives. Different constellations of such constituents may make up different kinds of narratives, which from a structural point of view may be regarded as different narrative programmes. In such narratives, the grammatical subject is not necessarily a person. As an example we may consider the following utterances: "the wind blew him away"; "a tree fell over him"; "he cut down the tree"; "the wind blew down the tree".

From these examples we see that the subject that accomplishes an act in one sentence undergoes an act in others. The grammatical subject (of the sentence in a narrative) is not necessarily a character that acts, and therefore Greimas replaced the term "character" with the term "actant":

This replacement of words highlights the process of actants changing roles throughout a narrative: an actant may acquire a character and become and actor or may remain an object of some actor's action. Narrative programmes become chained to one another in logical succession, thus forming a *narrative trajectory*" (Czarniawska & Hernes 2005b: 8).

Thus, the term actant applies not only to human beings, but also to animals, objects or concepts.

Actor-network Theory and Organisational Routines

The brief introduction to the vocabulary of actor-network theory should suffice to facilitate my exposition of the three articles I have subjected to a closer reading. I start with the article "Organizational Routines and the Macro-Actor" (Feldman & Pentland 2005), which examines organisational routines from the perspective of actor-network theory (by adherents abbreviated ANT, following mainstream contemporary organisation theory in preferring the economics of expression at the expense of the aesthetics of expression). The authors find that "[o]rganizational routines are particularly well suited for actor-network theory analysis because it allows them to be seen as quasi-objects, consisting of heterogeneous networks of human and physical actants" (Feldman & Pentland 2005: 91).

236

I have already mentioned that the ANT vocabulary is not quite easily accessible for "outsiders" – and apparently it is not even for insiders. The authors of the article on organisational routines declare at the beginning of their article that "[a]s newcomers to ANT, we have experienced some difficulties becoming comfortable with the terminology. We may have created (translated?) our own private interpretation of ANT to suit our purposes. Before proceeding, it is, therefore, useful to articulate how we are using the terminology", (Feldman & Pentland 2005: 92). The authors touch upon an issue more far-reaching than they seem to be aware of, and a few comments are required.

As we know, it is hardly possible to use any vocabulary without also interpreting it. Wisely enough, the authors mention the risk of "private" interpretations. But why worry? Isn't this a risk run by anyone publishing interpretations of any subject? Both yes – and no! No, because by making their interpretations *public* they, like all scientists, prevent their interpretations from staying *private*. On the other hand, yes! The authors' understanding of "interpretation" is too limited if they believe that their *explanation* of their terms will constitute their interpretation. Their interpretation is not mainly provided by their explicit definitions. The way they use their terms throughout the text, in their specific analyses and reasoning, is more important.

For those of us who still find the actor-network theory difficult to grasp, the authors' experience with it should have a calming effect: "As we have struggled with the complexities of ANT, we have been inexorably led to the conclusion that it's really rather simple" (Feldman & Pentland 2005: 92). Accordingly, they present their interpretations in admittedly quite simple terms:

First, actants can be anything – humans, machines or just symbolic references to abstractions (such as "our culture" or "our hiring process"). Second, actors have projects and interests – things they are trying to do. And finally, actants get enrolled (translated) whenever an actor mentions (or invokes or refers to) the actant as part of planning, performing or accounting for their projects. We found it necessary to preserve a distinction between actants (which can be anything) and actors (who have projects we can tell stories about and, hence, relative stability)" (ibid.).

After this presentation of what Feldman & Pentland consider the most essential terms of actor-network theory, we now must look at their use of this vocabulary, i.e. how it is used to improve our understanding of organisational routines.

The authors start by presenting their general perspective on organisational routines, developed more fully in an earlier book (Feldman & Pentland 2003). Organisational routines have two parts: "an ostensive part, which is the abstract summary of the routine, and a performative part, which consists of the diverse collection of specific activities (performances) that carry out the routine" (Feldman & Pentland

2005: 91). Their point – or ambition – is to show that "[r]ecasting the ostensive-performative distinction in the language of ANT gives us new insights into the construction of organisational routines, their role as macro-actors and their power" (ibid.).

Next, they distinguish between the *definition* of organisational routines and the *conceptualisation* of them. They agree with the most common ways of defining organisational routines, namely as repetitive, recognisable patterns of interdependent actions, carried out by multiple actors. But this agreement is not the main thing: "Conceptualizing routines is different from defining them, however, and there is more divergence in conceptualizations than in definition" (Feldman & Pentland 2005: 91). Referring to Nelson and Winter (1982), they state that "[o]ne common conceptualization likens organizational routines to individual skills" (Feldman & Pentland 2005: 92). This way of conceptualising routines emphasises the iterative, tacit and automatic aspects of routines. But the *real practices* of performing routines get hidden in a "black box'; the real practices literally become covered by this conceptualisation, according to the authors. Thus, one of their purposes is to

show how the ANT perspective helps us open the black box and understand the relationship between the performative and ostensive aspects of routines. Specifically, we suggest that the ostensive aspect as represented through a narrative enrols performances and the combination becomes a routine. These routines, in turn, become the building blocks of both organizations and organizational fields. Narratives, again, play a central role" (Feldman & Pentland 2005: 92).

To accomplish this narrative programme they first have to take a few analytical steps, by presenting the vocabulary of actor-network theory. I already quoted from the beginning of their presentation, where we were told that the ANT vocabulary is simple. It stays simple as the authors continue their presentation of some key ANT terms:

The relationship between actors and actants is also rather straightforward. People refer to ideas, things and each other as they go about planning, performing and explaining their work. These references occur in the context of narratives about the work ("I sorted the applicant pool by test score..."). This much is daily life. The first analytical leap occurs when we realize that these narratives create actants and the association between them (Feldman & Pentland 2005: 93).

In the example within the parentheses, referring to a routine or procedure of hiring people, the applicants are made into actants, because, according to the narrative, they are acted upon. And "by invoking actants as parts of narratives, people create associations between them" (ibid.).

Their terminological narrative, then, continues through two more "analytical leaps". The second analytical leap consists in the creation of actor-networks. If the narratives have commonalities, the

> associations between actants become stronger and more stable. These stronger and more stable actants become actors endowed with programs. [...] A third analytical leap occurs around the construction of "macro-actors". [...] In this leap, the many become one. Put simply, macro-actors are actor-networks that coalesce in such a way that the whole is seen as having projects. Hobbes' Leviathan is the quintessential macro-actor, as mentioned many times by authors in this volume (ibid.).

Having completed their terminological exercise, the authors can now reformulate their view on organisational routines as consisting of two parts or aspects, the ostensive and the performative:

> The ostensive aspect of a routine provides a way of connecting (translating) specific performances into what we have called an organizational routine. The ostensive aspect of a routine is an idealized narrative about the routine. [... However,] this narrative must not be confused with the activities or performances that it describes. Without the performances, the narrative makes no sense but without the narrative the performances are not connected. The narrative is what makes the performances cohere (ibid.).

The authors have now reached their "turning point" – the point where they turn to the real phenomena, the practical routines, and answer their own question posed in a sub-title (p. 95): *Why use ANT to understand routines?* They answer by reminding us that what is to be understood is the *real dynamic* of organisations. This is exactly what I've been looking for in organisational studies. How, then, do they conceptualise this real dynamic? One important aspect is that, to them, organisations

> are a sea of ongoing, over-lapping interdependent performances. By performance, we mean specific actions carried out by specific people in specific times and places. Performances are situated actions. In our view, performances are the foundation. Performances are the raw material for translations. They provide material that we can construct into narratives (Feldman & Pentland 2005: 95).

This emphasis on performances does not make the authors neglect narratives. In their perspective, reformulated in actor-network terms, they maintain that it is "the narrative that holds the performances together" (ibid.). Exactly this ANT perspective, emphasising the mutual relation between performances and narratives as constituting organisational routines, makes the authors see how easily one mistakes a stream of words for a stream of phenomena: "the narrative that binds together various performances has been mistaken for the routines and the performances have been overlooked" (Feldman & Pentland 2005: 96). The authors do not make this mistake, rather they realise that the actor-network theory

is particularly helpful in clarifying the ostensive aspect of routines. We see the ostensive aspects of a routine as a kind of abstract narrative – a typical story about how work is typically performed [...] In contrast to the traditional story, which suggests that organizational routines are simply followed or reproduced, our theory points to the central importance of subjectivity, agency and power (Feldman & Pentland 2005: 97).

Again, the advantage of the ANT perspective is in the combined perspective on performances and narratives: "organizational routines are powerful not because of any single performance by any particular actant but because of the network of performances that the ostensive aspect binds together across space and time" (Feldman & Pentland 2005: 98).

So far, so good, we might say. But still, we have been presented only to a certain improved general, theoretical framework for analysing and understanding organisational routines. They have not yet provided any concrete analyses, any specific examples. The authors implicitly seem to realise this, since they explicitly state that to understand their perspective on "the various ways that organizational routines are implicated in constructing macro-actors [...] it is easiest to take a specific example" (ibid.). Their example, a hiring routine, has already been mentioned. But what they present as an example of a hiring routine in practice is viewed quite distant from practice. It turns out to be a very brief re-presentation of an example presented in the subsequent article by T. Hernes in the same book.

Disappointingly, their re-telling of Hernes' story tells us very little new concerning their use of the ANT perspective on routines, neither in how the empirical material is presented by the example nor in how the theoretical perspective is tentatively exposed to it. Thus, their example does not show the usefulness of the ANT perspective in understanding routines in a better way, beyond what is already presented in general terms. Actually, my critical reading of how their example of a hiring routine works is indirectly confirmed by the authors in their summary of what the example tells us:

As this example shows, the routine takes on a life of its own that requires certain things of us. The analogy is perhaps to something like a power grid that we recognize as a macro-actor because it exerts influence over our actions. If we don't do what it requires, we suffer consequences (Feldman & Pentland 2005: 99).

This is a general insight, ok, but it is very far from being a *new* insight. Luckily, their article doesn't stop here. We are offered a second example, this time about the relationship between organisational routines and the whole organisation. Their focus on the organisation as a whole does not imply that the organisation is considered a closed entity. They emphasise that the organisation considered as a macro-actor is "leaky": both the organisational routines and the performances not associated with organisational routines transcend the boundaries of the organisation. The main point at this level of analysis is that the organisational routines themselves are turned into actants by the ways they are bound to the various kinds of narratives generated within the organisation. Examples provided are narratives about the boss (e.g. narratives of his/her preferences, likes and dislikes), about the mission of the organisation, about the stakeholders, the culture, etc. Also, at this level of analysis the relationships between the narratives and the organisational routines are mutually constitutive, but the narratives are made up by a more differentiated set of actors, who have quite different kinds of relations to the actual performances of routines. To demonstrate the usefulness of these perspectives, the authors choose an example of accounting routines.

Again they re-tell stories told in organisational studies made by others. One of the studies is about how two different accountability routines vie for domination in the same organisation. This competition is rooted in two different narratives about how the company should operate in order to be successful. Both narratives focused on the same three main issues, albeit with a different accent: flexibility, productivity and innovation. The story from this study is presented so briefly that I can hardly do anything but copy it:

> The narrative promoted by the CEO held that flexibility should be kept to a minimum because it is expensive, that productivity could be developed by subcontractors and that innovations should be integrated into the production system and standardized as quickly as possible. The narrative promoted by the factory manager [...] held that flexibility is in continuous demand by customers, that new technology supports productivity within the firm allowing for "productive flexibility" and that standardization is not possible in a constantly changing market (Feldman & Pentland 2005: 101-102).

In short, this story turns out to be nothing more than just another general version of a very common story, well-known to everybody who has an average level of knowledge from doing organisation studies of companies. The use of the ANT terminology adds practically nothing to the story, neither on the general, theoretical nor on the specific, empirical level. They do demonstrate that these kinds of stories may be retold in ANT terms, but not that this re-telling provides any new insights. My negative judgment is once again confirmed by the authors' general conclusion. Based on the above example, and another equally well-known example (from another sector than private industry), they conclude like this: "Understanding the relationship between organizational routines and organizations in this way enables us to see more clearly that specific routines are not inherent to the organization and need not be taken for granted" (Feldman & Pentland 2005: 102-103).

This conclusion might of course be considered good news. But it is far from new. Again, we are left with just another example of what is to be regarded as common knowledge within the discourse of organisation theory – and to a large extent also within the community of (experienced) practitioners. For my own part, it is still too early to conclude on Feldman and Pentland's attempt to use actor-network theory to improve our understanding of organisational routines. As they say:

> So far, we have considered the aggregation of performances into routines, and routines into organization. But there is another sense in which organizational routines are involved in the construction of macro-actors. In this view, organizational routines are the glue that holds many organizations together in an organizational field. [...] It is in this sense that routines become part of something even more powerful than the organizations described in the previous section" (Feldman & Pentland 2005: 103).

They draw the meaning of "organisational field" from the so-called "new institutionalism" perspective. An organisational field is not only constituted by organisations that interact with each other. Even organisations that belong to the same category of organisations, within e.g. the banking industry, higher education, or day-care centres, may be said to constitute a kind of organisational field:

> Organizations within this kind of field do not share routines directly with one another but they are united by the similarity in their routines and, indeed, may be required to have similar routines in order to be considered part of the field. [...] An organization considered to be part of the banking industry, for instance, will need to have routines for accepting and disbursing funds, for borrowing, for investing and so forth" (Feldman & Pentland 2005: 103/104).

To show what this means more specifically, they summarise an organisational history of the US broadcasting industry (Leblebici et al.1991). This study looks at organisations engaged in similar tasks, and according to Feldman and Pentland, it demonstrates the influence of organisational routines by showing how organisational fields change as the routines performed change. The study identifies three distinct configurations of organisational fields between 1920 and 1965. The most important part is the transformation from the second to the third configuration. This happens through a change from local stations sending programmes produced by networks also in control of advertising (the main source of income), to local stations producing local programmes supported by local spot advertising. Also, the practice of financing radio stations through selling records in addition to selling advertising became standard practice in this third period (1950-1965).

Having summarised this story, the authors claim that "[t]his summary focuses on some of the changes in *practices or routines* that define the transition from one field to another" (Feldman & Pentland 2005: 105-106). I have italicised the words *"practices or routines"*, because this re-naming of the "practices" into "routines" re-frames the organisational history of the US broadcast industry into a story that is meant to demonstrate, by a specific example, the usefulness of the ANT framework. But the legitimacy of this move can indeed be questioned, in particular because the authors themselves immediately add to the quote at the beginning of this paragraph, that:

Other practices (such as network contracting) were also important and provided the context for the practices described here. There are also *numerous contextual features* such as changes in technology (e.g. the rise of television) that are an important part of the story and are described well in the article by Leblebici et al. (ibid. [my italics]).

Thus, their conclusion that "[t]his portrayal of one particular organisational field suggests how powerful the *practices* of such a field can be" (ibid. [my italics]) is quite proper, but that does not justify renaming all these heterogeneous practices as *routines*, to make the story fit the framework of the actor-network theory. Neither can their re-telling of the US broadcasting history justify their conclusion that "[t]he role that organizational routines and networks of routines play as an actant in constructing organizational fields makes routines more important than they are often thought to be" (ibid.).

In the concluding section of their article, the authors correctly repeat that their primary focus has been on understanding how organisational routines contribute to the creation of various macro-actors, including organisational routines themselves, organisations and organisational fields. Also, the overall general conclusion they draw from their efforts that "routines have a potential to be a much more volatile part of organisational life than they are often thought to be" may be correct enough. But they still have not answered the question of why actor-network theory should be used to understand organisational routines. Thus, we have to search for more evidence for the claimed advantages of applying ANT to organisation studies.

Actor-network Theory Compared to Other Frameworks – an Empirical Test

One obvious place to search is the contribution of P. B. Hägglund, entitled "Explaining Macro-Actors in Practice". This is because the aim of his article is to make three different analyses of the very same case – a case of economic decline in a large company that sold qualified services to a large range of customers – by using three different explanatory frameworks: a *structural* framework, an *interpretive* framework and the framework of action-network theory. His ambition is to demonstrate how different frameworks bring different aspects of the organisational phenomenon into focus and thereby affect the quality of our understanding. Hägglund shows quite convincingly how the use of actor-network theory may provide an understanding of what happens that is not just complementary to the other frameworks he tries out, but even better. It is better not only because it is more specific, but because it focuses on the most relevant aspects and in a specific way.

However, the positive outcome concerning the use of the action-network theory in this case is largely due to the lack of qualities in the two other frameworks he tries out. Hägglund himself suggests that the structural framework is partly outdated because of the changes that have taken place within business organisations (Hägglund 2005: 258). The structural framework was developed mainly on the basis of organisational studies of "classical" industrial work organisations. Thus, it is indeed not very well suited to analyse a service industry company like the one that is the subject of his research. Nor is the interpretive framework he explicitly borrows from Silverman (1970) among those most "up-to-date". There exists in fact today a number of other, rather new theoretical approaches that are developed in order to analyse the service industry in particular, with all its particularities compared to e.g. classical industry (Berry & Parasuraman 1993). If Hägglund had compared the use of an ANT framework with any of these frameworks, the similarities between the frameworks might have been more striking than the differences. His comparison appears a bit like comparing one fresh fruit with two canned fruits, and concluding that the fresh fruit is the best one.

The *usefulness* of theoretical analyses is a core question to Hägglund. Not only their usefulness for a theoretical understanding, but their usefulness to practitioners: "to describe organisational action in a way that can be useful for managers, employees and their observers" (Hägglund 2005: 254). This is particularly interesting in our context, since he thereby explicitly maintains – or invokes – the ambition of creating actionable theory.

In fact, Hägglund makes the usefulness of theory into the main criterion for judging the three theoretical frameworks. He is explicit in rejecting the criteria that adhere to the theoretical discourse on organisations, which he portrays as a question of what we can *learn by* applying some theoretical framework to the study of some particular organisation(s) – that is, what new knowledge we can get. For researchers this is a very legitimate criterion, but according to Hägglund, *practitioners* may view it differently: "practitioners do not necessarily have learning at the top of their list of priorities when evaluating organisation theories" (Hägglund

2005: 263). According to Hägglund, people in organisations want to influence organisational action, and what they want from a theory is to help them accomplish such efforts.

Hägglund's point seems reasonable, also when he pursues his point a bit further, and adds that "[w]hat they seek is an influence that goes beyond themselves, and the ability to control objects and events at a distance" (ibid.). However, it is questionable to conclude from these reasonable arguments that the practitioners "want to be an important element of a macro-actor, and an optimal theory is thus one that helps them accomplish this. In comparing these frameworks, I have therefore chosen to use this criterion" (ibid.). Hägglund simply presupposes the answer by the way he formulates the question. By conceptualising the needs of the practitioners in actor-network terms and *presupposing* that the practitioners want to be an important element of a macro-actor, it is hardly surprising that exactly this theoretical framework and vocabulary is judged to be most useful to practitioners.

Hägglund generously admits that both the structural and the interpretive frameworks may be partially helpful to practitioners: "the former teaches how to reach for power, the latter how to resist it" (Hägglund 2005: 266). However, if we want to see and understand more of the whole picture of which we are a part, actor-network theory is what we should look for:

ANT focuses on [...] emerging and potential macro-actors in the organisation, and shows how they are formed in interaction between various local actors. It also accommodates the ever-increasing presence of non-humans in the organisation [...]. Along with these two advantages is ANT's focus on connections which prompts the analyst to start in the part of the organisation that is most relevant (most well-connected) rather than (re-)producing the top-down view.[3] This means that the action-network theory offers up a flat image of the organisational world, where the analyst is able to identify the horizontal connections and thus see the organisational world more as the individual actor sees it. [...] ANT is therefore a framework that recreates an organisational landscape resembling the everyday representation of the practitioners – at all levels of the organisation" (Hägglund 2005:266-267).

As we can see, Hägglund's reasons for judging action-network theory advantageous are not bad, and to some extent he has proved that these are the foci of actor-network theory in his preceding analysis of his case. But he totally overlooks that this is *his* judgment, not the judgment of any practitioner. He makes his judgment *on behalf of* the practitioners. We have not heard any single word from any practitioner on this issue, neither has Hägglund presented any empirical material showing the fate of actor-network theory within practical discourses of organisations, the discourse of the practitioners. Thus, the practitioners in fact become

---

3   That is, the view of the structural framework [ØP].

mere actants in his *theory of the practicality* of the ANT framework. By adding that "at the same time, the framework has the rigour and the precision demanded by the researchers" (ibid.), Hägglund confirms that he operates well within a style of writing organisation theory based on the presumption of the "double address-ee". This presumption makes researchers believe that the usefulness of organisation theory for practical discourses of work life can be judged adequately from within the theoretical discourse of organisation theory.

Our investigation of Hägglund's article as a second example of applying actor-network theory to organisation studies leaves us with the conclusion that yes, it is obviously useful for this purpose. But on whether this framework has particular advantages compared to other *contemporary* frameworks, more advanced than those chosen by Hägglund for his comparison, we still lack an answer – apart from the assurances made by the adherents of this approach. Finally, on the usefulness of this framework and its vocabulary for practitioners, we can at least formulate the challenge in a new way: so far, the practitioners exist mainly as actants within the framework of actor-network theory, they are not yet actors making use of it.

Actor-network Theory Compatible with Action Research Practice?

One critical question guiding this investigation of some examples of applying the actor-network theory to organisational studies is whether the framework of organisation theory in effect may work to keep organisational research "outside" the real events taking place in organisations. The reason for posing this question was my diagnosis of the current situation in the field of organisation studies: a seemingly unlimited growth of theoretical frameworks for interpreting data, combined with a limited repertoire of methods for generating the data.

Actor-network theory may not quite fit into this diagnosis. As the editors of *Actor-Network Theory and Organizing* put it in their introductory chapter, they have searched for contributions following ANT's precepts of epistemological pragmatism and ontological relativism. This means "in other words, less fuss about 'the method', but greater caution when apportioning the world into inherited categories" (Czarniawska & Hernes 2005: 13). In this respect, the contribution from David Vickers and Steve Fox is particularly interesting. Their article is based on a research method where the researchers are even more involved in the organisational events than is usually the case in action research projects. More accurately, one of the researchers worked as an HR manager in the company where he also (with the knowledge of his colleagues) conducted his research. He actively participated in the events of the post-acquisition process at the chemical plant that is the field of their study. The combination of actor-network theory and a method that makes the researchers experience the events from within, is a new combination. Thus, their contribution deserves particular attention.

The article of Vickers & Fox is entitled "Powers in a Factory". A business unit of a chemical plant, located at Burnsland in Scotland, had been sold (by a chemical company in the UK) to a transnational, US-based company, and a new site manager from the US arrived at Burnsland. Among his tasks was to execute the strategy decided upon by the US company, to rationalise production, which meant the closure of three out of nine production lines at Burnsland. Understandably, this was considered bad news among management and employees at Burnsland.

The article tells the story of how the specific controversies between the local operations manager, the HR manager and the local union representative on the one side, and the new site manager on the other side, played out. The local press, the local council and a local parliament member (MP) also figure in the story, partly as actors and partly as actants in this controversy. "The locals" won this controversy, as becomes clear from this short report on the result: "The three Burnsland production lines remained open for many months longer than the intended 'strategic closure' date and this delay enabled commercial managers to secure more product transfers to, and more investment in, Burnsland's remaining lines" (Vickers & Fox 2005: 136).

Against this background, the authors want to use elements of the ANT framework in order to understand the complexity of this organisation. They focus in particular on the notion of *core sets*. This concept was originally defined by Collins in his analysis of scientific controversies, designating the body of people involved (Collins 1981). Within actor-network theory this concept has been criticised for being too narrow, and the authors adopt a wider concept of the core set. They draw on Michael's concept of the core set and his account of the kinds of techniques used in the controversies played out in the power games among those involved (Michael 1996). These techniques they conceptualise in terms like *demonisation, demarcating rationality, intellectual and technological criteria* [of superiority], etc. These are different techniques for degrading and fighting your opponents in a controversy. In addition, the authors also make use of the conceptual apparatus in Callon's work on techno-economic network and irreversibility (Callon 1991) useful for their purposes.

Having presented their conceptual framework, the authors continue with some remarks on their method. One author participated fully in the power game. The authors put it like this: "Our research provides insight through fully immersed participant observation by one of the authors" (Vickers & Fox 2005: 132). Reading their story, however, the reader may realise that the expression "participant observation" appears a bit like a euphemism. The HR manager was active in the controversy for a period of two years, and his activities indeed influenced the result. Being aware that this kind of method may be controversial, the authors present arguments for regarding it as advantageous for research rather than as disadvantageous.

They start by reminding us that "no one has real-time, panoramic or analytical access to the 'real'" (ibid.). Furthermore, they claim that no insider can view the full context of the situation of which one is a part, nor can any outsider. Different actors will view reality in different ways from different angles, and the reality "as such" is accessible to no one. Thus there is no such thing as decontextualised knowledge. The question is rather how to contextualise the situation in a way that makes you aware of those aspects of the situation that are crucial for creating an appropriate understanding of it. To answer this question, the authors borrow the example of a canoeist paddling down the river from L. Suchman's (1987) *Plans and Situated Action*:

> Seen from the vantage point of the canoeist in the midst of the action, what is seen is not so much a rock and a boulder in the river but an opportunity and a danger: a way of going forward which has risks to the self and to others. Seen from the riverbank, the scene looks very different, picturesque maybe, the product of certain erosions perhaps. None of these views of contexts is impartial, but the canoeist's viewpoint is best for understanding the practicalities of her/his situated action (Vickers & Fox 2005: 133).

This way of arguing is similar to my arguments presented in the introduction to this article, on the differences between a discourse that is undertaken in order to *understand* something and one that is undertaken in order to *do* something. But in the present context, in which the question of the function of theoretical frameworks in general and the ANT framework in particular is the issue, the arguments presented by Vickers & Fox may add some new insight. What the example (or the parable) of the canoeist shows is that his *practical action frame* appears to be quite as important for understanding a situation as the *theoretical framework* applied to it. Different vocabularies and different conceptual systems make us see or recognise different aspects; that is true. Nevertheless, it is very likely that differences between perspectives derived *from within the specific, practical action frame* versus the perspectives derived *from some general, theoretical framework* are of greater importance regarding how to understand a phenomenon adequately, than the differences caused by applying different theoretical frameworks.

As a matter of fact, this thesis seems to be confirmed also by the article of Vickers & Fox. When they move *from* their initial remarks on their theoretical framework and method *to* the description of their case study, they describe their case almost without using any ANT terms at all. Although, as they say, the case is described in "broad terms", the story is told quite well. From an obviously overwhelming amount of details and experiences they have been good at picking those most relevant for making the reader understand the results of the controversies at Burnsland, and for understanding the complex patterns of relations and networks formed in the course of the events. This does not imply that the authors, including Vickers, who worked as HR manager, have not had any help from their acquaintance with actor-network theory in their work with coming to an adequate understanding of the case. The concept of the core set, and their differentiated understanding of this concept, obviously has been helpful in structuring their description of the case – this concept has structured their *plot*, so to speak.

But it is even more obvious that there would have been no such story to tell, if not for the direct experience from within the events by one of the authors. Without being one of the actors of the *core set* in this particular case, the particularities of this case, and the kind of patterns they form, would never have come to the fore as specifically as they do. The kind of experiences made, rather than the kind of concepts applied to them, is the reason why the complexity of this case does not escape the authors. The story is told not only from the "view" of the canoeist, but from his experiences. This is also the reason why the story can be told in a quite common vocabulary, far from being stuffed with ANT terms or the vocabulary of any other particular theoretical framework. In this respect it is significant that first when the story has been told once, in a "plain" way, some elements of the story become "viewed" through some of the concepts of the actor-network theory. This is done in a separate section sub-titled "The discussion" (the last section before the final "Conclusion").

In this section, the authors demonstrate that the concepts characterising the various techniques[4] used in core set controversies fit very well to what took place in the controversies at Burnsland. But this demonstration only shows that these elements of the ANT vocabulary are useful as categories for classifying the kind of actions and events that took place. It does not demonstrate that these concepts are imperative for becoming aware of these events or for understanding them. The point is that the undertaking of these classifications in a separate section does not add any new insights to what was already told in the preceding section, regardless of the authors' claims. As any reader can confirm from reading this section, we are just told – or shown – that even the events at Burnsland may work as empirical material to illustrate some of the concepts of actor-network theory. But we are not shown that these concepts were imperative in order to understand this empirical material. Thus, the conclusion is close at hand that in this case it is the *method* used by the authors that helps them enrich the ANT perspective, rather than that the ANT perspective helps them enrich their analyses of the events that took place over some years at Burnsland.

---

4   Cf. the earlier mentioned concepts of *demonisation, demarcating rationality*, etc.

Applied Actor-network Theory versus Critical Theory

The conclusion to be drawn from our investigation of three examples using actor-network theory as a new approach to organisation studies is that this approach does not seem to represent an exception to the rule. Firstly, all the three articles are written in a way in which the empirical material serves to give sense to the general concepts of the ANT framework. However, the use of these concepts does not serve to generate a new and even better and richer understanding of organisational phenomena than other contemporary approaches. Secondly, as we have seen in all three examples, their style of writing maintains the fiction of the double addressee of organisation theory. This fiction in turn maintains the illusion that organisation theory can be inherently actionable. This illusion serves both to legitimise the inherent abstractness of organisation studies and the neglect of the need to connect to practical discourses within organisational life if knowledge is to be made actionable.

To those who find it far-fetched to draw such general conclusions on the basis of just three examples from just one single anthology, I have no objections. I will be more than happy for counter-examples. To change my conclusion will cause no problem – the problem is to change the state of the art in organisation theory. The common features I have pointed to and criticised above are common to more than these three examples. They are common not only to more of the articles in the same anthology and to other organisational studies undertaken from an ANT approach, but common to innumerable organisational studies undertaken from any of the contemporary theoretical approaches in organisation theory. This practice with theoretical frameworks and style of writing can usually be recognised already by reading the abstract. Usually, they go like this: Hitherto this or that phenomenon has been neglected, overlooked or poorly dealt with in organisation theory; here comes an article that is written in order to make up for this shortcoming; it is based on a (new) theoretical framework that is particularly fit to catch and deal with this topic – and *voila*: a new piece of empirically based and theoretically informed knowledge is ready to be put in its place in the virtual jigsaw puzzle of organisation theory.

Considering the amount of energy and work invested in the production of all these jigsaw pieces, it remains a puzzle to me how little work and energy is invested in puzzling about the fact that organisation theory constitutes neither one nor many such jigsaw puzzles. Rather, the discourse on organisation theory is made of a number of more or less loosely connected discourses, within which the various images of what makes up the jigsaw puzzle that one's own text is intended to be a part of are (re)produced – a reproduction that takes place by the very way one's own text is written. This, of course, may give rise to the question of whether one's own text is written by oneself; a meaningless question to many, but not to those acquainted with actor-network theory. This style of writing is reproduced

250

through innumerable writing practices by actors who have writing projects. The texts under production may be regarded as actants following many but also quite similar narrative trajectories which are constituted by series of programmes[5] along the text's way from incomplete thoughts to a completed publication. Finally, these programmes serve the formation and stabilisation of the production of texts into networks of actants who take the shape of actor-networks, whose products carry so many similarities in the style of writing, due to the similarity in programmes, that it makes them appear as being written by a macro-actor.

This somewhat improvised use of the actor-network theory vocabulary to diagnose the dominant style of writing in organisation theory is not only meant to provoke new thoughts about all the questionable procedures that the production of scientific texts are embedded in and imprinted by, without really being questioned by those who write these texts. It is also meant as a combination of a tribute and a critical remark to those who make use of this vocabulary in their endeavours to create not just new knowledge, but critical insights. No doubt, many of the perspectives, concepts and insights produced by the intellectual endeavours associated with actor-network theory are quite original, express critical insights and still represent unexplored possibilities for renewing and improving the social sciences, also within the network of discourses called organisation theory. Therefore, it is particularly disappointing that so many of the attempts to apply this approach to organisation theory so often result not only in rather trivial insights, but also in trivialising the insights that have been presented in the original works where this approach was developed. Why has the attempt to establish ANT as an approach to organisation theory imprinted this approach as much by the established regime of writing organisation theory as by the writings from which it is inspired?

Instead of answering this question I will narrow it down a bit, in order to focus on an aspect that I think is one of the most critical in this respect. And this aspect is just about being critical, about the need for critical theorising, the need for some kind of *critical theory*. The writings of Bruno Latour, whose intellectual achievements have been decisive for the development of the actor-network theory, almost always seem to stem from a critical impetus – which is also why he appears as the main impetus behind the development of the ANT approach. Nothing escapes (t)his critical impetus, not even the adherents of the ANT approach. This may become clear from his introductory remark in a keynote speech at a workshop organised in 1997 to examine the past and in particular the future of this approach. The published version of his keynote is entitled "On recalling ANT", and it opens

---

5   The programmes are generated by editors, reviewers, teachers, supervisors, colleagues, technical procedures of journals and publishers, word programmes, rules of syntax, genre laws, etc.

with the following statement: "I will start by saying that there are four things that do not work with actor-network theory; the word actor, the word network, the word theory and the hyphen!" (Latour 1999:15).

Actually, the editors of *Actor-Network Theory and Organizing* quote this statement in their introductory chapter, at the end of a paragraph commenting the rather broad scope of various interpretations of what the expression actor-network theory designates. However, the editors do not appear to be driven by the same kind of critical impetus as Latour. They note that he expresses himself provocatively, and they also add the comment that "[o]ne might note that Latour never explained what was wrong with the hyphen, so we kept it" (Czarniawska & Hernes 2005: 10). But as a matter of fact Latour does, at least in the published version of this key note, and it requires no critical reading to discover what he says, he is very explicit about it. Latour comments on each of the four words and on the hyphen that connects the words "actor" and "network" into the expression "actor-network". When he arrives at the hyphen, Latour recalls that he has already commented upon it: "As I have indicated above, it [the hyphen] is an unfortunate reminder of the debate between agency and structure into which we never wanted to enter" (Latour 1999: 21). The earlier passage he alludes to is in fact more than just an indication:

> From day one, I objected to the hyphen because inevitably it would remind sociologists of the agency/structure cliché [...]. Most of the misunderstandings about ANT have come from this coupling of terms, one that is much too similar to the traditional divides of social theory (Latour 1999:16).

He goes on to elaborate his reasons for this objection to the hyphen, which comes down to the point that the intention with the term "actor-network" was not to present a new position or a new solution to the agency/structure problem in social theory – the aim was not to solve the problem, but rather to dissolve it:

> The original idea was not to occupy a position in the agency/structure debate, not even to *overcome* this contradiction. Contradictions, most of the time and especially when they are related to the modernist predicament, should not be overcome, but simply ignored or bypassed. But I agree that the hyphenated term made it impossible to see clearly the bypass operation that had been attempted (Latour 1999: 16).

As we can see, what Latour found to be wrong with the hyphen is rather obvious. Before commenting on the reasons why the editors may have missed this point, I will briefly present what Latour means with the "bypass operation", which is not obvious from the quotation above. This will also help to bring forth the literally more *critical* reasons why Latour worries so much about deleting the hyphen. A passage following later on in Latour's article suits my purpose well:

Actor and network – if we still want to use those terms – designates two faces of the same phenomenon, like waves and particles, the slow realization that the social is a certain type of circulation that can travel endlessly *without* ever encountering either the micro-level – there is never an interaction that is not framed – or the macro-level – there are only local summing up which produce either local totalities ('oligoptica') or total localities (agencies). To have transformed the social from what was a surface, a territory, a province of reality, into a circulation, is what I think has been the most useful contribution of ANT (Latour 1999:19).

The dissolution of the need for a concept of *structure*, by introducing the dynamic perspective of *circulation* in the sense of the quotation above, is what Latour considers the "bypass operation" undertaken by ANT: "may be the social possesses the bizarre property of not being made of agency and structure at all, but rather of being a *circulating* entity" (Latour 1999: 17).

Against this background, the reasons for Latour's objection to the hyphen become even clearer. According to him, the hyphen made it *impossible* to see clearly the bypass operation that had been attempted. The implication of this is that the term "actor-network" tends to lose its critical potential. Instead of turning the established debate on agency/structure down, as was the intention of the critical impetus behind launching this expression,[6] the debate just took another turn. The consequence is that the term "actor-network" never became the kind of *critical tool* that it was meant to be. This is more important to Latour than it seems to be for many of the adherents of ANT, because Latour never intended the terms and concepts he developed to end up as tools for creating a theory. Concepts should be *critical tools* that can be used on the one hand against those concepts of social science that are badly conceptualised (e.g. based on "false dichotomies"), and on the other hand as concepts that may help researchers come to understand the *specificity* of social phenomena.

As for the first of these aspects, concerning what concepts could achieve as critical tools, Latour's complaints about the fate of the term "network" is instructive. It once could be used as a critical tool, but not anymore.

While twenty years ago there was still some freshness in the term as a critical tool against notions as diverse as institution, society, nation-state and, more generally, any flat surface, it has lost its cutting edge and is now a pet notion of all those who want to modernize modernization (Latour 1999:15).

As for the second aspect, how to make use of concepts to capture the specificity of the phenomenon one tries to understand, Latour states very clearly that

---

6   The original French term was *acteur reseau* (cf. Law 1999: 5).

theory-building was never the purpose of his creation and use of concepts. Rather the other way round:

> Far from being a theory of the social or even worse an explanation of what makes society exert pressure on actors, it [ANT] always was, and this from its very inception (Callon and Latour, 1981), a very crude method to learn from the actors without imposing on them an *a priori* definition of their world-building capacities (Latour 1999: 20).

The quoted passages demonstrate clearly (as does the whole article) the *critical* dimension of Latour's writing. Rather than constructing new theories he tries to deconstruct the existing ones, and also to abolish or even demolish them – but always with the intention of making it easier for social scientists to get *access* to the events they try to come to a better understanding of by means of research. His critical impetus allows no exception for his own writings, and his own use of concepts: "I agree that we have not always been true to the original task, and that a great deal of our own vocabulary has contaminated our ability to let the actors build their own space [...]" (Latour 1999:20). He also realises that this critical dimension of ANT is not exclusive for this approach: "[...] ANT is merely one of the many anti-essentialist movements that seems to characterize the end of the century" (ibid.).

And he even goes a bit further, launching the more ultimate (self-)critical point that actor-network theory should not be regarded as a theory:

> But it [ANT] is also, like ethnomethodology, simply a way for the social scientist to access sites, a method and not a theory, a way to travel from one spot to the next, from one field to the next, not an interpretation of what actors do simply glossed in a different more palatable and more universalist language (Latour 1999:20/21).

The critical point Latour makes here, hits both the articles of Feldman & Pentland and of Vickers & Fox, as I have demonstrated above. But more important is that the critical remarks and points Latour puts forth throughout his short article reveal some significant differences between his project as regards the future of ANT and the project of the editors of the anthology on ANT and organising.

While the editors' project seems to be one of establishing ANT as a legitimate scientific approach within organisation theory, the project of Latour in his article is rather to de-legitimise the attempts to make ANT into an approach in its own right at all – for the reasons I have tried to show by quoting and commenting some passages from his text. Latour does not care about creating theories or approaches – he cares about creating a new, more specific and thus better understanding of those phenomena that catch his interest. The more general theoretical work that has to be undertaken in the course of the run is primarily working out a *critical* theory. Not in the sense of establishing some new kind of critical theory, but in the sense of writing texts that work as *critical interventions* in the scientific discourses he participates in. This critical aspect of his work is also what makes his style of writing very different from the style of writing that dominates organisation theory – including the articles collected in the anthology.

This is probably also why the editors seem to have missed Latour's critical point about the hyphen: if his text is read as a series of theoretical arguments and statements, many of his remarks may be calmly read as examples of his desire for making utterances in a provocative style – e.g. his introductory (and concluding) remarks about what is wrong with ANT. But if his text is read from a less theoretical and more practical point of view, namely as a series of attempts to make his text *work in practice*, as an intervention into a particular field of scientific discourse, his style of writing appears differently. It appears to be the rather successful result of a constant struggle against letting down neither his audience (readers) nor his critical impulses by the way he writes, the ways he tries to express his insights. This kind of struggle is indeed a personal one; any text will be imprinted by the author's struggle with the language of the text s/he is writing. If this struggle turns out successfully, the result will be a text imprinted by some kind of personal style of writing, or a personal signature, as in the case of Latour. If it turns out unsuccessfully, the result will be simply a bad writing style.

But the worst outcome is when there has been no struggling. In that case the text will not be imprinted by the person who wrote it, but rather by the style of writing that dominates the discourse of which the text is to become a part. In the case of organisation theory, this worst case unfortunately seems to be the most common case. Unfortunate not because it is absolutely required for any researcher to write publications in her/his own style – only outstanding researchers are able to stand out against the crowd – but because the contemporary style of writing organisation theory is imprinted by those questionable features I have presented and criticised above. Unfortunate also because the enterprise of organisation theory deserves a better fate – but luckily, fate may change.

Conclusion: Hopes for the Future

How, then, to change the fate of organisation theory? For obvious reasons there are no simple answers to this question, and no simple receipt for how to proceed. However, because the most obvious reasons are also those we tend to think of least, I will remind us of a few of them. Organisation theory, or the theoretical discourse on organisations, has to be considered a part of what is commonly designated as the field of organisation studies. Organisation theory is embedded in this field, and the fortune of organisation theory is highly dependent on the development of this field. Therefore, it seems apt to recall some main characteristics of this field. The characteristics I will highlight are truly "one man's impression", but this man is not me – it is one of the grand old men in this field, James G. March.

Recently, March put forth his judgment on the overall character of this field: "The field of organization studies is a large, heterogeneous field involving numerous enclaves having distinct styles, orientations and beliefs. It is integrated neither by a shared theory, nor by a shared perspective, nor even by a shared tolerance for multiple perspectives" (March 2007: 10). If this is the case, March continues, the field of organisation studies may be defined as a common field only by a definition that neglects this diversity. Thus, the field of organisation studies is a fictional unity, according to March. His judgment is that this myth cannot really be sustained by the teachings, the writings or the research which is permanently being carried out; the myth "is sustained by our hopes" (ibid.).

March's judgment is based on his diagnosis of the development of organisation theory and organisation studies since WW II until today. He delivered this diagnosis as a keynote address at the 2006 European Group of Organization Studies (EGOS) Colloquium, and after having stated that "forecasting the future is a fool's conceit", he also shared with the audience some of his views on – and hope for – the future. Among those things that will probably affect the factual development of the fictional field of organisation studies, he listed a number of general features that may have implications for the future development. The list ranges over a wide field, from the reduced economic, political and cultural centrality of the West related to the increased importance and influence on the global scene by Asian countries, via the continuing elaboration of IT and bio-technology, to "the earth's declining tolerance for human species" (March 2007: 17). The only point he elaborates a bit on, however, is the possible consequences from the increasing business school location of much of the research that will be carried out in the future.

March does not consider the business school context a neutral one. Without formulating himself explicitly in this way, he seems to fear a future development characterised by an unwelcome kind of homogenisation within the field of organisation studies. Neither does he make of use the vocabulary of actor-network theory, but he nevertheless sketches the contours of a macro-actor that appears to be the executor of the process of homogenisation: a Cyclops arising from the business schools' tendency to prioritise contact with economic disciplines rather than disciplines like psychology, sociology and political science, and to give less priority to such things as philosophies of science, interpretive social science and critical theory.

Those who may be wounded by March's view on the consequences of the stronger impact of the business school context in the future, may find that another of the grand old men in the field, W. H. Starbuck, rubs salt into the wounds when he comments on March's diagnosis of the field and the forecasting. Starbuck's assessment is akin to March's, but his emphasis is different: "The booming business school environment has allowed organization studies to develop and spread with little regard for its usefulness and relevance" (Starbuck 2007: 23). Starbuck emphasises that even though business schools are supposed to furnish business life both with people that are well informed on organisational issues and with knowledge of organisations that are useful to the world of business, the organisational studies undertaken by the scholars of business schools remain rather introvert.

According to Starbuck, organisation studies may be characterised by two main features. On the one hand side there are case studies dominated by stylised methods that allow researchers to maintain detachment (that is, methods that allow researchers to remain in academic settings). On the other hand side there is research emphasising statistical averages and large samples, researching events that "the general populace regards as commonplace, and the main purpose of research has been to reinterpret these commonplace events in language and concepts that intrigue academics" (Starbuck 2007: 24).

Interestingly, Starbuck's analysis coincides with my own in that he does not consider the worrying state of the art to be rooted in too much theoretical work, too much work spent on intellectual endeavours and theoretical analysis. He finds the problematic situation of organisation studies to be caused by the shortcomings in the *methods* that are used rather than in the theoretical work. As a matter of fact, he thinks there is an "underutilization of intellectual resources" (ibid.) in the field of organisation studies. This underutilisation he claims is due to the combination of the lack of interest in creating knowledge that is useful outside the academic setting, and the connected preference of creating "still-life images" of organisations as static systems at the expense of studies that focus on the real complexity and dynamics of organisations.

Starbuck even takes his analysis one step further, and puts forth a claim that is not only akin to, but identical with what is often claimed by action researchers: because both people and organisations are complex and dynamic, those who study them have to make what he calls incremental experiments if they want to really understand them. This point he (re-)turns into a critique of the dominant methods of organisation studies: "Those who rely on the passive observation cannot learn about the potentials of complex and dynamic systems, so they do not recognize or they misunderstand important aspects of what they observe" (ibid.). Then, in the end, he modifies his somewhat categorical statement by concluding that even

257

those who understand the complex dynamic of organisations poorly may very well succeed in making incremental improvements in the organisation.

Whether Starbuck would approve it or not, his viewpoints may indeed be interpreted as a plea for an increase of action research approaches to organisation studies as one of the most important ways to contribute to change the fate of organisation theory. Whatever my sympathies with such an interpretation, I would not subscribe to it unconditionally. Regarding the fate of organisation theory, we have to remind ourselves that whatever it will be, it will never cease to be made up by words being written. Thus, since what may be designated organisation theory is in fact made up by single, written pieces, I find March's suggestion of a way to proceed of equal importance: "Our task is to make small pieces of scholarship beautiful through rigor, persistence, competence, elegance and grace, so as to avoid the plague of mediocrity that threatens to overcome us" (March 2007: 18).

The two kinds of ways to change the fate of organisation theory which may be distilled from March and Starbuck may be regarded as complementary, and might even be combined. Both of their ways, and indeed the combination, would probably mean to take the straight and narrow way. As a way to change the fate of organisation theory, it may turn out that the result will be a narrow fate. However, when considering the alternatives, this is perhaps not the worst we might hope for?

References

Berry, L. L. & Parasuraman, A. (1993), "Building a New Academic Field – The Case of Services Marketing". *Journal of Retailing* 69(1):13-60.

Benhabib, S. (1992), *Situating the self: Gender, Community and Postmodernism in Contemporary Ethics*. New York: Routledge.

Callon, M. (1991), "Techno-economic Network and Irreversibility". In Law, J. (ed.) *Sociology of Monsters? Essays on Power, Technology and Domination*. London: Routledge.

Collins, H. M. (1981), "The Place of the Core-set in Modern Science: Social Contingency with Methodological Propriety in Science". *History of Science*, 19: 6-19.

Czarniawska, B. & Hernes, T. (eds.) (2005), *Actor-Network Theory and Organizing*. Copenhagen: Liber/CBS.

Elliot, J. (2005), "Becoming Critical: the Failure to Connect". *Educational Action Research* 13 (3): 359-374.

Feldman, M. & Pentland, B. (2005), "Organizational Routines and the Macro-Actor". In Czarniawska, B. & Hernes, T. (eds.): *Actor-Network Theory and Organizing*. Copenhagen: Liber/CBS.

Habermas, J. (1984), *Theory of Communicative Action: Reason and the Rationalization of Society*. (Vol. 1, T. McCarthy, Trans.). Boston: Beacon.

Hägglund, B. (2005), "Explaining Macro-Actors in Practice". In Czarniawska, B. & Hernes, T. (eds.): *Actor-Network Theory and Organizing*. Copenhagen: Liber/CBS.

Latour, B. (1999), "On recalling ANT". In Law, J.& Hassard, J. (eds.): *Actor Network Theory and after*. Oxford: Blackwell Publishers.

Law, J. (1999), "After ANT: Complexity, Naming and Topology". In Law, J. & Hassard, J. (eds.), *Actor Network and After*. Oxford: Blackwell Publishers.

Leblebici, H., et al. (1991), "Institutional Change and the Transformation of Interorganizational Fields: An organizational History of the U.S. Radio Broadcasting Industry". *Administrative Science Quarterly*, 36 (3): 333-363.

March, J. G. (2007), "The Study of Organizations and Organizing since 1945". *Organization Studies*, 28 (1): 9-19.

Michael, M. (1996), *Constructing Identities: The Social, the Nonhuman and Change*. London: Sage.

Pålshaugen, Ø. (2004), "How to do Things with Words? Towards a Linguistic Turn in Action Research". *Concepts and Transformation*, 9 (2): 181-203.

Pålshaugen, Ø. (2006), "Constructive Practice and Critical Theory – The Contribution of Action Research to Organisational Change and the Discourse on Organisations". *International Journal of Action Research*, 2 (3): 283-318.

Suchman, L. A. (1987), *Plans and Situated Actions: The Problem of Human-Machine Communication*. New York: Cambridge University Press.

Starbuck, W.H. (2007), "Living in Mythical Spaces". *Organization Studies*, 28 (1): 21-25.

Stacey, R. D. (2007), *Strategic Management and Organisational Dynamics: The Challenge of Complexity to Ways of Thinking About Organisations*. Essex: Pearson Education Limited.

Vickers, D. & Fox, S. (2005), "Powers in a Factory". In Czarniawska, B. & Hernes, T. (eds.) *Actor-Network Theory and Organizing*. Copenhagen: Liber/CBS.

10 Boundary Learning – Work complexities and reflexive practice in action research

Trine Deichman-Sørensen

Introduction: The socio-technical "hyphen"

This paper[1] is a contribution to recent debates on socio-technical principles and theory traditions as related to action research in work life, dealing with developmental work and practice learning. The focus will be on the relational interface and interactions taking place in various forms between human and nonhuman elements and between social and technical organisation. I will discuss open-ended, almost paradoxical and heterogeneous learning processes as contrasted to more conventional thinking about learning as linear, telos-oriented, transparent and homogeneous. Hence, the hyphen, always a part of the term "socio-technical", is the central construct of my concern. My point is to make a (de)tour from politics to learning. I hope to show that there is much to gain in turning our attention from singularised goal options to multiple choices of directions.

I wish to shed light on the importance of the "hyphens" of distinctive, multiple relations concerning practice-based learning in work life. An abortive developmental project, focused on "work-based training" in a technology firm, will be used illustratively. Hyphens indicate not only the conditional character of a given texture of work, but also a wide field of choices of combinations that may co-exist. The focus of my exploration is thus how learning crumbles and dissolves when our engagements in work become straight-lined and one-dimensional.

The basis of my argument is taken from Philip Herbst, one of the pioneers within both action research and socio-technical design. Today, his argument is practically forgotten, replaced by less constructive newcomers and derivations. I start by discussing two such "latecomers". The first is Yrjö Engeström's contribution on work co-configuration based on activity theory principles. The second one is presented by the Norwegian sociologist Øyvind Pålshaugen, and addresses democracy at work linked to developmental organisations of social dialogues. Both represent benchmark conceptions in current discussions. I will compare their mod-

---

1   This chapter has been partly written within the strategic research programme (2003-2007) at the WRI, Oslo. It was first presented as a paper at the 4th International Conference on Researching Work and Learning, Sydney, December 2005.

els, concentrating on two contributions from the authors: on the one hand an article on "Discourse democracy at work: On public spheres in private enterprises" by Pålshaugen (2002), and on the other hand some aspects of Engeström's theories and design models related to his notion of co-configuration work (2001, 2003).

In the two contributions I believe we can find a lost and forgotten playground of "in-between" learning principles, as expressed in the works of Philip Herbst. I believe Herbst's almost forgotten theories of co-genetic triadic logics and "in-between" learning principles represent a developmental model that is critical to revive in times of economic reductive thinking. I will write about this as "boundary learning". Herbst's theories counter all kinds of social amnesia whilst repeatedly pursuing deep-structured organisational sustainability, including substantial democratic values. The comparison will form a background on which I can demonstrate my fieldwork experiences from the angle of a contextual conception of complexity. This itinerary is then mapped on to Herbst's theory on co-genetic logics and Laurent Thévenot's description of pragmatic regimes of engagement forms.

Socio-technical design ambiguities

Since action research methods were initiated in the 1940s, several techniques of socio-technical design have been developed. Enterprise development models based on workers complicity in collaborative efforts of strategic decision making in firms is one important example. With a solid foundation in Norwegian and Swedish industrial policies springing from social democratic politics of the 1960s and continued by the neo-liberalism of today, this model, centred on social collaboration techniques, has proved to be robust. This has made it into one of the major successors of the industrially oriented action research tradition springing from the British coal mine experiments in the 1950s (e.g. Trist et al. 1993). Nowadays, similar principles have become central to European politics in developing novel social partnership models.

During the last decade, so-called activity theory models with a quite different descent from Russian social psychology have emerged. Among these, the most famous one is Engeström's theory on expansive learning taking place within and between activity systems. Although with a different descent, this theory is based on socio-technical design principles as well, perhaps even more so.

In what follows, I will compare the contributions from Pålshaugen and Engeström. The comparison will hopefully reveal to the reader the appearance of a different discursive playground of "in-between" learning principles. This I shall call "boundary learning", drawing on some works of Laurent Thévenot and Philip

Herbst, in the search for adequate re-conceptualizations of reflexive practice inside working life complexities.

Pålshaugen and Engeström seem to share some basic principles of vital importance. Firstly, both models are anchored in interventionist methodology. They are both basically action research. Secondly, each model is also directed at cooperative work efforts that enhance organisational development and learning. Collaborative efforts are parts of both. Thirdly, in order to achieve their aims, each model also seems to emphasise the establishment of a supplementary developmental organisation implemented through "change laboratories" (Engeström) or "dialogue conferences" (Pålshaugen).

The two approaches are different, however, to the degree in which they emphasise the work organisation or the supplementary organisation. The social partnership model, seated in social dialogues, emphasises the supplementary organisation. The activity system model emphasises incongruities of cognitive and operational directions in the work organisation(s). This divergence of direction between the two models makes a difference with respect to where learning gets started, carried out and targeted.

Putting it bluntly, what is at stake is the feat of razor-blade balancing between principles of social *democracy* and principles of social *engineering*. Pålshaugen's essay argues for work place democracy as something that enhances *both* democratic values *and* economic value added to the firms. Engeström pursues improved work-task-coordination enhancing organisational efficiency which consequently supports citizen rights as connected to clients or other third parties involved. Thus, Engeström promotes some kind of "consumer democracy" values with business process re-engineering origins "reinterpreted" (Lahn 2002). Accordingly, in both models the implied concepts of learning seem to remain constrained by some outer or higher order organisational objectives, albeit more or less ambiguously stressed and sorted out. Still, these disparities and disjunctions between the two models provide valuable access to some basic principles of learning dynamics and configurations. I shall elaborate a bit further.

Pålshaugen's position is important for two reasons, mainly related to the theoretical foundations of action research. Pålshaugen is among the few to present *the discursive formation of enterprise development* in a systematic account (Pålshaugen 1998, 2001). In the European discourse on action research, his writing on the construction of public spheres in private enterprises probably marks a decisive step to leave behind socio-technical modelling of "spearhead" work organisations (cf. van Ejnatten 1993, Gustavsen 2001). His article confirms the idea of making social-participative discourse models the paramount principle to care for. In making this turn, however, the dialogues for social learning in enterprises also fall prey to the politics of celebrating the better argument, an arrangement

263

which next also seems to get socially encapsulated. It is solely *within* the enterprises among the *social partners* (virtually or in reality) that these discussions or negotiations are supposed to take place.

A second point of Pålshaugen's is also important, namely his accentuated political democratic interest, including his concern for *individual engagement* to become an integrated part of enterprise development. Pålshaugen claims that collaborative enterprise development today has to adapt to the prevalence of an individualised culture. Individual motives must be integrated in order for collaborative strategies to become efficient, sound and adjusted. He thinks public discussions in enterprises can make a kind of collective ground for further individualisations. Still, the way he theorises this paves the way for the opposite of individualisation. Individualisation is propounded (paradoxically) in ways that have the opposite as a consequence.

Consequently, there are three aspects I find problematic. *Firstly*, the notion of social-dialogues-in-enterprises is restricted to speeches carried by human agents only. No discourse formations linked to nonhuman elements – for instance work technologies – are acknowledged. Demands and voices external to the democratic dialogues of social negotiations are in principle neglected and overruled, not taking part in the "the-enterprise-as-a-whole" negotiations. *Secondly*, the dialogues in question may intend to cover, incorporate and evaluate all sorts of issues, technological questions included. But these promises only hold provisionally. The time framing as such appears to become the most important issue. From this angle, presence is all there is. The procedures prescribed only allow for stepwise, forward-directed negotiations to take place, thereby gradually banishing a number of arguments. Hence, under the pretence of being an all-encompassing discourse on corporate social responsibilities of governance transparency, a series of consecutive asymmetries is produced. *Thirdly*, these procedures, which are meant to enable public reasoning to take place, also imply the prescription of a demarcation line between the private and the public. Only private opinions passing the "discursive test" of carrying collective relevance and acceptance remain as active and partaking members in the consecutive collaborative effort. Language games that are fit and robust for enterprise development promotion do not permit "private grammars" or "private speech" (Pålshaugen is a Wittgenstein expert, cf. Pålshaugen 2001b).

Engeström, on the other hand, worries primarily about the preservation of organisational quality benefitting possible client groups. Differently from Pålshaugen, Engeström highlights discursive mediations of work arrangements, stressing the importance of interrelated connections and tensions between instruments, role interpretations and common rules in organisations. His study of a medical practice in Finland illustrates, for instance, the variety of conceptions and practices that doctors may have, depending on whether they fill managerial functions or are bio-medically directed in their work, on whether they are socio-medically or psychiatrically educated, or on whether they conceptualise according to system-interactive requirements in virtue of holding positions that are task integrative (cf. Engeström 2001). Essential to Engeström's conception are the tensions generated from the socially distributed division of labour. This provides potential driving forces for organisational development and change to come about.

Still, even this conception turns out to be somehow instrumentally fixed. We are told about organisational "dialect" variations. But they tend to be treated more like some sort of temporarily given linguistic modifications of a standard discourse to be achieved – in parallel somehow to his repetitive re-instantiation of the same analytical model of fixed poles in one case to another. Hence, his major emphasis on providing a "landscape of expansive learning" principally seems to imply the *endorsement of technical efficiency*. On the other hand, his texts also carry some interesting metaphors of description that need to be taken seriously, for instance the way he describes "learning" to require the tracing of "moving horizons" of objects. Unfortunately, though, he seems to lose this notion as his argument progresses.

An issue of special concern to Engeström is the following: basically, he says, there are no contradictions involved in having a forward-oriented learning system that simultaneously represents a mélange of horizontal movements. We can agree to that, and this is exactly the point where Herbst's theories are well suited (I will return to this). In practice, it seems to be the other way around in this case. Referring to a description made by a colleague of his, this "mélange of horizontal movements" seems to turn into a state of "messiness" that it is important to avoid:

> The actors are like blind players who come eagerly to the field in the middle of the game, attracted by shouting voices, not knowing who else are there and what the game is all about. There is no referee, so rules are made up in different parts of the field among those who happen to bump into one another. Some get tired and go home (Engeström 2002:3).

Differently from Engeström, I find this description close to what essentially is at stake in learning settings. When they work, such settings are essentially informal and chaotic in character. So it is actually a good description when the players involved are said to be thrown into the game of a "force field" of actions for sorting out new rules among those who happen to bump into each other. Additionally, under such circumstances people will often stay, absorbed in the effort of developing their matters of concern.

Engeström, however, seems to hold on to the idea of system transparency, emphasising that learning processes have to be accountable from their "germ cells" of actions to the final achievement of a revised and remodelled organisation. Seemingly, the heterogeneities in play are to be dismissed if not thoroughly ordered and mastered within the framework of change laboratory techniques or by means of other instruments implanted. At the end of the day, even this model seems to be heavily *reliant upon prescribed, extraneous system and procedural formulas.*

I also want to comment Engeström's statements on "following the object". Citing Karin Knorr Cetina, he points out that objects serve as centring and integrating devices for regimes of expertise. Seemingly, even closer to her conceptions, he points out that these objects are heterogeneous, yet enduring entities, thus projective and transitory, representing a "moving horizon". These characteristics are most noteworthy, indeed. Engeström seems to argue that the research objects maintain a methodological status that resembles, somehow, his notion of "boundary-crossing zones", essential to the expansive learning happening across activity systems, alluding in this case, however, to the well-known semiotic figure of "boundary objects" presented by Susan Leigh Star (Guissemer & Star 1989; Star 1989). Unfortunately, though, this figure soon gets lost. When tracing these objects, it is hard to fathom whether these objects really differ from the clients muddling about, or not. The "moving horizons" of the research objects seem to turn into the transparency the client objects themselves were presumed to hold. In fact, these are the key knowledge holders. His first sentence, then, seems to be the only one to hold: objects serve as centring and integrating devices for regimes of expertise. Consequently, the point made by Knorr Cetina, accentuating the *dynamics of an open, mutually constitutive relation between research objects and researchers* (cf. Knorr Cetina 1999), *is ultimately dismissed. His ground conception of a socially distributed division of labour takes primacy.* Put differently, the claimed transitory character of the objects appears to pass transitorily.

Concluding this part of the discussion I maintain that we have to qualify a discursive understanding of work place organisation and development; this is an action research methodological stance initiated, I believe, by Pålshaugen. I also share his conviction that enterprise development is gradually becoming more dependent upon the degree to which personal engagements in working matters are pursued and acknowledged. However, I differ from him for the same reasons. On the other hand, I appreciate Engeström's description of parallel existent activity systems in enterprises as well as his maintaining the importance of learning processes to be kept closely connected to operational work issues. I also find his "landscapes of expansive learning" and "tracing the trajectories of the knowledge objects" to be valuable metaphors. To follow up these metaphors, however, it seems necessary to leave behind the merely hierarchical, linear conceptions of work organisational development and learning.

Multiple engagements in the world of work

Pålshaugen's theory on work place democracy and Engeström's conception of expansive learning based on co-configurations of activity systems in tension share the common interest of harmonising socially distributed viewpoints. In the former case this is for the benefit of the enterprise as a whole, and in the latter case to the advantage of concerned third parties.

Surely, all action research projects dealing with work-based learning depend upon some sort of complexity reductions. Yet, most often such reductions appear to be taken too far. Action research projects in work life seem to attend to the idea of bringing about organisational efficiency as their prime task, thus favouring forward-directed progress of work. This, in turn, reduces the developmental interests or matters of concern available. In this way valuable learning gets lost. Planned actions of unidirectional developmental work constitute an inappropriate and misleading approach today, blocking work with the real challenges of handling complexity in work life. I owe my stand on this to an unsuccessful action research project dealing with work-based learning in an enterprise. I will now present its context.

The action research project in question was based on three basic design principles. Firstly, it was designed in order to have important assets gained through inter-organisational learning among similar firms of proximate locations. Four companies participated together with two higher educational or research institutions, the regional university college and the Work Research Institute. Secondly, the participants were to be operators on the shop floor level as well as be management representatives. The funding for this project was premised on the activation of social partnership principles. Thirdly, the project was supposed to be embedded in work task operations, literally closely connected to workers' daily experiences and assumptions.

The two prior requirements relate to action research principles as presented by Pålshaugen. The first and third request virtually link to the activity theory principles of Engeström. In this particular project setting, however, the common mission vaguely agreed upon was never put into practice, at least not reconciled and connected. On the contrary, this task almost fell apart into dispersed, disaffiliated activities differently exposed in each firm as regards ambitions, design and direction. Here are some reasons.

It was hard to establish a common aim of action and learning among the firms involved. Firstly, their interest in mutual learning and collaborations was insufficient and too abstract when confronted with immediate and pressing, compulsive adjustment demands. All firms, mostly seated in the microelectronic industry, were heavily exposed to competition. They had to adjust to customer requests in rapid succession, thereby continually restructuring their production process technology and work organisation design. For some companies even the ownership affiliations changed swiftly. Hence, there was hardly any common ground for this project to reside in, far less any stable situation. Two common demands for action research projects were missing. Secondly, the premise that the project should build on social partnership ideas and practice was only partly kept and honoured. Ultimately some firms, i.e. their management groups, only wanted to run this project solely for the purpose of tariff bound qualification demands and negotiations. In one of the firms, the operators were expelled also from taking part in the project-directing group. Thirdly, the technology used in production was partly similar, partly different. There was no common client to relate to as in Engeström's case. Only ISO system requests could possibly represent this common but ideal and abstract "demanding customer". Even here, though, to learn from each other dealing with similar problems of adaptation soon faltered, reportedly due to parallel instabilities in other areas of concern.

But despite being dispersed and partly crumbling, this project did in fact accomplish some real learning. Taking part in diverse *ad hoc* networks on organisational matters, these people often "bumped into each other", apparently creating alternative, supplementary rules of the game on an informal basis. These network associations seemed to foster a certain sense of regularity, providing space for themes instantly occurring from inside or outside the work organisation, simultaneously crossing the *ad hoc* agendas of the project-based networks.

Leaning on the French sociologist Laurent Thévenot and his conception of pragmatic regimes, I shall call this sense of regularities the distillation of series of incommensurable work life engagements. Pragmatic regimes, he says, rest in evaluations that co-configure – different from Engeström's co-configuration work, though – human and non-human elements into *distinctive orders of worth*:

Among human beings coordination rests on the connection between human behaviour and the orientation towards some kind of *good* that delimits the relevant *reality* to be taken into account. … But the notions of good that have been elaborated to make sense *and reality* of human conducts are quite diverse, depending on the way attachments to the environment are handled and evaluated. I have argued that "the good" and "the real" are linked together in a variety of ways within what I have called pragmatic regimes of engagement. The argument is that people – but also things – are evaluated through their involvement in different modes of activity and that *evaluation* and the *realist* conditions for an *effective engagement* with the world necessarily go together… The distinction between realism and evaluation is much tighter than is commonly imagined in social sciences… objects and people are caught up and evaluated – that is, "engaged" – in a world of multiple regimes (Thévenot, 2002: 76, emphases made by author).

No wonder, then, our project nearly fell apart. In fact, people were dealing with crossing aims of attention and considerations, engaged in a world of multiple regimes. The common "good" to get achieved in this project – "work-based learning in the enterprise" – actually represented several objects of concern, each depending upon idiosyncratic priorities. Some were industrial-technological, others financial, and still others organisationally communitarian. A fourth type specifically emphasised educational goods, a fifth engagement form was constructed on the basis of domestic orders of worth, and a sixth one dealt with global certification system standards. Partly building on Thévenot's (2002) conceptual distinctions, I shall next return to the way these engagement forms were conducted and conceived.

Typically, working out these orders of worth for the most part took place backstage, effectuated by the projects' or networks' discussions as well as inflicting "disturbances" upon these, but they were never officially put on the top agenda for "proper" negotiations in meetings. These rules of regularities at work rather "propped up" the process developing, some members of the team argued, deviating them from staying result-oriented and forward-directed. In other words, only due to organisational disorder and dissatisfaction did this "messiness" of criss-crossing regularity orders come to the fore.

Thanks to this and to their serious engagements in work, people in this project paved the way for a probable re-conceptualisation of action research premises. Indeed, they were engaged in the multiple forms of the probable by means of bringing in their basic assumptions and questioning – setting off and coupled with differing technologies – as related to complex work and learning conditions.

We have to return to Philip Herbst's classic writings on socio-technical design to find a similar conception of horizontal complexity of multiple engagements in the worlds of work as regards action research conceptualisations and premises:

First and foremost, Herbst was the first to emphasise the importance of building in slack in all sorts of organisational work, be it work settings or education. He talks in support not only of sharing tasks within and across work teams, but also of boundary zones "with respect to which there is no general agreement as to whose job they are, or with respect to which disagreement exists between the work team and management" (Herbst 1974: 145). Slack – or some degree of "disorder" – is a prerequisite for organising, he states. Besides, it may effect vital educative achievements not otherwise allowed.

Secondly, in line with Thévenot, Herbst also accentuates the common rule of investments in forms. All through his life this constitutes his leitmotiv, especially as related to his conceptualisations of what he calls "co-genetic triadic logic" building on *The Laws of Forms* by George Spencer Brown (1969). In the light of the linguistic turn in action research, emphasised later on, this "behavioural logic" or "contextual logic" of his (it carries many names) represents no less than a distinctive theory on discursive mediations of socio-technical engagements – if discursive mediations cover something more than mere social dialogues taking place, that is.

I find Herbst's theories genuinely reflexive. Herbst was not concerned with constructing technical procedures, far less any technical repetitions thereof as seem to be the case for some of his contemporary or later colleagues. Essentially, his prime interest was in finding methods for improved *diagnostic* descriptions and orientations. This makes a crucial difference as regards forward-directed learning, a matter to which I shall return.

Thirdly, his engagement in making a better future was never restricted to forward-directed procedures and orientations alone. In fact, he was deeply concerned with mapping out basic premises and principles for autonomous systems to come forth when dealing with increasing complexity in working relations. His famous "minimal critical specification" design principles underpin a work organisation order of multi-perspectivism as the basis for promoting enhanced organisational effectiveness. His approach was radical, searching to distillate basic "roots" of work organisational premises.

Fourth, and finally, Herbst is one of the few action researchers to give a theoretical account of the contingent character of forms, generalisations and theories. Any theory can only have local validity, never universal validity, he claims. This too makes a conceptual difference of great importance in dealing with the foundations of action research.

I shall try to elaborate on these points related to a needed shift in action research approaches, starting with a presentation of the generalisations rudimentarily displayed in the disrupted action research project mentioned.

Work and learning regimes in tension

In the lack of a common endeavour to accomplish – apart from the abstract will of mutual learning and cooperation – no substantial negotiation on organisational constraints and potentialities took place in the project. Within limits, having fixed objects of concern favours the immediate efficiency of the procedures and research models suggested by Pålshaugen and Engeström.

However, important contextual issues seem thereby to get lost. Object tensions are far more than socially distributed. Likewise, goal option divergences are not sourced in social roles in accord with a certain regulatory division of labour. These terms are essential elements both in Pålshaugen's work place democracy model and in the co-configuration model of work integration based on Engeström's activity system theory. Concerning the truncated project, then, the diverse ordering systems therein put on view definitely demonstrate the significance of role enact-ment and distributions as well. But people's investments and articulations here also indicate conflicts that may arise from the opposite fact either of role positions being shared amongst all or role differences becoming blurred, dependent upon the framing in question. Finally, these forms of coordination also demonstrate the role independence played by system technologies as such in addition to examples of personally anchored role interpretations most often inhibited or neglected.

The regime of educational worth

For learning efforts in work life to qualify as educative they are supposed to im-prove, at the very least, people's work performance, preferably recognisable for others to approve. A different opinion stresses the importance of enhancing work comprehension in general, possibly with respect to the logics and designs of con-trol systems in use. In either case we are dealing with conventions of informal learning. At the other end, some would say that declaring a process to be educative is sufficient to become one. Connected to this, while entering the domain of formal training, are claims for the attendance of competent guidance. Others require the transfer of formal knowledge as well. Finally, some would require the learning processes to be sanctioned through an official institution or a certificate as being the only thing that makes education sound and complete, the ultimate form of qualifying evaluation.

Generalisations thus at stake within the regime of educational worth are them-selves criss-crossing and in tension, especially as regards learning in work life. Nonetheless, all of them support evaluations by means of *standards of proficiency,* as required for a regime qualification with educational worth related to didactics undertaken or individuals' capabilities for investments.

Practically all forms of engagement listed above were represented in our project, indicating the vagueness of the educational goods in flow. Some mea-sures were rather creative in outline, that is, activating workers' initiatives and self-directedness as well as e.g. billboards, spreadsheets and logbooks for quite untraditional applications. Others were relatively conventional. Underneath was a conflict between information-directed and experience-based learning principles. Negotiating this clash of methods was the main issue at stake in the project, still another thing that remained unresolved. A third aspiration, connected to the idea of spontaneous on-the-job training, underlines the conflict in question. For some, the main objective was the training of operators to become some sort of flexible tools akin to and annexed to the machinery – an arrangement, then, ultimately not residing in qualifications of an educational kind.

271

The regime of industrial worth

The majority of firms involved in the project represented highly automated, textually mediated production systems. Principally, their priorities were put on investments in calculative, intelligent technology to ensure predictable system processes of reliable production. Here, a "good" production system refers to evaluating its organisation – people and tools alike – against the extent to which the organisations are rationally ordered by means of stabilising procedures able to control future events. The qualifying criterion remains the *maintenance of technical efficiency* in all parts of the organisation. In this case of severely complex compound production systems, this was provided and supplemented by inbuilt series of apposite standard measures in the production apparatus.

This regime blurs the distinction between people and things. As ultimately promoting full automation in production, manual work is saved and made redundant while, on the other hand, in some parts of the production, demands on mental surveillance get intensified (cf. Zuboff 1988). In order to possibly transcend this gap of opposite orientations, then, successively more and more operations are put under standard control, only to entail a system rationality almost bordering on system implosion.

We have been told from people working in that kind of standardised work that they find these things weird or incomprehensible, as representing something that ends up out of any technician's or any technical control at all. Manoeuvres related to standardisations for the future, they argued, will undermine common capacities and capabilities for innovations.

The industrial regime is for the most part educationally reductive, transforming skill disciplines into modules, knowledge into competencies, and education into training. On the other hand, though, full qualification according to the rules of this order either imposes breakdowns or its transcendence into reflexive, co-configurative orientations – a meta-qualification beyond or in-between the various regimes present.

Work-based training and education of market worth

My interrupted action research project was also plausibly expected to pay off. Several investments carried out within or in relation to the project were made for the firms to comply effectively with this demand. Some companies were concerned with finding strategies for taking care of their labour supply, as they were in an unfortunate resource situation due to a high turnover rate. In order to accommodate to fluctuations in the market, these firms even induced contra-market principles of free regulations, founding a resource bank amongst themselves and neighbouring enterprises, including labour as well as tools. Other companies were employed in developing firm-specific training programs for the same reasons. In the latter case more than in the former one, this tended to transform these workers' status into a kind of locally bounded tenant labour. From one management group we were in fact told that this was intentional, partly because of their experience with local union problems. These people also justified their choice of training investments in economic terms by means of keeping the costs limited. In a third case with a strong union, the firm was actively engaged in the employees taking supplementary training courses leading to certificate tests, sometimes even to the extent of founding training expenditures for people laid off.

The regime of market worth differs in significant ways from the regimes of educational worth or of industrial worth. We notice, for instance, that the roles constructed are customer-related but some are even extra-market directed. *The returning point is always evaluations of cost benefits and expenditures. Principally, be they "costs" or "investments", in each case these are evaluated by means of price.* This makes the foundation for redefining human labour into "human capital", and moreover to some sort of private holdings of "intellectual capital" mainly belonging to the firm only as extrapolated in some literature currently debated (cf. Edvinsson and Malone, 1997). In the latter case, proficiency is translated into firm investments appropriated and sorted out by means of intellectual capital balance scores.

So, investments in this realm confront us with a suggestive situation. The debate on high cost and low cost education – the so-called "high road" and "low road" – apparently was lost and passé long before it started (Crouch et al. 1999). Ultimately, price-directedness annihilates all standards of communality of valuations, like for instance professional standards or group-differentiated tariffs – other than the common good as related to getting a "good" price, that is.

Work and learning organisations of globalisation worth

Today, gradually more standards of work organisation accountability get formalised and uniformed, and some are even of global extent. The well-known ISO certification systems represent one of these, distributed mostly among small and middle-sized enterprises all over the world, while others of similar allocation are industry-directed. Although these systems rest in economic globalisations, the evaluations enacted are different from those of market worth. At the same time the practice systems connected also diverge from those of industrial worth. Rather than centring upon price on the one hand or reliability as connected to technical efficiency on the other, evaluations in the case of globalisation worth are directed at the promotion of accountability. *The principle of transparency, including certain external revision procedures of signs of recognition, makes the texture for this to install a common good.*

The qualification of work systems through transparency changes the inner and outer fabric of the organisation. It inaugurates *management systems* as the central coordinating figure and focus of concern, internally at the expense of evaluations as connected among others to professionalism or budget, and externally by means of the organisation to get subjected to evaluations and norms set by designated revision authorities, including acceptance or rejection of protocol systems locally employed.

Members of the project group pointed out four additional and related consequences. Apart from the sign value added by virtue of its common recognition in the market, they found ISO certifications helped to sort out and clarify fields of responsibilities inside the organisation. A second asset found was the common ground made amongst firms with respect to overall customer-led production, including its indirect encouragement to set forth inter-organisational mutual learning amongst otherwise non-affiliated industry partners. On the negative side they pointed to difficulties emerging when boundary zones in-between work domains became blurred, turning these into problematic zones of incessant adjustments, negotiations and refinements. Organisational slack making pragmatic solutions possible, got lost.

Finally, some people also voiced a certain anxiety as regards qualifications of personnel, worried that the possibility of organisation-based qualifications were going to make current standards of individual proficiency redundant. Certifications of proficiency may move from the hands of people to become global standard measures of revisions linked to enterprise design and organisation, they reasoned. With respect to the latter we have to add that these discussions took place long before the so-called Europass was launched, which, likewise motivated by the idea of transparency promotion, translates national skill certificates into Trans-European standards of commonly adjusted competence schemes. Yet, this strand of negotiations currently taking place, concerning the flexibility of labour and education, has only just started. It still remains "on its marks" to get formalised and implemented.

Co-ordinations of communitarian worth

Undertakings directed at organisational learning represent a fifth domain of work-based learning. These kinds of activities are deeply rooted in Norwegian politics, which has been dominated by social partnership ideas since World War

274

II, in the beginning adhering to social democracy, later on adjusted to principles of neo-liberal social corporate governance. Despite differences, the theme of harmonising social interests runs as a thread throughout this span of time. From a present day point of view, we may call it a long-lasting era of communitarianism.

Communitarian principles and arrangements differ from those of industrial politics as related to market worth. Basic principles are *trust endorsement* and *consensus making*, as required for politics that originate in corporativism. Through communitarianism market principles are set aside. The same happens to principles with respect to civic effects relying upon conflict negotiations incessantly taking place (Slagstad 1998). A "good" regime of coordination is in this respect harmonisations of interests *beyond limits*. Ground figure of co-operation is counting on "safety in numbers" (Fuller 2002) by means of which it also departs from the virtues of "safety of numbers", which for the sake of comparison represents central qualities of the regime of industrial arrangements.

Among engagements thus connected we find "zones of proximate learning", applying a term by Engeström, either related to "change laboratories" seated in collaborative efforts related to a joint mission among professionals, or related to "dialogue conferences" linked to social partnership principles as presented by Pålshaugen. Both emphasise negotiations among equals. Connected by a common cause, be it the clients' best interests or "the enterprise as a whole", the social dialogues in question each prefer communal membership to interest representations. In a manner of speaking, social partnership interests incarnate the speech of the global village. That is to say, the term communitarianism, initially of American origin (e.g. MacIntyre 1990, Etzioni 1997), entails a re-socialisation based on deeds associated with local communities; accordingly, modern interest articulations as dependent upon civic arrangements like public opinion institutions are abandoned. Typically, governance network principles tend to supplant political disputes as these kinds of qualifications tend do disappear into the void of economic globalisation. In short, politics are levelled.

To some extent members of the project team were enclosed by this kind of thinking and arrangements, having created a regional network association a few years before as a successful niche industry started to grow. Little by little this network incorporated the whole communion region becoming the main institution of practical politics – or governance – in the area. People in the group experienced this network as a bulwark against fierce market competition, as well as an arena for business innovations to take place, including one concerning public administration. Additionally, no less important, a semi-structured social scene was established, encouraging informal talks taking place amongst otherwise peripheral associates . – Not all inhabitants in the community were equally regarded as members, though. Literally, this regime of coordination rests upon blurry distinctions expelling all discourses on oppositions. In order to let the "social dialogue" among "associates" flourish, interest conflicts that may exist between "employees" and "employers", or people possibly wishing to voice civic protests or "citizens' opinion", are pretended to no longer exist. Consequently, the social roles constituting the entrance ticket turned out as excluded from membership. No wonder, then, people were confused about their tasks and roles in the play.

Engagements of Domestic Worth

The last form of engagement to get mentioned here is also one characterised by matters of proximal learning. Thévenot calls these kinds of engagements qualifications of domestic worth, grounded in *habitual accommodations and learning*. Thévenot explains their characteristics as follows:

> The familiar handling of used things departs for normal conventions or conventional prescriptions. Such dynamics of engagements have nothing to do with conventional forms of judgement or the subject/object division implied by normal planned action. They have instead to do with perceptual and kinaesthetic clues about familiar and customized "paths" through local environments that involve modifying the surroundings as well as the habits of the human body.... The kind of good that governs this cautious handling of human characters and specified things is not the fulfilment of planned normal action but rather has to do with taking good *care* of this *accommodation*. (Thévenot, 2002:71ff., emphasises made by author)

In contrast to co-ordinations of communitarian worth, then, these are engagements primarily qualified *from below*. With respect to daily work surroundings, these kinds of engagements are recognised for instance in bringing flowerpots or family pictures to the office. We also may find reminiscences of domestic behaviour at work as related to incidents of "disorderly", familial conduct. A third kind is represented by affairs of personal accommodation as related to task operations connected to new work demands. I shall give two examples from the project. One woman, employed on a daily basis in soldering circuit boards, once casually told the group she always felt triggered immediately to grapple with the problem of solving the puzzles represented by novel board designs. To her, this resembled the kind of excitement she felt for a nice knitting recipe brought home. Another group member, who worked in human relations, compared his work to PID controllers, a picture of which he memorised from school days' physics. He said that to him, this PID figure represented a kind of ground gestalt recipe by means of which he was able to tackle and comprehend his work's complexities.

Typically, these people were "at home" at work, indicating not only the way people and things are entangled but also the manner in which these kinds of life histories – people's personalities, that is – continuously are worked on. There are, in other words, no recipes to follow other than the ones developed on our ways. Work performance as personalities alike are founded on the *repeated practice of distributed activities* – as *series of new beginnings*, just as we might expect it from the labour of domestic worth.

This also makes work activities essential to personality formation, which in turn makes a *sine qua non* for self-directed learning or planned action in work or in society to take place. Herbst, interested in autonomous work systems, is a thinker who was quite well aware of this matter of concern. In his short but famous article, "The Product of Work is People", he states:

> We may then become aware that it is not, after all, how much or how little we have achieved that matters, but how we went about achieving it... After everything else is gone, that which we have become remains, whether we recognise it or not, as the product. (Herbst 1972/1974:213)

"Whether we recognise it or not", he claims. Regardless of which, *habitually* we are formed through products and processes we are taking part in.

"Inverse socio-technical design" of boundary learning

Regularly, socio-technical design principles are criticised from two opposite sources. On the one hand, work principles of this kind are criticised for sustaining technological culture dominance with respect to all work life relations (Sejersted 1998), and, on the other hand, there are some who criticise autonomous group functioning as it is tested out mainly in industry for representing time-consuming and expensive arrangements (Adler & Cole 1993). My focus here is another one. I shall concentrate on the *methodological* aspects of concern related to Herbst's way of thinking, not so much the possible prescriptions connected. The latter is either something that is already achieved as transported, although changed, into for instance TQM principles, or it refers to something that is outmoded linked to an industrial era nowadays out-dated. As regards action research methodologies, I believe a lot remains to be gained from rereading his work from a methodological point of view, of which my presentation here is only a provisional start.

Herbst's main concern was related to work operation descriptions focussing on task relations and the boundaries in between. Whereas this was originally connected to working *teams*, today probably *themes* of directions constitute the coordination form that counts. We have to shift our focus from work descriptions based on coal mine experiments to his theoretical accounts as connected to co-genetic dynamics and logics, as represented in his early writing in particular linked to his elaborations on education. So far mostly the opposite is the case (cf. Blichfeldt et al. 1978). In his later works Herbst actually called for an "inverse socio-technical design" to take place in the manner of which shifts in attention from work to education or from organisational design to gestalt theories preliminarily convey a course of direction.

The basic methodological account of Herbst that helps me to read work complexities in a different manner, associated with education, is ultimately based upon his conception of *primary distinctions as related to contextual logics*, initially derived from Spencer-Brown. Simplified, this notion first discussed in his book on *Alternatives to hierarchies*, then as "behavioural logic" (1976), entails the following, formulated in his essay, *What happens when we make a distinction: An elementary introduction to co-genetic logic* (published posthumously):

The point of departure is the world before there was any subject or object. Or more correctly, the time before there was any time.

When a distinction is made, a boundary comes into being together with the inside and the outside of the form. What is generated in this way is a triadic go-genetic unit and the distinction made that is represented by the boundary. At this stage, we have nothing more than a form in an empty space.

In its most general form what has become generated in this way is a unit consisting of not less than three elements, which we denote by [n, m, p]. In this case the primary distinction that generates the form (the inside) together with the empty space (the outside), and the boundary separating and distinguishing inside and outside, is only one particular realisation of the primary distinction, which was first formulated by Spencer-Brown in a different way. A triadic unit has the following four properties:

1. It is Co-genetic
The three elements that are generated come into being together

2. It is Nonseparable
We cannot take the components apart. And also, we cannot have them initially apart and then put them together, (…) what we have here is not a modular or a mechanical structure.

3. It is Nonreducible
There cannot be less than three elements. (…) The nonreducible property is the converse of the co-genetic property that says that all three components come into being together.

4. It is Contextual
None of the components have individually definable characteristics. In fact, they have no intrinsic characteristics that belong to them. This is because they are not separated, (…) each is definable in terms of the others. Thus if we wish to *define the boundary* we can do so in terms of the inside and outside as *that which is crossed by moving from the inside to the outside* (Herbst 1995:67 ff., emphasis added)

According to Herbst, this logic leads to the conception of two basic operations: an "Identity Maintaining Operator", referring to mechanistic, modular ways of thinking, and an "Inversion Operator", referring to relational constitutions of objects (and subjects). Herbst's point is that it is *only through inversions* that modular states of being are made possible – that is, as an exception to the rule – or more correctly, as referring to *particular conditions* where these kinds of (non)configurations are met. He calls it the "zero state" of atomistic relations, the most fragile one, one that in the main borders on breakdowns, an exceptional state of relations that soon will become "metamorphosed into potentially any one of other process networks". Inversions make the rule for any forms of the probable to come into being:

> The act of creation is an act of negation. It is a negation of the original state, and it is through the act of negation that a finite, bounded, and segmented world is produced. Hence, it is only by the negation of the negation that we are able to return to the original state, that is at the same time the same as the state that we left and also not. For it is said that the man who has done the outward journey and later returned no longer is the same as he was before he made his journey. (Herbst 1995:74)

Now, then, if we shall take these statements of his seriously, it is only through *inversions of the texture,* be it at work, in education or in literature, including the texts by Herbst, that the "original" state of affairs – or engagements – becomes *real* and *comprehensible*. We have to start at "the time before there was any time" – at the border of the open or "empty" space emerging when confronted with peculiarities of particularities – looking upon these textures as *constructions of certain orderings*.

Essentially, this heirloom left by Herbst indicates that he wanted his texts to be read historically, as something rendered probable and constrained by circumstances. His legacy is to maintain making distinctions, an appeal for us to continue on his journey. He also labels this procedure an act of "mapping".

Retrospectively, it is quite easy to read his ways of sorting out work organisation probabilities as formal mapping constructions – easier today than in the heydays of Fordism. His "operational unit paradigm" represents a methodology of questioning the ways in which work is coordinated from different angles or by different coordination schemes. Configuration units as "work domains", "activity systems", "variance control systems" or "task dependency patterns" all represent particular forms of work engagements: the "work domain" with respect to the degree to which *roles are differentiated*; the "activity system" with respect to the degree to which work is *carried out separately or in teams*; the "task dependency patterns" with respect to the degree to which work is *coordinated in chain, convergently, cyclically or divergently*; and the "variance control system" with respect to *coordination (or work directional) effects as resulting from type of variance, frequency, average amount of disruption and so forth* (Herbst 1974, Chapter 10: "Production Tasks and Work Organization"). All these types provide *forms of work organisation probabilities, themes of work directions.* They are nothing but *metaphors of work ordering manners.*

Somehow analogous to the descriptions made by Garret Morgan in "Images of Organizations" (1986), these forms of work relations provide elementary principles for Herbst to reconstruct bureaucratic work organisations, based on segmented labour, into multi-perspective matrix-organisations. It is important that these are ways of ordering *practical* matters where each individually may in principle get *qualified and questioned* according to norms of values of a common set of rules. All work organisations make distinctive relational constructs of general arrangements – of probabilities. In this sense, each mode of coordination provides distinctive forms of inner and outer stabilisation, including making space for organisational slack to work on for future perfection.

This double-faced character of inherent forms is more explicitly worked out within the frame of Herbst's discussion on educational matters. Similarly, he here demonstrates that each manifestation of forms represents at the same time a closed systems as much as an open one. His "design of educational organizations" (1974: Chapter 13) stresses: "each subject is capable of structuring and illuminating the whole world of knowledge. Each subject displays a different structure of the whole" (p. 193). They are, in his view, themes of coordinations *displaying the world somehow similar to gestalts' modes of hiding or exposing things*:

The model requires that the world can be seen not just as a single Gestalt but several Gestalts, depending on which viewpoint is taken, together with their interrelationships.

Every conceptual model, as soon as it is formulated, becomes a closed system and also carries within itself the possibility of self-transcendence. (…)

The problem lies in the inherent limitations of the processes of perception and conceptualisation. A structure or figure becomes visible in so far as we suppress and make invisible the background from which it stands out. Thus, perception is not possible without distortion of what is seen, and conceptualisation is possible only by virtue of what is left out. To go beyond this we would need to see figure and ground simultaneously. However, if figure and ground become one, then there is no figure to be seen, no object that can be got hold of, and no basis for conceptualisation. Conceptually, the step beyond takes us over the edge of the knowable, *which is at the same time both possible and inconceivable* (Herbst 1974:197, emphasis added)

Consequently, gestalts not only manifest themselves differently. Their inherent limitations also border on implosion, perhaps turning into the gestalt of "the atomistic state" of "zero level of the structure" in which the structure under certain conditions "will break down and become metamorphosed into potentially any one of the other process networks" (1995:75). This is the point of new beginnings, of new inversions to evolve.

"Any theory that is based on pre-specified conditions can have local validity, but not universal validity", Herbst concludes in his essay on "What Happens When We Make a Distinction". In another of his later essays on "Contextual Design" (which I believe is still unpublished, dated 1985), he argues in favour of "minimal critical specification design" principles as related to work co-ordinations based on theme specifications. Like in the book on *Socio-Technical Design* (1974), there are three basic organisational principles: 1) the principle of non-hierarchical structure, 2) the principle of multi-functional capacity of individual and organisational units which enter into a collaborative mode of functioning, and 3) the principle that none of the participant individuals enter into exploitive modes of function in their relation to one another.

Compared to his earlier work, in this later paper he seems to have become more engaged in making inversions, adding new ways of coordinating variance. Reporting on a developmental project based in complex work organisations, he emphasises the following: *"it was possible to look at every problem from the view of production efficiency, cost efficiency, work environment and trade union interests"* (1985:12). This kind of multi-perspectivism evolving from work complexities, he adds, represents a *socio-technical inversion in which environmental issues are reversed to become inside matters of concern.* This is the only way for an organisation to become self-referential and robust, that is. This type of organisation has finally returned home, we probably could say, following up his journey metaphor. Today, demands on horizontal integration are a hallmark of modern organisations of work. Correspondingly, making inversions – staying focussed but open-minded – is a prerequisite for these organisations in order to learn – to survive. The alternative to learning is organisational collapse.

His point, therefore, was never to fuse social and technological matters but to learn from their forms of integration, to keep them distinguished, but entangled in chains of probabilities. I believe his main interest remains working *diagnostically*. His interest remains an enduring search for forms of the probable that entail differentiations – or inversions – to be maintained. Organisations are to him nothing but networks: all components are to be conceived of as nodes, not individual elements. In virtue of their relatedness, possibilities of inversions are always laid bare. In "The Evolution of World Models", he formulates this diagnostic approach as follows:

What is seen now is that it is the means and methods that we apply that create the future. It is in the choice of methods and means that values become operative, and it is by understanding what the effects on the future will be of actions performed today that rational actions become possible. (Herbst 1974:209)

I believe this approach to creating the future on the basis of deciphering conditional facts of the "probable" makes a lasting and common theme in his writing. Forward-directed learning primarily depends upon tracking, including mapping, the objects in question in a horizontal manner – to reverse and learn from conditional constrains.

Conclusions

My interest in this paper has been to look for implementable steps in the direction of developing a spatial understanding of learning, more in accordance with the horizontal complexity of modern work. I have wanted to show there are several engagement forms at play at work, each constrained according to which values or regimes of worth that are put into operation. A truncated development project put me on this track, including re-convincing me that common individual learning performance forms the prime basis for organisational learning, as confirmed by Thévenot as well as by Herbst.

The learning organisation put forth differs in essential ways from those presented by Pålshaugen and Engeström, respectively – the points of departure for my argument. Both seem to me to close off learning at a certain stage of the processes, favouring instead individualised target objects, whereas for Herbst the knowledge or learning object seems to constitute a kind of "expansive learning" always in the making. Consequently, thereby both Pålshaugen and Engeström evaporate the idea of multi-perspective modelling as a building block in all organisational development. This was essential to Herbst, also in action research. Pålshaugen loses this kind of perspective by making political procedures akin to decision-making processes within political parties the central figure of his concern, thus supplanting in effect his own idea of public opinion formations as the basis for work place democracy. There is no outside to his conception of procedures, which rather constitutes processes of public opinion development. All his opinion formations remain enclosed in the enterprise, withdrawn from public reasoning. In fact, the source for this viewpoint is political, even anti-democratic in origin, I believe. The predecessor to the dialogue conference model, on which his social dialogues build, is the so-called search conferences of similar design, initially originated by the action researcher Fred Emery, who also belonged to the group that founded the Australian

Communist Party. What strikes me by reading Pålshaugen is the reiteration of the logics of democratic centralism.

Multi-perspectivism is maybe closer to Engeström. He fails, however, to acknowledge fully the multi-perspectivism to all social roles adhered within complex work organisations. Seemingly, his interest is to hold on to certain ways of organisational coordination and learning that turns out to exclude individual schemes of accommodations, perhaps even at the expense of organisational learning. Furthermore, his interest in "expansive learning" basically seems to neglect and overrule intrinsic power relations. Therefore, even his conception turns out as relatively closed off and unidirectional, closing down the "moving horizon" of his objects.

All in all, neither Pålshaugen's nor Engeström's theories seem to have the organisational slack built in for learning and individualisations to take place. Neither one provides, I believe, an infrastructure of accommodations and learning. Today, perhaps, Herbst's multi-perspectivism represents the only action research model at hand to do so. In contrast to him, seemingly, the benchmark conceptions of Pålshaugen and Engeström are suffering from the possibility of imploding or falling apart.

References

Adler, P. S & Cole, R. E. (1993), "Designed for Learning: A Tale of Two Auto Plants", *Sloan Management Review* 34(3): 85-94.

Blichfeldt, J.F., Haugen, R. & Jangård, H. (1979), *Mot en ny skoleorganisasjon*, Oslo: Tanum.

Crouch, C., Finegold, D. & Sako, M. (1999), *Are Skills the Answer? The Political Economy of Skill Creation in Advanced Industrial Countries*, New York: Oxford University Press.

Edvinsson, L. & Malone, M. (1997), *Intellectual Capital: Realizing Your Company's True Value by Finding its Hidden Brainpower*, New York: Harper Collins

Engeström, Y. (1998), "The tensions of judging: Handling cases of driving under the influence of alcohol in Finland and California". In Y. Engeström & D. Middleton (eds.): *Cognition and Communication at Work*. Cambridge, Melbourne: Cambridge University Press.

Engeström, Y. (2001), "Expansive learning at work: toward an activity theoretical reconceptualization", in *Journal of Education and Work*, Vol. 14, No. 1: 133-156.

Engeström, Y. (2003), "New Forms of Learning in Co-configuration Work", Keynote Presentation, *Proceeding Book I, p. 1-12, 3rd International Conference of Researching Work and Learning*, July 25-27, 2003, Tampere, Finland.

Ezioni, A. (1988), *The Moral Dimension – Towards a new economics*. New York: Free Press.

Fuller, S. (2002), *Knowledge Management Foundations*, Boston: Butterworth & Heinemann.

Gustavsen, B. (2001), *Creating Connectedness – The Role of Social Research in Innovation Policy.* Amsterdam: John Benjamins.

Herbst, D.P. (1985), *Contextual Design: Towards the development of socio-technical learning networks*, unpublished paper AFI-dok 8 / 85, Oslo: Work Research Institute.

Herbst, D.P. (1995), "What Happens When We Make a Distinction: An Elementary Introduction to Co-Genetic Logic" in T.A. Hillsdale (ed.): *Development of person-context relations*, Hillsdale, NJ: Erlbaum.

Herbst, P.G. (1974), *Socio-technical Design: Strategies in Multidisciplinary Research*, London: Tavistock Publications.

Knorr Cetina, K. (1999), *Epistemic Cultures. How the Sciences Make Knowledge*, Cambridge, MA: Harvard University Press.

Lahn, L. C. (2002), Boundary crossing in working life – between developmental transfer and fashionable imitation, Paper *Symposium Developmental transfer – novel solutions to transfer problems, 5th ISCRAT Congress, Amsterdam*, June 18-22, 2002.

MacIntyre, A. (1990), *Three Rival Versions of Moral Enquiry.* London: Duckworth.

Morgan, G. (1986), *Images of Organization*, Beverly Hills, CA: Sage.

Pålshaugen, Ø. (1998), *The End of Organization Theory?* Amsterdam: John Benjamins.

Pålshaugen, Ø. (2001), The Use of Words. Improving Enterprises by Improving Their Conversations, in P. Reason & H. Bradbury (eds): *Handbook of Action Research. Paricipatory Inquiry and Practice,* London: Sage.

Pålshaugen, Ø. (2002), Discourse democracy at work: On public spheres in private enterprises, in *Concepts and Transformation* 7(2): 141-192, Amsterdam: John Benjamins.

Sejersted, F. (1998), *Teknologipolitikk*, Oslo: Universitetsforlaget.

Slagstad, R. (1998), *De nasjonale strateger,* Oslo: Pax.

Spencer Brown, G. (1969), *Laws of Form,* London: Allen & Unwin.

Star, S.L. & Griesemer, J. (1989), "Institutional Ecology, "Translations", and Coherence: Amateurs and Professionals in Berkeley's Museum of Vertebrate Zoology", 1907-1939, in *Social Studies of Science,* 19: 387-420.

Star, S.L. (1989), "The Structure of Ill-Structured Solutions: Boundary Objects and the Heterogeneous Distributed Probem Solving", in M.N. Huhns & L. Gasser (eds.): *Distributed Artificial Intelligence,* Vol. 2 pp. 37-54, London: Pitman.

Thévenot, L. (2001), "Pragmatic regimes governing the engagement with the world", pp. 56-73 in T. R. Schatzki, K. Knorr Cetina & E. von Savigny (eds.): *The Practice Turn in Contemporary Theory,* London & New York: Routledge.

Thévenot, L. (2002), "Which Road to Follow? The Moral Complexity of an "Equipped" Humanity", pp. 53-87 in J. Law & A. Mol (eds.): *Complexities. Social Studies of Knowledge Practices,* Durham & London: Duke University Press.

Trist, E, Murray, H. & Murray, B. (1993), *The Social Engagement of Social Science Vol. II. The Socio-technical Systems Perspective,* London: The Tavistock Institute.

van Ejnatten, F. (1993), *The Paradigm that Changed the Work Place, Analysis of STSD,* Aasen & Maastricht: van Gorcum.

Zuboff, S. (1988), *In the Age of the Smart Machine. The Future of Work and Power,* Oxford: Heinemann.

Arbeit, Bildung & Gesellschaft
Labour, Education & Society

Herausgegeben von Prof. Dr. György Széll, Prof. Dr. Heinz Sünker,
Dr. Anne Inga Hilsen und Dr. Francesco Garibaldo

Bd.   1   György Széll (ed.): Corporate Social Responsibility in the EU & Japan. 2006.

Bd.   2   Katja Maar: Zum Nutzen und Nichtnutzen der Sozialen Arbeit am exemplarischen Feld der Wohnungslosenhilfe. Eine empirische Studie. 2006.

Bd.   3   Daniela De Ridder: Vom urbanen Sozialraum zur kommunikativen Stadtgesellschaft. 2007.

Bd.   4   Heinz Sünker / Ingrid Miethe (Hrsg.): Bildungspolitik und Bildungsforschung: Herausforderungen und Perspektiven für Gesellschaft und Gewerkschaften in Deutschland. 2007.

Bd.   5   Anja Bastigkeit: Bildungsbiographie und elementarpädagogische Bildungsarbeit. 2007.

Bd.   6   Antônio Inácio Andrioli: Biosoja versus Gensoja. Eine Studie über Technik und Familienlandwirtschaft im nordwestlichen Grenzgebiet des Bundeslandes Rio Grande do Sul (Brasilien). 2007.

Bd.   7   Russell Farnen / Daniel German / Henk Dekker / Christ'l De Landtsheer / Heinz Suenker (eds.): Political Culture, Socialization, Democracy, and Education. Interdisciplinary and Cross-National Perspectives for a New Century. 2008.

Bd.   8   Francesco Garibaldo / Volker Telljohann (eds.): New Forms of Work Organisation and Industrial Relations in Southern Europe. 2007.

Bd.   9   Anne Marie Berg / Olav Eikeland (eds.): Action Research and Organisation Theory. 2008.

Bd.   10   György Széll / Carl-Heinrich Bösling / Ute Széll (eds.): Education, Labour & Science. Perspectives for the 21st Century. 2008.

Bd.   11   Francesco Garibaldo / Philippe Morvannou / Jochen Tholen (eds.): Is China a Risk or an Opportunity for Europe? An Assessment of the Automobile, Steel and Shipbuilding Sectors. 2008.

Bd.   12   Yunus Dauda: Managing Technology Innovation. The Human Resource Management Perspective. 2009.

Bd.   13   Jarmo Lehtonen / Satu Kalliola (eds.): Dialogue in Working Life Research and Development in Finland. 2009.

Bd.   14   György Széll / Werner Kamppeter / Woosik Moon (eds.): European Social Integration – A Model for East Asia? 2009.

Bd.   15   Benedicte Brøgger / Olav Eikeland (eds.): Turning to Practice with Action Research. 2009.

www.peterlang.de